CITIZEN YOU!

HELPING YOUR GOVERNMENT HELP ITSELF

Edited by
MIKE LOEW

Written by
**MIKE LOEW, JOE GARDEN,
AND RANDY OSTROW**

Designed by
ALICIA KUBISTA

THE NEW PRESS

NEW YORK
LONDON

Requests for permission to reproduce selections from this book should be mailed to:
Permissions Department, The New Press, 38 Greene Street, New York, NY 10013

Published in the United States by The New Press, New York, 2004
Distributed by W. W. Norton & Company, Inc., New York

ISBN 1-56584-915-9 (pbk.)
CIP data available.

The New Press was established in 1990 as a not-for-profit alternative to the large,
commercial publishing houses currently dominating the book publishing industry. The
New Press operates in the public interest rather than for private gain, and is committed
to publishing, in innovative ways, works of educational, cultural, and community
value that are often deemed insufficiently profitable.

www.thenewpress.com

Printed in Canada

10 9 8 7 6 5 4 3 2 1

CONTENTS

GRAPHICS BY
Alicia Kubista, Mike Loew, and Chad Nackers

COVER DESIGN BY
Mike Loew

IDEA CONTRIBUTION BY
Todd Brunner, Josh Saunders, Chad Nackers,
John Krewson, and Colin Robinson

SPECIAL THANKS TO
Colin Robinson, Sarah Fan, Abby Aguirre, Fran Forte, Aziz Ansari,
Dave Denson, Jim Hoffman and 911research.wtc7.net, Andrew Boyd and
Billionaires for Bush, Kate Brunner, Carol Kolb, Peter Koechley, Sean Mills,
Daniel Greenberg, Matthew Rohrer, Susan McCullough, Seamus Rohrer,
Regan St. Pierre, Gabe Adams, and Fabrice Scotto

CITIZEN
YOU!

Citizen
YOU!

Welcoming Remarks by
Presidential Appointee
George W. Bush

"I believe in America. America's made my fortune. And I raised my daughter in American fashion. I give her freedom, but—I taught her never to dishonor her family."

So begins that great tribute

to the American Dream, *The Godfather*. Every American can identify with that little Italian undertaker with the daughter who got beat up. All across this great land of ours, Americans just want to do their civic duty, to support their troops and their brave leaders, to fight terror, to work hard and make a living. And all of us want to prevent our families from getting beat up, and all of us want a "godfather" who will unite the forces of good and deliver God's just retribution to the evil ones. Back in the time of *The Godfather*, the danger came from roving bands of Italian, Mexican, or Negro youths. Today, it is terrorist foreigners and their evil traitor friends.

I believe in the optimism of the American people, in their values and morals. Everybody wants a tomorrow full of hope, progress, homeland security, and money. That's what makes Americans strive to better themselves, and with *Citizen You!*, this vital volume of helpful hints, we "godfathers" in the White House hope to help you become a better citizen—a citizen better able to love your country, your God, your Presidential Appointee, your military, your children, and your spouse of the opposite sex (not necessarily in that order).

As God has shown Me the one true way, so shall we show you, in brief, easy-to-follow chapters written in plain words, full of pictures and charts. As God has asked Me to put my trust and faith in Him, so we, your leaders, think it would be a good idea if you put your trust and faith in us. Considering I'm doing God's will, Americans should pretty much just take My word for things, and leave the details to the experts here in the White House. That arrangement has always worked for Me. In fact, it even worked for Me when I was a lush and a coke-snorting party monster before I stumbled across God. That's how great He is, and how much He loves Me. And America, too.

My fellow American citizens, I know that you love God, and that you love Me, and that you will do right by America. Your country needs you to be a good citizen and pay attention and pull your weight right now so that I can get on with making the world safe for you by crushing evil everywhere. I've got a tough job ahead of me, and I need to concentrate pretty hard, so I will appreciate your cooperation. For those who can't or won't cooperate, there's the new powers granted to me under the USA PATRIOT Act. For the rest of you, there's this book, which pretty much covers all the bases. And don't forget, I have spoken with God, and he made it clear to Me that your very lives and the lives of all your loved ones depend on Me being able to finish the job I have started. So be sure to vote for Freedom™ and safety in November, and not for treachery, evil, and death.

Thank you, and God bless America.

Civic
DUTIES

Welcoming Remarks by
His Excellency,
Supreme Court Justice
Antonin Scalia

For some reason, the American people, the lower courts, even my own mother-in-law can't seem to grasp the burden of responsibility that falls upon the shoulders of each and every one of us the moment we take on the sacred mantle of "citizen." The Constitution of the United States of America is very clear on this subject, despite what some of my learned brethren on this exalted bench might claim. Therefore, I will explain this principle in the simplest manner possible, so that the American people, limited as they are by their second-rate intellects, can begin to grasp it.

Imagine our government as an extremely complicated jigsaw puzzle—an interlocking system that requires all of its components in order to see the full picture. Separately, each piece of the puzzle is meaningless. If you lose one piece, you might be tempted to throw the whole thing away. In an ideal world, we assemble this puzzle in a tranquil environment, on a perfectly smooth and level surface. But this is not an ideal world. We don't have a card table big enough for the puzzle, so we have to set it up on the living room rug, and there's a dog running through the house like a maniac, knocking pieces all over the place.

In that event, some pieces from another puzzle may get mixed in with yours, or some pieces may get lost under your living-room sofa. Now, hypothetically, you can either throw the puzzle away or make do with what you have. While some pieces of our democracy, such as due process, the right to an attorney, and the presumption of innocence may have gotten lost under the couch of 9/11, we would be foolish to throw our whole system of government away just because a piece or two are missing. Rather, our duty as citizens is to embrace the genius of our Founding Fathers, take a piece of another puzzle, and jam it in there with all our might, pounding away until we've made it fit through sheer determination and brute force.

While notions such as individual privacy and search warrants may have been lost, we have other pieces we can replace them with. If we have "illegal enemy combatants" stored under lock and key, with no legal counsel and no access to our system of justice, that does not mean that democracy has failed. It just means that we have found a good substitute for civil liberties until we get around to vacuuming the living room. *And we will vacuum the living room.*

Puzzles don't put themselves together. They need the guiding hand of a higher power to assemble them properly. It is every citizen's duty to submit to the will of the government so that we can put the puzzle that is America together correctly, as defined by the extreme right wing of this court. We must all stand together and keep quiet about the fact that it doesn't look anything like the picture on the box, or that one of the pieces sticks up around the edges, or that the kitten has a puppy ear from another set. If you don't keep your mouth shut, citizen, prepare yourself to be pounded into place like that errant piece of the puzzle. As crowded as those detention camps are right now, there is always room in this great land of ours for one more prisoner.

Thank you. You may go now.

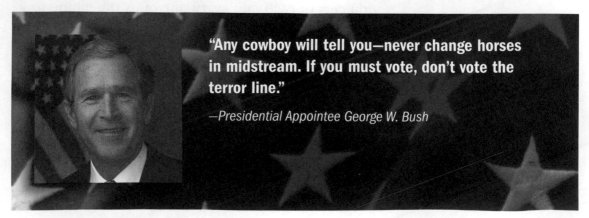

"Any cowboy will tell you—never change horses in midstream. If you must vote, don't vote the terror line."

—*Presidential Appointee George W. Bush*

★ **CITIZEN KID!**

How a Bill Becomes a Law

with Presidential Appointee George W. Bush

It used to be that a law was passed because someone saw a need for it in society. What could possibly be wrong with that? Plenty! See, the needs of the majority of the people aren't always the same needs of those who can afford to help me serve our country. Who makes laws to help these guys? That's where I come in! I see our Congress not listening to these corporate executives and billionaires, so I do what I can for these people—because remember, democracy is for everybody. So how does it happen? How do we help the little guy that can't get help?

First, I meet with these important, successful people, who tell me how a new law could help make their lives even better. It all sounds like a good idea, so I get Dick Cheney to write up some legal mumbo-jumbo.

The next step is to figure out a good name for my bill. Bills are full of all sorts of words and nonsense, the kind of stuff no one has time to think about. That's why it's important to come up with a punchy name, something that fools people into supporting it. Let's say I want to give a big tax break to my good old campaign-contributor buddies. I'll call it something like the "American Friendship Act." Hey, who's going to think there's anything wrong with friendship? Or maybe my pals in the chemical industry want to set all of our nation's rivers on fire. I'll call that one the "Cleansing Our Rivers Act." Ooh, I'm good!

Now that I've got a comforting, deceitful name on there to hoodwink the stupid American people into thinking I'm actually on their side, I can move right ahead on ramming that bill through Congress. I don't go in there to debate it, boys and girls. I just take my bill, jab it in their fat faces, and shout that if they're not with me, then they're with the terrorists. That line always works great! Then I just kick back at my ranch and wait for the votes to roll in. My people behind the scenes will make sure that your congressman knows exactly how to "vote his conscience," if he knows what's good for him. A few days later, Senate Majority Leader Bill Frist breaks out the rubber stamps for everyone, and you know what happens next. George W. Bush always gets his way.

Guess what, boys and girls? They signed my bill! Now it's a law, and there's nothing that you or anyone else can do about it! *Oh, yes!*

Our Founding Fathers, who had a deep and misguided distrust of tyranny, limited the exercise of federal power by separating it among three branches of government: the executive, legislative, and judicial branches. This had to change. By taking control of both chambers of Congress and the Supreme Court, the Republican Party has turned this rattletrap collection of spare parts into a single, streamlined machine of governmental progress. We contend that there still is a separation of powers—we have them, and you don't. Let's take a closer look at how these three branches of government do our bidding:

Executive Branch

The Presidential Appointee and his handpicked cabinet make up this branch, which does all the real work of running the country. The agenda of the Presidential Appointee is in no way influenced by the American people, who gave some other guy half a million more votes in 2000, but by his wealthy campaign contributors, his father, and fellow members of Skull and Bones, his elite secret society from Yale University.

MAKING A DIFFERENCE— EIGHT MORE YEARS

Since Presidential Appointee George W. Bush was not officially elected in 2000 but appointed by the Supreme Court, the presidential two-term limit does not apply to his first four years in office. Therefore, we will not have to appoint another Bush family member as president until 2012—unless, of course, another major terrorist attack occurs on U.S. soil, in which case martial law will be enacted and all bets are off. This is just one example of how we're *making a difference*.

Legislative Branch

This branch's main purpose is approving the federal laws that the Presidential Appointee creates. The legislative branch also appropriates money for invading other countries, brings and tries impeachments against Democratic presidents, and conducts the appearance of investigations that whitewash any questionable actions and suppress any evidence of deceitful wrongdoing by the Presidential Appointee.

Judicial Branch

This branch is responsible for appointing the Presidential Appointee to power. The American people now have no right to choose a president. This branch also upholds the Presidential Appointee's laws after they are unanimously approved by the Legislative Branch. Finally, the Judicial Branch is responsible for upholding the spirit, if not the letter, of the Constitution, unless John Ashcroft tells them not to.

★ SUPREME COURT APPOINTMENTS

Choosing a Supreme Court Justice is a contentious process at best. We try and try, and no one's ever happy. You wouldn't believe all the griping about who's against abortion or who hates blacks. There's all sorts of qualifications that have to be met, backgrounds that have to be checked, and allegations of sexual harassment that must be viciously dismissed. That's why we're so excited about our pick for a new Supreme Court Justice as soon as that withered old Jewess kicks the bucket: Sean Hannity. There couldn't possibly be any problem with his judicial past, because he doesn't have one! He's always talking about the problems with the courts, though, so he seems pretty knowledgeable. Sean Hannity is just a straight-shooting, no-nonsense kind of guy, and best of all, he could out-scream all of

those old farts combined. That's just the kind of henchman we need. So here's hoping that one of the bad guys drops dead real quick, so Sean can let freedom ring from the highest court in the land.

★ THE NEW FREEDOMS!

You're always going on and on about your loony liberties, you liberals! With all your grumbling and groaning, you'd think that we were holding you all back from taking a trip to the corner store and renting DVDs. That ain't the case, buddy, and you know it. Who needs these liberties, terrorists or you? Alright, fine, if you want liberties, you got 'em. But this Bill of Rights is new and improved! With the bold, refreshing taste of the New Freedoms for a New Generation, you'll find that your life doesn't have to change much at all!

FREEDOM FROM INCONVENIENCE!

FREEDOM FROM DISCOMFORT!

FREEDOM FROM RESPONSIBILITY!

FREEDOM FROM UNCERTAINTY!

FREEDOM FROM WORKPLACE SAFETY!

FREEDOM FROM GARBAGE COLLECTION!

FREEDOM FROM LIBERAL LIBERTY LA-LA LAND!

HOO-YAH! What are you waiting for, America? Grab a tall, cold glass of liberty!

Last year, there was a bit of a hubbub about the outing of Valerie Plame-Wilson, the CIA agent whose husband, Joseph Wilson, claimed that our brave leader George W. Bush was lying when he said Saddam Hussein was trying to buy uranium from Niger. (That's a country in Africa. Take our word for it; it's right next to Libya.) If you pay attention to the liberal media, Plame-Wilson's secret identity as a CIA agent was leaked as an act of revenge by a mysterious White House chief political advisor, whose identity may never be known. We need to ask, was it really that big of a deal? Plame-Wilson was only an undercover analyst who tracked and attempted to halt the proliferation of weapons of mass destruction around the world. She wasn't out on the front lines fighting the real terror, Saddam Hussein.

What is so important about what an analyst does? They simply look at vast streams of data and process it to come to a logical conclusion. Why do we even need the analyst? We still have all the data, and we can do all kinds of things with that stuff. We can make data say anything we want about WMD, educational test scores, prescription drug costs, military casualties, or the federal deficit. It's true that with her cover blown, Plame-Wilson's network is now unable to generate any new data, but that's fine, too! We did just fine with twelve-year-old data on Iraq's WMD program, didn't we? In fact, why do we even need data at all? Sometimes you just know what to do, deep down in

your heart. There were definitely weapons of mass destruction in Iraq, no matter what the "facts" might claim.

We are interested in tracking WMD, but only when it increases our profit margin. Iraq has been a very profitable WMD hunt for our business partners, and Valerie Plame-Wilson paid the price for her husband challenging our business plan. In any business, you have to keep an eye on your competition, even if the competition is an abstract concept like truth. Thanks to Joseph Wilson's assertion that George W. Bush's terrifying fantasy of a nuclear bomb–wielding Iraq was based on a crude forgery that had been discredited years ago, his wife became the competition.

Bad idea. You don't challenge George W. Bush and his terrifying fantasies. In response, Karl Rove, Bush's chief political advisor, declared that Joseph Wilson's wife was "fair game." And then, some unnamed White House chief political advisor—NOT, we hasten to add, Karl Rove—leaked the undercover identity of Valerie Plame-Wilson to conservative journalist and longtime Rove ally William Novak. Do

you see a direct connection? A smoking gun? Were you there? We didn't think so.

Nevertheless, these are very serious allegations. The Bush administration is doing everything they can to sweep them under the rug so Americans can stop worrying about the danger their government poses and go back to worrying about the very real dangers of al-Qaeda. In the spirit of the highly memorable *Just Say No* anti-drug campaign, we are launching our own catch phrase: *Who Cares!* Where did the leak come from? *Who Cares!* Did this leak damage the well-being of a dedicated government agent who was working to contain weapons of mass destruction? *Who Cares!* Did it compromise the safety and security of the nation? *Who Cares!* Go on, give it a try. It's good for you, good for us, and good for your country.

MAKING A DIFFERENCE: YOUR REGULATORY AGENCIES

The environment, as well as your health and safety, are very important to the Republican Party. Seriously. So when it comes to the governmental agencies that are supposed to protect these things, we've gone to the experts. In the past, "the experts" were Ivy League brainiacs whose weird theories made it impossible for any hardworking American to conduct their business. We don't need these fussy old chickens clucking about "worker safety" or "the ozone layer." The foxes are guarding the henhouse now. Our crafty new leaders have the real-world knowledge needed to make life easier for big business and run regulatory agencies.

Who could be a better choice to lead the Environmental Protection Agency than Utah Governor Mike Leavitt? During Leavitt's three terms as governor, some tree-huggers say that Utah's environmental-enforcement record tied for worst in the country. Utah's air quality and toxic releases were second worst, just behind those of George W. Bush's Texas. The way we see it, Utah's environmental record was second *best.* Then there's Gale Norton, our Secretary of the Interior, who is in charge of our national parks and public lands. As a lawyer, Norton represented Delta Petroleum and lobbied for NL Industries, courageously defending their right to poison children with lead paint. Now that's a gal we can count on. Our head of forest policy, Mark Rey, was a lobbyist for the timber industry for two decades before joining the Bush administration. His experience in making it easier for corporations to cut down our national forests has been invaluable. John Graham, our pick to lead the Office of Information and Regulatory Affairs, has bravely fought for years against regulations for harmless substances such as dioxin, pesticides, radon, and asbestos. This list of our right-minded appointees who do what's best for (a very small group of extremely wealthy) Americans goes on and on!

The great thing about all these folks is that they don't waste any time consulting anyone before making a decision. Whether it's blasting off mountaintops to get at the coal underneath, or dumping billions of gallons of saltwater into our topsoil from methane well operations, they know the right thing to do and they do it. This dynamic leadership of our appointees is just another example of how we're *making a difference.*

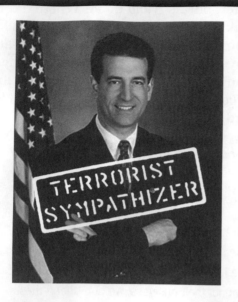

then why wasn't it good enough for you, Feingold? Sorry we didn't make the language pretty enough for you. Next time, we'll put a poem in there so you'll be happy with it, you pathetic protector of individual rights and freedoms. We hope, for your sake, that you fall in line before you get Wellstoned.

MAKING A DIFFERENCE: SPEED-READING FOR SENATORS

After years of getting nowhere by playing nicey-nice with Congress, the Bush administration has finally found a better way to get things done. We're cramming 1,000-page pieces of legislation down the throats of your elected representatives, then giving them only twenty-four hours to decipher these sweeping changes to our Constitution before being forced to vote. This tactic worked for the USA PATRIOT Act and Dick Cheney's energy bill, and it will continue to work for America. To help our slow-witted legislators get on the fast track with us, we're offering speed-reading lessons to all members of Congress, free of charge. In these classes, we teach them to take note of the important words in proposed legislation—like "justice," "terror," "Mars," and "steroids"—and teach them to skip the filler, like "imprisonment," "military tribunal," and "martial law." If there are at least four "terrors," two "justices," and a "steroid" in the bill, then it should be passed. It's that simple—and just another example of how we're *making a difference*.

When the time came to do something meaningful to protect America, every member of Congress—men and women, Democrats and Republicans—stood by their Presidential Appointee. All senators and representatives voted "yes" for the USA PATRIOT Act, giving us the power we needed to scrutinize every American so we could pick out the bad apples. All of these legislators did exactly what we told them to do. All except one. One man, or more specifically, one Jew, did not love his country enough to support our evisceration of the Bill of Rights. Russell Feingold, a Democrat from Wisconsin, tipped his traitorous hand by casting the sole "no" vote for the USA PATRIOT Act, ensuring him the title of Least Patriotic Senator and the number-one spot on our Enemies List. Feingold tried to cover up his treason by giving the usual liberal excuses about the "sacred trust of protecting civil liberties." Hey, if the USA PATRIOT Act was good enough for that commie Billary Clinton,

★ THIS TRUCK AIN'T STOPPIN'

We've smashed through congressional gridlock and are rolling ahead! Our tax cuts for the rich, free passes to polluters, and attacks on the Bill of Rights are no longer stuck in the traffic of partisan debate. With Congress completely controlled by the Republicans, the only thing the House and Senate fight over now is who can make our Presidential Appointee the happiest! Congress has become an unstoppable eighteen-wheeler that is delivering the goods to the American people. Do you need tax relief? POW! It's there in a heartbeat, even if you didn't ask for it. Are you scared that a homosexual is going to try and marry you? WHAM! We just change the Constitution so that can't ever happen! You better not try to stand in our

way. When you're hauling twelve tons of governmental fury on the road to the New World Order, you don't have time to stop or swerve for nothin' or nobody. We're so cranked up, we can drive all night. Our big, thick tires scatter the gravel of resistance behind us, and the bug-like corpses of our enemies are splattered all over our windshield. So get on board or get left behind! *YEE-HAW!*

★ JOIN THE TAX-CUT ARMY!

If you are one of the elite Americans who would really benefit from more Bush tax cuts, then we need you! If you really

want to go the extra mile for the cause, and if you put together a construction worker or lumberjack costume last Halloween, then give your local Republican campaign office a call. We need large crowds of supporters to participate in our tax-cut rallies, but they must be "dressed down" and resemble "real worker types." Leave the $1,000 suits and ties at home, fellows, and lose the diamond earrings and pearl necklaces, ladies. That way, when the cameras show a large crowd of people cheering for more money to go to the rich, it will appear as if "the people" are cheering for your tax cuts. If you don't have any convincing proletarian clothing and don't know where to buy it, we can probably work something out. Tell you what, we'll provide the blue jeans and flannel shirts if you provide the spirit!

As the nation's guardians of fiscal responsibility, we've tried our hardest to control unnecessary government spending. That's no small task when you've got to pay Lockheed Martin, the Carlyle Group, and Halliburton enough money to wage an unending War on Terror on multiple continents. However, with everyone breathing down our necks after turning the largest surplus in our nation's history, $281 billion, into a $521 billion deficit, we'd like to address some of the criticism we've received. It's the least we can do.

Eighty-seven billion dollars sounds like a pretty huge expenditure for Iraq—especially when we're giving huge tax breaks to the wealthiest one percent of Americans at the same time—but only if you put a price on your own personal safety. Don't you feel safer now that Saddam Hussein is not crouched in a hole

somewhere, growing his evil beard longer and longer, while plotting to destroy our great nation? Come on, don't you? Eighty-seven billion dollars is a small price to pay for that peace of mind, but we admit, there might be a little we could trim here and there. No questions on the military spending or the huge reconstruction contracts for our friends' companies, of course, but what is this—a postal system? Why does Iraq need a postal system? No one can read those chicken scratches they call writing anyway. School lunches for Iraqi children? Give us a break. If Ronald Reagan single-handedly won the Cold War by cutting funding for school lunches, we should have no problem putting down a handful of insurgents if we're not shelling out money on fancy pita bread for a bunch of brats who don't even speak English. So don't worry, we're keeping costs under control. Plus, if you weren't paying attention, there are no new expenditures scheduled for our military operations in Iraq *or* Afghanistan (until right after November 2, 2004, for some reason).

When it comes to fighting terror, we're saving money in Iraq as well as saving money on the shores of our own homeland. A lot of that money would just be wasted if we spent it here, anyway. With all the cargo that gets imported to the United States, any port security we instituted would undoubtedly fail, so why bother throwing money away on that? We've also cut $900 million in funding for fire-fighters, local police depart-ments, and emergency rescue units. Our courageous "first responders" can go hold a bake sale. Finally, we've got the best anti-terror system in the world right now with the Homeland Security Advisory System, and it doesn't cost a dime. With just one press release containing the words "Orange Alert," every citizen transforms into an eagle-eyed G-man, on the lookout for terror and responsible for his own safety.

We're extending that sense of self-reliance across the board. Take education funding, for example. Just what do kids need a "Head Start" for anyway? That's for their mothers or nannies to provide. Why waste any money on the Environmental Protection Agency, when trees grow back on their own just fine? We've cut the Federal Aviation Administration's budget for "modernizing" the air traffic system by $393 million. Hey, learn how to fly, pilots,

> *Why does Iraq need a postal system? No one can read those chicken scratches they call writing anyway.*

and take a gun on board with you while you're at it. The Internal Revenue Service says they're struggling to crack down on abusive tax shelters and outright cheating, so we definitely cut their funding. If those IRS eggheads aren't smart enough to catch ambitious tax evaders, tough.

The vast majority of you have to make sacrifices in order to support the tax breaks for our ruling overclass that will get the economy back on its feet. The Bush budget for 2004 eliminates sixty-five programs and cuts back sixty-three others, adding up to an incredible total savings of $4.9 billion! With the federal deficit hitting $521 billion this year, that $4.9 billion we saved at the expense of the public's health and welfare will really help to make an extremely tiny dent in that big, bad deficit. Thanks, Citizen You!

But there's one depart-ment that we'll never cut the funding for, and that's the Department of War—sorry, we mean the Department of Defense. The Bush administration hiked military spending to a record-breaking $401.7 billion for 2004. Nuclear weapons programs in the Energy Department account for another $19 billion, and like we said, expenses for the occupation of Iraq and Afghanistan will not be made public until November 2004. We figure that military spending for 2004 will come out to around, oh, $521 billion or so. But could there be anything more important than gigantic military budgets during this global age of terror? What better way is there to defeat a terrorist waving a deadly box-cutter than with a $2 billion

B-2 Stealth bomber in low Earth orbit? What could deter a suicidal terrorist from setting off a homemade bomb on a New York City subway car more than a $4 billion Trident submarine loaded with nuclear missiles roaming beneath the waves of the North Atlantic? You can see that we've got our priorities in the right place. Protecting and maximizing profits for the manufacturers of weapons of mass destruction—that's *our* definition of fiscal responsibility.

★ VOLUNTEERING—IT MAKES AMERICA WORK!

Staggering unemployment rates in this country can mean only one thing: opportunity! This is your chance to revitalize the long-dormant spirit of unpaid volunteerism that courses through the veins of America. It is this spirit of civic involvement that will help most of you through the rough days of belt-tightening ahead *and* give you a reason to get out of bed in the morning. So what can you do to make your community a better place? Here's some suggestions to help you kickstart your new life as a volunteer:

★ Clean up the environment at your local country club. Often, the manicured putting greens and sweeping fairways of otherwise beautiful golf courses are littered with detritus such as torn scorecards, discarded mini-pencils, and swizzle sticks. Contributing just ten hours a week, picking up litter on your hands and knees while dodging flying golf balls, can help stressed-out CEOs "get away from it all" in a serene, tidy setting.

★ Volunteer to read classic American stories to children, such as the heartwarming tales of Horatio Alger and Little Black Sambo.

★ Visit the elderly on a regular basis, and bring them any pills you have lying around the house, since they can't afford any themselves. Expired prescription drugs, vitamins, allergy medications—don't bother keeping track of what everything is, since they won't know the difference anyway. It's all bound to make them better— that's why they call it *medicine*.

★ Start a neighborhood watch group. Enlist the help of neighbors that are just like you to keep an eye out for neighbors who are not just like you, strictly speaking, and who may not share your values or skin tone. These neighbors are statistically more likely to be dangerous criminals and a threat to your children.

★ If you own a car, you can bring people together by carpooling. Offer a ride to people you would not normally pick up, such as your mother and father at the airport when they come to visit you. Or take your grandmother to a doctor's office for her CAT scan without asking her for gas money. Volunteer to drive your family to a relative's home for Thanksgiving dinner. Pick up your child from soccer practice without even being asked. What the heck, pick up another child while there and drop him off somewhere too.

★ Volunteer to help those who are less ambitious than you. The next time a homeless man begs you for spare change, give him something more valuable—a word of advice. Suggest that he take a shower, shave, and seek gainful employment. You'll walk away with a spring in your step, knowing you've done all that you can to put that man on the road to self-improvement.

★ Help autistic and learning-disabled students whose schools are no longer able to care for them due to cuts in special-education funding. By taking these children into your home and keeping them busy with housework and yard chores, you will help them immensely. These unusual children are much like wild beasts; hard physical labor makes them docile.

CAN I VOTE, PLEASE? A NEW VOTERS' GUIDE

Are you wondering if you are eligible to vote in the 2004 presidential election? We congratulate you for having the democratic initiative for even asking that question in the first place. Here, then, is a clip-out card that you can use to get an answer to your unusual request. In case a sudden and unreasonable urge to vote descends upon you, remove this card from your wallet and ask yourself:

> ★ **Are you under the age of 18, or over 65 and retired in Florida?**
>
> ★ **Have you ever committed a felony, or are you related to a felon, or do you have the same last name as a felon, or can you define the word "felony"?**
>
> ★ **Has your family been in the country for less than two generations?**
>
> ★ **Did you oppose our government's decision to invade Iraq?**
>
> ★ **Do you have any opinions of your own that George W. Bush has not provided you with?**
>
> **❑ YES ❑ NO**

If you answered "no" to all five questions, then congratulations! You may vote freely in the next election. If you answered "yes" to any of these questions, it's better that you stay at home on November 2, 2004, unless you enjoy being arrested.

What Are Civil Liberties?

A Campfire Chat with Sheriff Clint McJustice, the All-American Cowboy

"Civil liberties" are on a lot of lips lately. There's been a whole mess o' talk about them blowin' away like tumbleweeds, or bein' denied to a bunch of Irabians. The way I see it, this all sounds like a bunch o' city slickers sufferin' from diarrhea of the jawbone.

I'm mighty ashamed when I hear the liberal media talkin' about how the government ain't got no right to spy on its own citizens. Maybe you don't remember a little something called September the 11th? By ten o'clock in the mornin', our whole goddamn Eastern Seaboard looked like beef day at an Injun agency. Looked to me like everyone was so busy eyeballin' the government that no one was keeping an eye on the terrorists. So let's circle the wagons, little cowpokes, and chew the cud about these so-called civil liberties that have become a real cactus in our government's saddle.

What are civil liberties?

Civil liberties refer to the first ten amendments tacked on to the U.S. Constitution by our fancy-pants Founding Fathers. The main one gives us the right to keep our six-shooters. The rest are a big ole pile o' steamin' cow flaps.

I hear that we have the right to an attorney and can't be imprisoned without being charged with a crime. Is that true?

Sure you do. But you know who don't have them rights? Foreigners. They weren't born in the U.S. of A. so they don't get the same freedoms as God-fearin' Americans. And if someone was born here, but still looks like a foreigner—wild, woolly, and full o' fleas—then they don't get our freedoms neither.

Do we have the right to avoid unlawful search and seizure?

When you're tryin' to head off the next terrorist attack at the pass, there's not always time to get some judge's okay to rustle through somebody's undies without them knowin'. Like my good buddy Blind-Eye O'Beedience says, "you can't ketch a calf if you don't throw your lariat." Even if you aren't up to anything illegal, isn't it worth the small inconvenience of having your house turned upside down if it means you're off our suspect list? Don't you want to see them bad Irabians get caught?

How about the freedom to assemble? Can we still do that?

That depends. Now, nobody's goin' to stop you from assemblin' at a rodeo or a Boy Scout jamboree. But if some people assemble for the sole purpose of belly-achin' about the government, they might just be terrorists. Sorry to disappoint you, but bein' a terrorist ain't allowed no more in these parts. We might secretly put a member of our posse in there with 'em to keep an eye on their treachery, or we might just have Tom Ridge and the boys blaze in there with enough hot lead for a real corpse-and-cartridge occasion.

Can we protest our government's decision to go to war?

Now why would you want to do a damn fool thing like that? When those terrorists get a good look at the danger end o' my scattergun, they take to the tall timbers right quick. Then all I gotta do is call in the flyboys to drop 25,000 pounds o' napalm on those woods, and we can have ourselves a good ole-fashioned Irabian barbecue. After that's settled, all of us good Americans can bunk down, safe and sound, and ketch some real peaceful shut-eye.

Can we criticize our Presidential Appointee?

Now you can shut yer bean hole right there, pardner, before I dress you up with a hemp necktie and make you the guest of honor at a string-up party in my cottonwood out back. Are you in cahoots with al-Qaeda? Our Presidential Appointee is one straight-shootin' son of a gun, and he don't need no back talk from a yellow-bellied yearling. This crazy world turned into a real buckin' bronco after 9/11, and George W. Bush is the one cowboy who can take terror by the horns and ride it all the way into the sunset.

Now if you want to poke fun at a president, why don't you take a good look at that sorry sack o' spit that disgraced the office before W. mosied along? That dough-belly couldn't ride nothin' wilder 'n a wheelchair. He was so weak he couldn't lick his upper lip, and that's why we got all the terrorist problems we got today.

Well, youngsters, I hope I've answered all your questions about civil liberties. If you have any more, you might want to keep 'em to yourselves. Now if you'll excuse me, I've gotta jingle my spurs over to Fort Freedom™. Seems like a bunch of Choctaw squaws and their brats are beggin' for food over there, so it's time for me and the blue-shirt boys to grease up the Gatling guns and have ourselves some fun. So long, li'l dogies, and don't stray too far from the herd. I'll be keepin' an eye on you.

MAKING A DIFFERENCE: OUR SHADOW GOVERNMENT

Immediately after 9/11, the Bush administration laid the foundations of destroying what is left of our representative democracy by enacting a shadow government in an undisclosed location under a mountain somewhere. Congress was not advised of this shadow government, especially not congressional Democrats. Hundreds of loyal henchmen of the White House are now being shuttled back and forth to this remote bunker, preparing for what comes next—just another example of how we're *making a difference*.

A Guide to Civil Disobedience

You might be surprised that we actually want people to learn about civil disobedience, but we recognize the value of protests in a free America. One of the pivotal moments of the 2000 presidential election was the spontaneous protest of concerned voters in Florida, who flew in from Republican campaign offices across the country, stopping the illegal counting of votes for Al Gore. However, protesting the government is serious business and must be done in an orderly and completely pointless fashion in order to avoid anyone getting hurt. We don't want anyone breaking the law, even peace-loving, tofu-licking, feminist homosexuals who belong in jail, so here are your guidelines for organizing safe and legal public protests:

1 Research and obey all state and local statutes governing traffic obstruction, sidewalk usage, vandalism, illegal signage, public obscenity, improper noise levels, and ferret-leashing requirements.

2 Be sure to include several large, homemade, goofy-looking papier-mâché puppets in your protest parade. This is a great way to ensure that onlookers take you seriously. Puppets are best constructed while high on "grass."

3 Speaking of which, try "toking" on your "grass" during a protest. This will make you more pliant and obedient to commands from authority figures.

4 Be sure to have a small drum, tambourine, or cowbell for all protest participants to beat on. The sound of a hundred people with no musical training banging out a hundred different attempts at rhythms simultaneously will always draw supporters to your cause.

5 If you wish to mock the noble efforts of the Department of Homeland Security, wrap multiple layers of duct tape over your mouth, eyes, nose, and hair.

6 Obey all orders given by police officers.

7 Obey all orders given by police officers' horses.

8 If a man with an unusually short haircut and shiny dress shoes, who has never attended a meeting of your organization before, suddenly begins shouting, "Hey, let's torch that Starbucks!" during your protest, do what he says. He'll have all sorts of great ideas that will land you in jail—a sure-fire way to get your cause the media attention it deserves, and a badge of achievement for any real protestor.

9 Instead of public protests, consider writing letters to your elected officials instead. These letters have the benefit of being able to be screened for anthrax, as well as being easily thrown into trash cans.

10 If you fail to follow these guidelines, which will lead to the police assaulting you with boots, fists, batons, pepper spray, tear gas, fire hoses, attack dogs, horses, rubber bullets, concussion grenades, and stun guns, be sure to turn off and put away all your video and/or photographic cameras. You don't want any damage done to such nice equipment.

★ PREPARING FOR THE NYC GOP CONVENTION

We know some of you liberal protesters are champing at the bit to disrupt the Republican Convention when it comes to New York City in September 2004. We're making every effort so the convention can go on uninterrupted and the protestors can wave their signs and shout their slogans to their hearts content. After all, like George W. Bush always says, we love free speech.

First, all protestors will be rounded up and made into felons who can't vote. They will then be dumped into "free-speech zones" located in appropriate locations such as southern Staten Island and Far Rockaway, Queens. Free-speech zones are much like dog runs (without grass) where free-speech enthusiasts can indulge in their love of free speech with other like-minded individuals.

All protest signs must be pre-approved by the U.S. Protest Sign Inspection Board twelve months in advance. If you have not already submitted your required sign approval forms, it is too late. Once constructed, these signs must all be screened for anthrax, which may take up to an additional six weeks at a cost of $175 per sign. Protestors will then be issued a list of acceptable slogans to chant and a government-appointed "protest buddy" to ensure compliance with all local rules and regulations. Protests will begin two days after the convention is over and will last for approximately forty-five minutes. Please, enjoy your right to free speech responsibly.

Throughout time, untold billions of people have perished in floods, earthquakes, hurricanes, volcanic eruptions, and other homicidal disasters. We don't need to call the United Nations inspectors to figure out who is behind these acts of murder. All signs point to one culprit—the planet Earth itself. Presidential Appointee George W. Bush vows to bring the killer Earth to justice for these crimes against humanity.

Containment of the Earth doesn't work. It will merely find and exploit new weaknesses on our part. Therefore, America must strike preemptively against the Earth, *before* it can harm us again.

Bringing the Earth to justice will be a difficult task, particularly when the Earth cares so little for its own safety. In order to keep the Earth from embarking on more suicidal missions, we have begun several preemptive programs. For example, our "Safe Logging" initiative will protect our nation's forests from being burned down in forest fires by clear-cutting them first. This ensures that the Earth cannot commit arsonous planetcide, destroying itself and taking as many innocent American resort homes with it as it can.

It is initiatives like this that will enable

us to see justice served, but we cannot do it alone. Attacking and destroying the Earth will require the cooperation of all loyal Americans. We all must conduct our own acts of punishment against this wicked killer. Disable the catalytic converter in your car. Bury some lead in the ground. Turn the other way when you see someone dumping pesticides on children's playgrounds. If you have any doubts about these civic duties, grimly remember Hurricane Andrew or Mount St. Helens, then go pour gasoline in the nearest river. And most importantly, vote for Presidential Appointee George W. Bush in 2004. A vote for Bush is a vote against our evil planet.

MAKING A DIFFERENCE: REDISTRICTING

We learned the painful lessons of playing bipartisan footsie for eight years under Bill Clinton. Now, we're ready to move ahead, erasing the problem of a cumbersome second party through political redistricting. The state of Pennsylvania lost two seats in Congress after the 2000 census, sending Republican legislators scrambling to redraw district lines in order to favor our Grand Old Party. Our patriots in Harrisburg pulled out all the tricks, like forcing two Democratic incumbents into the same district and splitting strong blocks of Democratic voters into two separate districts. Good job! Our boys in Pennsylvania were given lemons, and they made electorate-stacked lemonade. It's just another example of how we're *making a difference*.

★ TIME TO CHANGE THE FLAG?

Anyone born after 1959 is probably used to the fifty stars that decorate our flag. Heck, we've grown fond of them, too, so it may come as a shock that we're thinking about making some changes to Old Glory. See, we want to ensure that the voice of the people is heard loud and clear, and doggone it if California doesn't mess all that up. What with their high population and even higher concentration of Hollyweird loonballs, it's tough for the average guy or gal to be heard. It's like having one smart kid in the front row that blows the curve and makes it tough on all of us. At least New York City is balanced off by the dumb kids at the back of the class, like Buffalo, Rochester, and Schenectady. We figured the best way to sort this out was to do some redistricting, if not outright border swapping, so that the voting out west is more fair and balanced. Therefore, in October 2004,

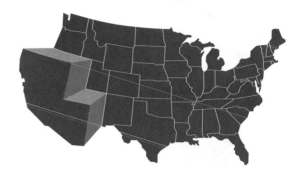

California will be folded into Nevada and Arizona, creating the new state of Calivadizona. This way, the homosexuals of San Francisco, the pot-growing hippies of Humboldt County, and the liberal celebrity elite of Los Angeles will have their votes canceled out by the cowboys of Nevada and the blue-haired retirees of Arizona. Governor Arnold Schwarzenegger will assume control of the entire area. So get ready for a whole new flag, America, and a new state song, Calivadizonians!

★ OUR NEW VOTING MACHINES

"I am committed to helping Ohio deliver its electoral votes to the President next year."

—Warren O'Dell, CEO of Diebold, Inc.
in an August 2003 fundraising letter

This nation cannot allow another presidential election like that of 2000. The electoral victory of George W. Bush must be accomplished by an unbelievably large margin that can be backed up by error-free, computerized voting machines manufactured by Diebold, Inc. All we want to do is help America vote the right way, but there are still some cavemen out there who want to hold us back. These naysaying primitives have raised a big stink about possible problems with the secret computer code of our electronic voting machines. They're crying that these ingenious devices are susceptible to computer hackers and that the lack of paper documentation can lead to massive vote fraud. In response to these incendiary accusations, we would like to say, "Whatever."

Frankly, we've already spent too much

money on these systems to just chuck the whole thing out the window, so you'll have to trust us that our new voting machines will work fine. Just fine. Hardworking Republican technicians are working intently on fixing any bugs in the system, which should be completely cleared up by the 2008 election. In the meantime, we're fast-forwarding production on several alternative electronic voting machines to make everyone happy. Here are some of the innovative designs that you'll be seeing soon:

ATM/Voting Machine

With a simple software update, we can transform existing ATM machines into ballot boxes. You'll be able to vote at your corner convenience store, without having to wait in long lines or brave police barricades. Under this system, you may cast one vote for each $10,000 you have in your banking account. If you are a successful voter that has over $5 million in your account, you qualify for an auto-

matic seat in Congress! You may be ineligible to vote if you have insufficient funds in your account. If this is the case, your inability to vote should give you the motivation to go out and make more of yourself, so that you can participate in democracy next time.

Voting Video Game

Freedom Voters™ is a fun new video game/balloting system that allows people to cast their vote while challenging their hand/eye coordination. Plus, it's our way of saying to young people, "Hey, voting's cool!" The test version is complete, so this thrilling new way to vote will be in many polling places and arcades by November 2, 2004.

Your skill and accuracy in blowing up the enemies of Freedom™ will determine how your vote is cast. On Level One, you pilot a B-2 Stealth bomber and drop 5,000-pound bombs on a bunch of Taliban goatherders in Afghanistan. If you finish this level (don't worry, it's really easy), you win the reward of casting a vote for George W. Bush! If you get the high score on your local Freedom Voters™ machine, you can also vote for a write-in candidate, provided their name does not contain more than five characters. The game gets progressively harder. Only the best players will be able to conquer Level Thirty-Three, where they must defeat Osama bin Laden. This level boss takes the form of a huge, demonic monster, sprouting a dozen metallic tentacles that whip hijacked airplanes at you. If you can take out this intimidating foe, you "unlock" Democratic candidate John Kerry. Good luck!

Voter-Intent Scanners

This is some of our most cutting-edge technology, and you don't even have to leave your house to use it. On Election Day, teams of Republican voter-agents will knock on your door with small, handheld units that will scan your finger-prints, voice patterns, and retinas. Using this biometric information, we can ascertain what your vote will be. Your information is safe in our machines. We can't say exactly how it works, but it's computer chips or something.

For the districts in our nation's less-than-desirable areas which will not be receiving any of these new systems, we have taken steps to educate voters on how to use their antiquated voting technology correctly. Every polling place will have an appointed Voter Helper—a large, reassuring man who will accompany you inside the voting booth to prevent any confusion about how to cast your ballot.

Whatever method you ultimately use

to cast your ballot, you can sleep soundly, knowing that you paid lip service to our democratic process, and that ultimately, the Supreme Court will be making the hard decisions anyway. Good luck, everyone! Let's make this a clean, contention-free election. James Baker III is a busy man, and he doesn't have time to go through all that rigmarole again.

AN ANNOUNCEMENT TO ALL RESIDENTS OF THE UNITED STATES BORN TO AN ARAB PARENT AFTER 1970

The U.S. government would like to apologize to all young Arab Americans for any inconvenience caused by the necessary implementation of Homeland Security measures and any periods of imprisonment without charges or deportation they may have caused. We know many of you are law-abiding American citizens going about your rightful business. It's just bad luck that you are in the demographic that our research shows is most associated with terrorism. Our condolences are extended to you and your families, but we can no longer afford to take chances. Please report to your nearest INS offices within the next twenty-one days. A warrant will be issued for your arrest should you fail to do so. You will need to bring the following items:

★ **Your passport**

★ **Your "go-bag"**

★ **Any necessary medical supplies**

★ **$700 processing fee**

★ **Details of next of kin**

So You Want to Run for Class President!

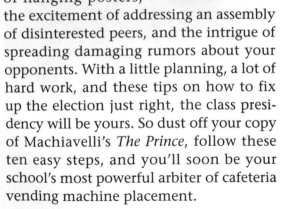

VOTE FOR ME

First of all, good for you! Running for high school office is the first step down the rewarding road of your political future. You'll learn the thrill of hanging posters, the excitement of addressing an assembly of disinterested peers, and the intrigue of spreading damaging rumors about your opponents. With a little planning, a lot of hard work, and these tips on how to fix up the election just right, the class presidency will be yours. So dust off your copy of Machiavelli's *The Prince*, follow these ten easy steps, and you'll soon be your school's most powerful arbiter of cafeteria vending machine placement.

1 Get to know your vote counters. This is not to imply that they should actively work to change the election results, but everyone knows that accidents do happen, so you should work to insure that they happen in your favor.

2 Make sure the student government advisor, who oversees and regulates all election processes, is also the chairman of your campaign.

3 Get access to a list of students who have been sentenced to detention or found guilty of lacking "school spirit." Make sure their names are scrubbed from the eligible voter rolls.

4 Just to be on the safe side, remove all probable class troublemakers—easily identified as African American and Hispanic students—from the eligible-voter rolls. These people don't know how to work a voting machine properly anyway.

5 Enlist school security to monitor the halls, making sure that the people you removed from the voter rolls, or anyone resembling those people in skin tone, don't congregate and attempt to rush the ballot boxes in an attempt to vote.

6 Have the ballots printed in a secret code language that only you and your supporters can understand. Claim that you are "fostering appreciation of other cultures."

7 Demand that ballots in which the voter's intent is in question are all counted as votes for you.

8 Make sure that a close family member of yours, such as a brother, sister, or cousin, is the student who reads your school's morning announcements over the PA. Before the votes are fully counted, have your loyal family member announce your victory.

9 If the election results are so close that a recount is deemed necessary, enlist the biggest, most frightening members of your school's football team to descend on the recount room to protest loudly, screaming and beating their chests until this travesty of democracy is stopped.

10 If you still don't gather enough votes to win—and we'll be quite surprised if you don't after using all these handy tips—take it all the way to the Parent-Teacher Association. Make sure that the PTA is stacked with your parents, your parents' friends, and members appointed by your parents. These people can be counted on to decide the true winner.

Now, Mr. President, your real work begins! Start with cutting funds for school lunches and effeminate extracurricular activities, then funnel those profits into your private coffers. You can use that money to fund special projects like the establishment of an extra-legal detention room, where traitorous students who oppose your "election" can be sent without appeal. Or, you can shell out tons of money to your friends for nonexistent services to your school. For example, instead of using class money to build a big float for Homecoming, tell your buddies to form a "Private Float Committee." You can then pay your friends $5,000 to drive their pick-up truck in the parade and call it the class float, plus they can charge the school $50 per gallon of gasoline used. Hey, the sky's the limit! Whatever you say goes, Mr. President!

MAKING A DIFFERENCE: SPEED UP YOUR TAXES

Here's a news flash—no one likes doing their taxes. Between the piles of forms, the impenetrable tax codes, and the long wait for refunds, it's enough to drive you crazy. Now here's the good news! We're privatizing the inefficient IRS. It's time to take those buttoned-down bureaucrats out of their taxpayer-supplied ergonomic chairs and toss them out on the street! Besides, ever since we kicked off our unending Global War on Terror, your taxes don't pay for social services much anymore. Instead, your money is used to stamp out the fires of terror wherever we think we see smoke. Who helps the firemen, or in this case, the military-industrial complex? Halliburton! So why not skip the middleman and put your tax dollars right where they're going in the first place? Now you can give directly to the HRS—the Halliburton Revenue Service—and they will put the money where it's most needed. It's just another way the Bush administration is putting the American taxpayer right where it wants them—and one more example of how we're *making a difference.*

Notwithstanding a terrorist cell known as the Dixie Chicks, you'd think that Texans would be more than proud to have their former governor George W. Bush occupying the White House. You'd think they would realize that the GOP had their best interests in mind when they redistricted the state of Texas to better reflect the desires of white voters. But a certain group of yellow-bellied, brown-skinned Democrats from the Texas State Legislature turned tail and ran for Oklahoma the moment it was time to vote on erasing their say in government. They tried to hide like scared little school-girls in a Holiday Inn until the voting time was past. Looks like everything is bigger in Texas—even traitors. Shoot, if it had been Democrats making a stand at the Alamo, that whole state would be speaking Spanish right now!

★ OUR KILL COUNT IS HIGH

One of the great successes of George W. Bush's stewardship over the state of Texas was the fact that he presided over 152 state-sponsored executions in only six years. No other governor can even come close to that kill count. Despite the presence of conflicting DNA data, docu-mented prosecutorial misconduct, and the fact that a number of those executed were retarded adults who still believed in Santa Claus, the Texecutioner still found a way to send all those evildoers to the pits of hell. As Presidential Appointee, George W. Bush is bringing that same vision to the Oval Office. Our brave leader now has the power and authority to elim-inate all the evildoers in the entire world! Since he first occupied the White House, Bush has repealed executive orders that outlawed the assassination of foreign leaders. He's ordered our military to kill tens of thousands of people in Iraq and

Afghanistan. He has smashed the pathetic governments of these countries, throwing them into chaos, with plans for plenty more in the pipeline. If there was an electric chair large enough to put all of the world's sinners in it, you'd better believe that our Presidential Appointee would strap them in there.

★ THE SPACE WHITE HOUSE

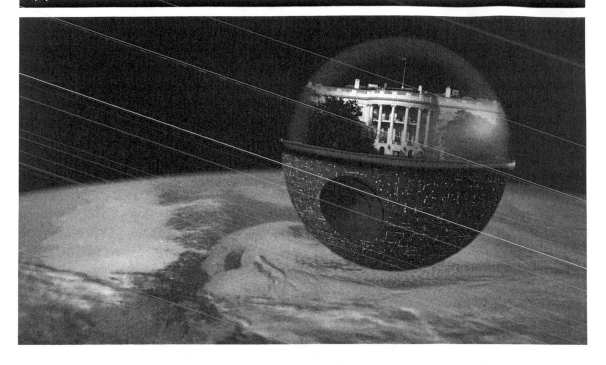

The Presidential Appointee is just like you and me, only more so. He has a lot of stress, and he needs to unwind. Sometimes you just need to get away from all the nonsense and phonies in Washington, D.C. During his first eight months in office, George W. Bush spent a long, leisurely month on his Texas ranch, or what we like to call the Western White House. Then along came September 11, and all that leisure time you get when you're the Presidential Appointee evaporated. Suddenly, the Western White House wasn't far enough away. How's a man supposed to relax with people calling him all the time and the liberal media hounding him about where Iraq's weapons of mass destruction are? That's why we've begun construction of a White House in space. This Space White House will have all the amenities of the one on Earth, only with more robots and lasers. This impregnable executive headquarters/orbital weapons platform will afford the Presidential Appointee, as well as Dick Cheney, the peace of mind they need to make the complicated decisions that affect us all. This is why we are striving to put a base on the moon, a man on Mars, and a White House in high Earth orbit. Where better to look down on it all, put things in perspective, and ponder the Grand Architect of the Universe's great plan for these United States?

Support Our
TROOPS

Welcoming Remarks by
Secretary of War
Donald H. Rumsfeld

You know, I've been doing this an awfully long time, some say way too long, and I think I've got the military running about as smoothly as it's going to run right about now. Griping and complaining, you know, outsiders and professional worrywarts, they don't really register with me. Still, it would be nice every now and then for our people in uniform to get some encouragement from the people at home. You can take an army only so far on its stomach—then you have to give them something for the heart, and then let them stand up for a while. Stretch their legs and give the stomach a rest. It gets pretty rough down there. I know; I've seen some of the rashes and abrasions.

Of course, when your stomach is a gaping hole spilling out bloody guts, it's not hard to reach up an root around and find the heart, but I really think that dealing with this subject metaphorically is much more suitable than talking about it in realistic terms, as I'm doing right now.

Really, what we're talking about here is not supporting *the troops,* because we're looking out for them pretty darn well, but rather supporting *the military* as a whole, and the commander in chief, and yours truly. The public supports us; we support the troops. It's nice to talk about the public supporting the troops, but really, *the public?* They're not going anywhere. They're not the ones going bravely into battle to fight and die, bringing freedom to every nook and hidey-hole bunker, whatever you want to call it, in the Middle East. I'd love to see the public board a transport plane to Baghdad. We'd blow the whole military budget just on airsick bags.

I've seen a whole lot of military budgets come and go, and they all have one thing in common: they are all, bar none, unimaginably large and full of money. And I've watched them balloon, explode really, into these giant, behemoth weapons programs that boggle the mind. I, for one, don't even try to fathom where all the money goes. I don't really want to know. You don't really want to know. So I don't think anyone in his right mind would argue that we're not supporting our fine soldiers. We pay them, we feed them, we clothe them. We do everything short of burp them, bathe them, powder and diaper them, and I swear I've met some generals for whom we do even that!

> ## "You get more with a kind word and a gun than with a kind word alone"
>
> —Al Capone

I've visited our troops overseas and I haven't seen anything but the best and latest equipment. I grew up in Chicago, and, like Al Capone said, "You get more with a kind word and a gun than with a kind word alone." We've got the firepower, but some in the press write about unsanitary conditions in the mess halls and the hospitals—not Iraqi hospitals, mind you, but our own!—and the public assumes it's true. Well, let me tell you, Dick Cheney would not stand it for a minute to have his friends at Halliburton, who run things for us in Baghdad and elsewhere, give anything but the best to our troops. I've visited those facilities, and there weren't any puddles of blood or feces on the floor, at least when I showed up. As far as cutting veterans' benefits, hey, we have an economy to run, as well as a war. Our military personnel know that sacrifice is part of service, and so do private citizens, which is what our soldiers become once they've been discharged and they take off their uniforms. Besides, it's Congress that controls these things. Who knows what *they're* up to? I don't ask them, and they don't ask me.

The strength of the American system depends on an overfunded, unaccountable military, ready to serve at the whim of the commander in chief. End of story. The job of every citizen is to salute us, and provide a stiff backbone to shore up any weakness that may exist in the reasoning behind, or the intelligence behind, or the logistical preparations for this war or that war or what have you. So far, I'm pretty darn satisfied with the way things are going. I want to congratulate not only our brave soldiers, but every loyal American, for suppressing the natural urge to question military policies that seem completely insane to the layman, like when I went to Baghdad in '83 to glad-hand Saddam, then we turn around and blast him all to hell. You're right; it makes no sense. For me it does, but for you, no. My heartfelt thanks go out to all Americans for ignoring all the inconsistencies, blunders, and criminal activities that have cost us so many lives, and so much of our precious national treasure.

May God bless our men and girls in uniform, bless the United States of America, and smite our enemies and rivals.

★ MAKING WAR EASIER

Everyone knows that our great nation is unsurpassed at building weapons that are so devastating our enemies think they're fighting Martians. But did you know that old-fashioned American ingenuity is bringing people together, as well as killing them? The Babylon Project from the Defense Advanced Research Projects Agency (DARPA) has developed an amazing one-way language translation device that is currently being used by our troops in Iraq. Our soldiers can speak English phrases into the electronic device, which recognizes the phrase and then emits the Arabic translation through helmet-mounted loudspeakers.

Currently the device has a vocabulary of only fifty preset phrases, but that's more than enough for our soldiers to tell Iraqis what they should do. Some of the phrases include:

💥 *"DROP THE WEAPON!"*

💥 *"FACE DOWN AND SPREAD 'EM!"*

💥 *"WHERE IS THE OIL REFINERY?!?"*

💥 *"PULL DOWN THE STATUE!"*

💥 *"TAKE THE ANCIENT SUMERIAN VASE; I DON'T CARE!"*

💥 *"WHERE CAN I PURCHASE PORNOGRAPHY?"*

💥 *"STOP ASKING FOR DIRECT ELECTIONS!"*

💥 *"SHI'ITES, RETURN TO YOUR HOMES!"*

💥 *"YOU'RE FIRED!"*

💥 *"WHERE DO YOUR DAUGHTERS UNDRESS?"*

And, perhaps the most touching phrase of them all:

💥 *"MY NAME IS GI JOE. DO YOU LIKE THE DEMOCRACY I'VE BROUGHT YOU?"*

Business is gushing forward on the new oil pipeline being built across Afghanistan by giant petroleum companies. Now that's a victory you should celebrate! Aren't you happy for us? This pipeline will transport the massive oil reserves of the Caspian Sea region, which are worth trillions of dollars to a few lucky people, through Afghanistan to the booming markets of Pakistan, India, and China to the east. When John J. Maresca, vice president of international relations for Unocal, told the United States back in 1998 that the government of Afghanistan would have to be replaced in order for Unocal's business to proceed, we heard his call to free the pipeline. Now, with former Unocal advisor Zalmay Khalilzad the new U.S. ambassador to Afghanistan, and former Unocal hireling Hamid Karzai the new president of Afghanistan, the pipeline is once again

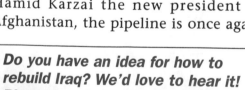

free to roam across Afghanistan. We can all be proud of our brave troops for installing this new Afghani government that is so friendly to petrochemical corporate concerns! Now Unocal says they're not interested, so who else wants in?

Our military never did get around to capturing Osama bin Laden in Afghanistan. That must have slipped our mind. And it looks like we forgot to clean up those Taliban guys, as they're busily regrouping across the country. Oh, fifteen of the nineteen 9/11 hijackers were supposed to be from Saudi Arabia, and not one of them was from Afghanistan? Looks like we bombed the wrong country. Whoops, opium production soared over there, too. Didn't see that one coming. Gosh, we even forgot to put any humanitarian money for starving, war-ravaged Afghanistan in our initial 2003 budget! I guess when George W. Bush said that we would never turn our back on Afghanistan, what he actually meant was "We'll bomb the hell out of you and then forget you even exist."

Finally, although oil pipelines can proudly go forth across Afghanistan, women outside the capital of Kabul should not proudly go forth across Afghanistan, unless they enjoy being brutally raped and having acid thrown in their faces.

But how about that new pipeline! Wow! Thank you, troops, for making our dream of what Afghanistan could become a reality! And thanks to the American people for actually believing in all that other stuff we told you we were going to do!

★ MEET OUR WEAPONS

We want you, the common taxpayer, to feel good about supporting the troops! Since all of you civilians are footing the bill for our war budget, we thought we should make sure that you're pretty darn impressed with our technological accomplishments. Below, you'll meet just some of the incredible weapons of the U.S. armed forces. This is what 53 percent of your tax money pays for!

Depleted-Uranium Ammunition

Depleted uranium (DU) is a waste product of nucular power plants. Instead of just dumping all that radioactive waste in the ocean, nucular power companies discovered they could sell this incredibly dense and heavy material to the U.S. military to use as ammunition. These shrewd businessmen took toxic trash, made taxpayer-supplied cash, and now we use it to zap humans into piles of ash.

Back in the 1991 Gulf War, we referred to DU ammunition as the "silver bullet" because it was so effective at killing our werewolf-like Iraqi enemies. A few years later, the DU ammunition created more hairy, grotesque, misshapen little monsters. You see, these magical bullets keep on killing long after they've been fired! DU shells and bullets ignite upon impact, vaporizing the uranium into tiny particles of radioactive dust. This radioactive cloud becomes widely dispersed. Once inhaled or swallowed, the uranium particles lodge in the body

and emit radiation forever. We've turned Iraq, Afghanistan, and Yugoslavia into contaminated war zones that will remain radioactive for the next 4.5 billion years! The radiation gets into the soil, the water supply, the food chain, and just goes to work. Astronomical cancer rates, unbelievably hideous birth defects, and premature death are just some of the benefits of using DU ammunition on defenseless enemy populations. However, this radia-

MEET OUR TROOPS!

We know that all of you are looking forward to a terrorist Red Alert as much as we are. Do you know what happens when we go to Red Alert? We get to go on a camping trip! Well, you get to go camping. We'll be up there in the guard towers, looking down at all the fun you'll be having. Civil disobedience will not be tolerated.

In preparation for the forced relocation of citizens into concentrated camps under armed guard, the U.S. military has been holding practice drills for years in urban areas. If you really want to support our troops, why not volunteer to be a civilian role-player for one of these martial law simulations? Beg for your constitutional rights! Kick and scream! Struggle against your plastic wrist restraints as Marines herd you into the relocation camps! We're always looking for animated, theatrical people who can make these urban warfare simulations feel real for our soldiers. These drama queens will be the first to go into the camps anyway.

tion does not affect Freedom™-loving American troops, only evildoers. The 300,000 Persian Gulf War veterans who have now developed incapacitating illnesses are all fakers.

The B-2 Stealth Bomber

 Two billion dollars go into each one of these dark, glittering gems of Nazi/extraterrestrial/American know-how. The B-2 is a low-observable, long-range heavy bomber capable of penetrating sophisticated air-defense shields. To avoid radar, the Stealth bomber has no true right angles that radar can track. The plane's exterior is layered with radar-absorbing material that also acts as a light refractor, making the aircraft difficult to see when in flight even by the naked eye. The engines also have special exhaust ports to lower heat emissions, so even infrared sensors cannot detect the aircraft. A squadron of B-2 Stealth bomber pilots can fly off right after breakfast from their airbase in Missouri, drop bombs on Central Asia, and be back in time for lunch. All of this dazzling technology ensures that the schools, Red Cross buildings, and wedding parties of the enemy will never know what hit them!

Mark-77 Firebombs

Back in the good old days of the Vietnam War, these weapons were known as "napalm." If you're a big hippie, you might remember the photo of the naked Vietnamese girl running away from her bombed village, her clothes and skin burned away by napalm. Well, these new Mark-77 firebombs can

do a whole lot more than burn the skin off small children! We're talking about total vaporization of dug-in troops and light vehicles. "The generals love napalm," said Colonel Randolph Alles, a Marine commander who used Mark-77 firebombs during Operation Iraqi Freedom™. "It has a big psychological effect."

A 1980 United Nations convention banned the use of napalm against civilian targets. We didn't sign that treaty, because we don't use napalm anymore— just Mark-77 firebombs. See, napalm is a gooey mixture of gasoline and polystyrene that sticks to human skin as it burns. Our new and improved Mark-77 firebombs are filled with a mixture of *kerosene* and *polystyrene-like gel*. Mark-77 firebombs are like, totally good for the environment!

Cluster Bombs

 These weapons are made up of over 200 individual bomblets, about the size of a can of Pepsi, which disperse upon impact to fill an area the size of two football fields with explosive shrapnel. However, some of these bomblets fail to explode, leaving behind a little surprise for anyone walking, toddling, or crawling through the neighborhood later on. Yes, these little babies kill a lot of little babies, which might be one reason why cluster bombs have been banned by more than 100 nations in a treaty the United States has refused to sign. Hey, just because some kid doesn't know the difference between Rockeye CBU-99 submunitions and lollipops doesn't mean we shouldn't drop them. Besides, those little cluster bomblets scattered around the battlefield keep U.S. troops on their toes as well. All of us, whether we're soldiers at the front or citizens in the homeland, must be eternally vigilant.

Mini-Nukes

Those old H-bombs of ours are just too clunky, and they sure make a big mess. We need small, sleek mini-nukes for this stylish new age of terror. Think of them as the i-Pods of Armageddon. These weapons are only half as powerful as the atomic bomb we dropped on Hiroshima. So instead of 66,000 people dead and 69,000 injured instantly, these mini-nukes only give you 33,000 dead and 34,500 injured instantly. We're interested in using small nucular bombs known as "earth penetrators," which can destroy underground enemy shelters holding chemical and biological weapons—the greatest security threats of the new century. What's the best new way to take on these threats? With a nucular explosion that will suck up the chemical and biological agents and disperse them across a wide area, mixed in with plenty of good old-fashioned radiation, of course.

Another exciting mini-nuke is the portable nucular weapon, also known as the "suitcase nuke." We're planning on buying lots and lots of these. Ideally, all members of George W. Bush's cabinet would have their own personal suitcase nuke they could carry with them at all times, for maximum nucular readiness. Don't worry, they're all very responsible people. We wouldn't want any of these portable nukes falling into the hands of terrorists, now, would we?

The wonderful thing that all of these weapons have in common is that our brave troops can use them at great range, immune to any counterattack from the inferior weapons of the enemy. We don't even have to look at the filthy subhumans we're vaporizing, much less grapple with them hand to hand!

COMPASSIONATE CONQUEST

We're addressing the problem of civilians being shot at U.S. checkpoints in Iraq with a new program to avoid unnecessary deaths. For their own safety, all Iraqi civilians now must crawl on their hands and knees at all times while outside of their homes. In crawling mode, they will be moving slowly enough to avoid any impression of being a threat, and it will be clear that they are not carrying any weapons if both of their hands are on the ground. There will be penalties if Iraqis do not follow this crawling code of behavior. If any uppity Iraqis such as respected Shiite clerics refuse to crawl on their hands and knees and attempt to stand up, they are handcuffed, hooded, and slapped. This vigorous slapping campaign inspires a healthy respect for our overwhelming force, keeping the Iraqi masses on their knees for the foreseeable future.

We can all be proud of our military and their incredible success in Operation Iraqi Freedom™. Never before has an army so completely dominated its opponents, even more so than when Germany invaded Poland at the beginning of World War II. Our long-standing perseverance and tenacity in facing the Iraqi threat is the reason for our total victory.

Our ingenious multistep war began in 1991, when we decimated the Iraqi army in less than a hundred hours. After the war, Iraq went from relative affluence to massive poverty. Its GDP fell by two-thirds in 1991, due to an 85 percent decline in oil production and the devastation of the industrial and service sectors of the economy. Then, we clamped down with twelve years of sanctions on Iraq, an effective method of "wearing down" the enemy. Blockading food, medical supplies, hospital equipment, and everything else killed more than a million Iraqi civilians during the 1990s, 600,000 of whom were children. We'd like to think that all of these Iraqi children dying every day weakened our enemy's morale just a wee bit! The lack of a national economy, electrical power, water and sanitation service, health care, medicine, and food didn't hurt either. Starving the Iraqis out for twelve years really gave our soldiers an extra edge, which they used to slice right through the Iraqi lines in March 2003.

Denis Halliday, a former UN Assistant Secretary-General, once said of our Iraq sanctions, "There can be no justification for the death and malnutrition for which sanctions are responsible. We are in the process of destroying an entire society. It is as simple and terrifying as that...." He then resigned after thirty-four years of service to protest the sanctions. Don't let the door hit you on the ass on your way out, Denis! If you can't see the obvious benefits of sanctions for our goals in Iraq, we'll give you a special pair of goggles that let you see the world in Rumsfeld-Vision™.

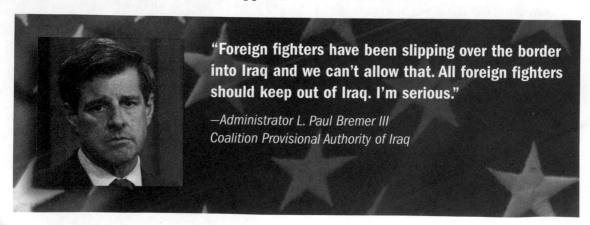

"Foreign fighters have been slipping over the border into Iraq and we can't allow that. All foreign fighters should keep out of Iraq. I'm serious."

—Administrator L. Paul Bremer III
Coalition Provisional Authority of Iraq

★ QUOTE QUIZ

"We are aggressively striking the terrorists in Iraq, defeating them there so we will not have to face them in our own country."

—Presidential Appointee George W. Bush, November 3, 2003

STUDY QUESTIONS

Reread and analyze this quote by our leader. Break the sentence down into components and consider the meaning of each point that George W. Bush makes:

1 Are we still aggressively striking, or rather, being struck against aggressively? Or are we just hiding behind our fortifications and trying not to get killed?

2 Are U.S. soldiers still on the offensive, or are they getting ambushed with roadside bombs while trying to drive between the airport, the gas station, and the oil well?

3 Are these terrorists that we're fighting, or a local, homegrown Iraqi resistance?

4 Are these the same guys who blew up the World Trade Center?

5 Will our troops in Iraq somehow defeat and contain all the would-be terrorists in the world?

6 With our borders still wide open, couldn't anyone still infiltrate our shores?

7 The 9/11 terrorists supposedly lived in the United States for years; couldn't there still be some others left, waiting to kill us?

8 In addition, if we're aggressively striking the home of the terrorists, doesn't that only add to their motivation to commit terrorism against us?

ANSWERS

1 STRIKING

2 OFFENSIVE

3 YES, AND YES, THAT TOO

4 YEAH, SORT OF

5 YOU BET

6 JUST TRY IT

7 OF COURSE—THOUSANDS

8 THEY CAN'T BE TERRORISTS IF THEY'RE DEAD

Match up each question with the correct answer. Study these answers carefully. Then try it again. Don't just *read* the quote, *believe* in it! If you repeat George W. Bush's words enough times in your head, everything will make perfect sense.

Do you have an idea for how to rebuild Iraq? We'd still love to hear it! Seriously, send us your suggestions!

Ideas for Iraq
33 Patriot Avenue
Washington, D.C. 91101

Hey, there, Mom and Dad! Haven't heard from your kid in Iraq for awhile? Here's a beautiful form letter from your son or daughter serving in Operation Iraqi Freedom™! Most of our troops in Iraq are too busy shooting at cars full of Iraqi civilians who fail to stop at checkpoints to put pen to paper, so we compiled this letter for them and their families. Using the latest in group-averaging software and public relations emotional profiling, we composed a letter that will warm the patriotic cockles of your heart. Just circle the appropriate relationships, fill in the blanks, and enjoy:

GET TOUGH

Unfortunately, the number of accidental deaths and suicides among our troops in Iraq is rising along with our combat casualties. Nobody likes to die, but our war fighters and their families can take comfort in our leaders' "get tough" attitude. When George W. Bush told the cowardly Iraqis who are shooting at our soldiers to "bring it on," he also meant the same thing to weapons misfiring, unexploded ordnance exploding, sandstorms that make our Humvees flip over into ditches, and devastating psychological problems. We won't be intimidated by bad luck or meteorological noncooperation with our mission, and certainly not by some infantry grunt feeling "bummed out" about his role in Operation Iraqi Freedom™. So keep your chins up, widows!

Hi Mom and/or Pop and/or Sis and/or Bro!

It's your old son/daughter/brother/sister _____! How are things back in _____? Things are going great here in Iraq! What a beautiful place. Only two guys in my unit were killed today. Oh, and one guy couldn't take it anymore and blew his own head off. Oh yeah, and three other guys lost a total of two arms, a leg, and an eyeball. But you should see all the improvements that are happening over here! Today I saw two Iraqi kids selling sodas from the side of the road to thirsty drivers. Watching them dart in and out of the traffic through the clouds of diesel fumes, wearing no shoes, to sell sodas all day and night for a couple of pennies, really is an encouraging sign that small businesses and the entrepreneurial spirit are taking off here! Oh, I guess we have to go pick up the pieces of a helicopter and its squad now, so I love you and say hi to _____ for me and GO OPERATION IRAQI FREEDOM™!

Your patriotic servant to his country, Private _____

★ BOOSTING YOUR MORALE

All across Baghdad, American soldiers have put up billboards that read "Baghdad Is Getting Better" above a scenic view of the Tigris River and arching palm trees. Here is a wallet-sized card with the same image that is being used to cheer on our troops and the Iraqi people. Clip it out and save it in your wallet. Whenever you hear about one more American soldier being killed in Iraq, pull out this card and take a good look at it to keep your Freedom™-loving spirits high! (Consider having the card laminated, as daily use of the card may cause it to crumple and tear.)

★ TEAM SPIRIT

The liberal media loves to talk about how George W. Bush skipped out of Vietnam and got assigned to the Texas Air National Guard ahead of hundreds of other guys. They snicker at how Dick Cheney had "other priorities" than military service during Vietnam, and at many other Republican "chicken hawks" who skipped out of military service. Are you questioning our leaders, liberal media? Here's a question for you—have you pansies ever watched the all-American game of football?

As in football, some individuals are suited for the hard work of grinding out yardage, hitting each other as hard as they can without shattering their kneecaps. Some people are strong and bright enough to lead their team as quarterback on the field. Other individuals have the intellect and sense to stay on the sidelines and coach their team on what to do. Above them you have the owners, sitting high above the fray, watching from their luxurious skyboxes, following their investments carefully. Somewhere above them all, perhaps in a passing blimp, fly men like Dick Cheney, one of the grand architects of the universe, watching all games unfold beneath him. It would be a shame to waste such powerful minds as this on getting a few measly yards when they could be plotting the complete destruction of the opposing team and their entire hometown, using neutron bombs so that their resources remain intact for us to capture.

Get on the winning team, everybody. Stop questioning our coaching. Our leaders may not have personal experience in military conflict, but they play like hawks, not chickens, and they know how to lead this team to win the Super Bowl every year.

PRIVATE JAMES DOBSON
U.S. ARMY
AGE: 23
BORN: MARCH 10, 1980
DIED: SEPTEMBER 25, 2003
HEIGHT: 6'1"
WEIGHT: 189 LBS

James Dobson is one of our fallen heroes of Operation Iraqi Freedom™. While patrolling the streets of Baghdad, Private Dobson's Humvee was struck by an improvised explosive device that the enemy had hidden in the body of a dead goat on the side of the road. Dobson was severely wounded, losing three limbs and an eye, but was evacuated alive to U.S. Army medical facilities. After extensive surgeries, Dobson recovered and slowly gathered strength for two months, until he suddenly developed an unusual goat-borne virus, became ill, and died. His family remembers James as a beautiful son, a loving big brother, and an American hero.

PUBLIC NOTICE: While in the care of U.S. Army medical facilities, Private James Dobson incurred charges totaling $741.60 for his food expenses. Since Dobson passed away before the law on charging wounded soldiers for their hospital food was changed, his family is now responsible for this bill. The U.S. government is currently looking for his parents, Curtis and Ruth Dobson, age 54 and 51, or his fiancée, Alicia Walker, age 22, who are all believed to reside in the Chicago, Illinois, area. If you have any knowledge of the whereabouts of these people, please contact the Military Bill Collection Service at 1-800-USA-BILL.

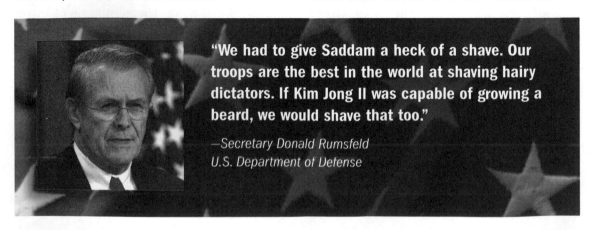

"We had to give Saddam a heck of a shave. Our troops are the best in the world at shaving hairy dictators. If Kim Jong Il was capable of growing a beard, we would shave that too."

—Secretary Donald Rumsfeld
U.S. Department of Defense

★ HIDING OUR DEAD

Although the basic realities of war have never changed, the U.S. military has recently made incredible strides in finding more sanitized ways to phrase those realities. During the Vietnam War, soldiers that were killed in action were placed in "body bags." Sounds icky, doesn't it? Like taking out the garbage. In the first Gulf War, that term was replaced with the more polite-sounding "human remains pouches." But we still weren't satisfied. Our new and improved name for where we stick the fallen heroes of Operation Iraqi Freedom? *"Transfer tubes."* Doesn't that sound nice? So clean and tidy. A tightly sealed transfer tube ensures that all of those dirty dead soldier parts stay inside, unlike a drippy bag or pouch that could leak blood and brains all over the floor.

In fact, the new transfer tubes will soon be incorporated into a worldwide, pneumatic tube–powered corpse delivery system. This network of pressurized subterranean tubes, constructed by Halliburton, will whoosh transfer tubes filled with dead soldiers from our various theaters of conflict overseas directly to Dover Air Force Base in Delaware every day. The underground system will be hidden from any prying news cameras, and President Bush will have a great new excuse to not attend the homecomings of any dead soldiers—he might get hit by a transfer tube shooting out of a pneumatic corpse-pipe at 600 mph!

Although no one will see these dead young Americans, the public will be able to view this exciting new human-remains transfer technology in the Tube of the

U.S. ARMY

Unknown Soldier at Arlington National Cemetery, presented by Pepsi™. Don't worry, there won't be any mutilated eighteen-year-old bodies inside the tube! Citizens will see a clean, shiny, spotless transfer tube—the perfect showcase for our clever military, without all the mess.

OUR PLAN IN IRAQ

We have already turned over control of parts of Iraq to other members of our mighty Coalition of the Willing. And hopefully, other countries will soon find the will to free Iraq. For example, the Turkish Army has historically been a very powerful force for human rights, democracy, and peace in the world, so we would love to see them in Iraq. Unfortunately that hasn't happened yet, but perhaps after the fortuitous terror bombings in Turkey, the Turkish government will see the wisdom of sending occupying troops into a neighboring country full of people who hate them. The Turkish Army also has intimate knowledge of Iraq, as they conducted their own, earlier version of Operation Iraqi Freedom™, which lasted from the year 1534 to 1918. Perhaps the U.S. Army could even learn a thing or two from the Turks.

Get Ready for a Massive Burst of Comfort!

Are you tossing and turning from all the negative headlines coming out of Iraq? Then it's time that you snuggled up to the Massive Ordnance Air Burst Pillow (MOAB-P). America's biggest bomb is now available as a luxurious body pillow for your sleeping comfort. Instead of high explosives, this pillowy replica is packed with high-density visco-elastic foam. Give it a hug—it hugs you right back! MOAB-P allows war-weary Americans to stretch and cradle their entire body in weapons-grade comfort. And for the kids, don't forget Tickle Me MOAB. This adorable plush version of our most devastating nonnucular air-dropped weapon doesn't explode when tickled—it actually giggles, delighting the children with its merriment! Look at your loved ones as they snuggle into bed with their MOAB-P or Tickle Me MOAB. Doesn't it give you a warm feeling knowing that we can drop the biggest conventional bomb ever made in human history on whosoever would dare to harm a hair on their precious little heads? Aren't you glad that *your* MOAB pillow is waiting for you in *your* bed? Buy your MOAB pillow today and enjoy the sleep of the righteous!

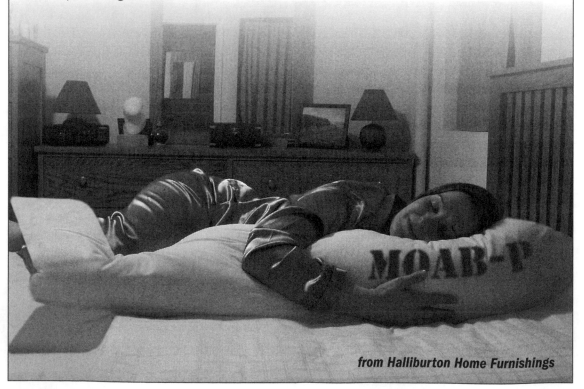

from Halliburton Home Furnishings

★ PROFITING FROM WAR

For most people, war means death, destruction, and loss. It takes a special kind of person to make war into a profitable business that enriches him and his family. America is blessed to have several of these special people as our leaders, who can always find the silver lining in the dark clouds of war. George H.W. Bush, his loyal son George W. Bush, Uncle Dick Cheney, and their friends in the bin Laden clan love making war into a fun family activity. While the rest of us might sit down with our families to play Monopoly™, these shrewd men sit down to play war—except the money is real, and instead of plunking down little green plastic houses, they plunk down smart bombs on Oriental Avenue.

The Carlyle Group is an international firm that makes billions of dollars investing in weapons manufacturers that equip the U.S. armed forces. Former President George H.W. Bush is their senior advisor. Back on September 11, 2001, the annual investor conference of the Carlyle Group was held at the Ritz-Carlton Hotel in Washington, D.C. Some of the Carlyle staff in attendance were former U.S. Secretary

of Defense Frank Carlucci, former Secretary of State James Baker III, and members of the bin Laden family such as Shafig bin Laden, Osama's brother. George H.W. Bush had been at the conference the day before. As these businessmen watched the World Trade Center crumble and the Pentagon burn, they all knew that everything had changed for their profit projections. The United States was going to be buying a lot more Carlyle-supplied weapons from then on. George W. Bush leapt into action and gave his father's Carlyle Group even more lucrative weapons contracts, ensuring that he will inherit billions from the Global War on Terror

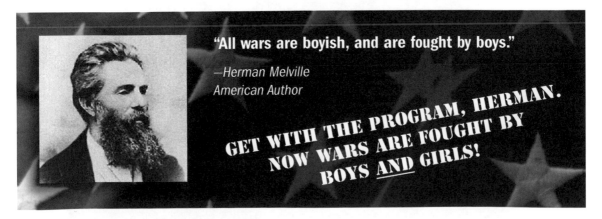

"All wars are boyish, and are fought by boys."

—Herman Melville
American Author

GET WITH THE PROGRAM, HERMAN. NOW WARS ARE FOUGHT BY BOYS AND GIRLS!

and Operation Iraqi Freedom™. The bin Ladens, an ultra-wealthy Saudi family that made their fortune in the construction business, knew that they would win lucrative contracts building a sprawling network of American military bases throughout the Middle East and Central Asia. For the Bush and bin Laden clans, 9/11 was a blessed family event.

Don't forget good old Dick Cheney, the president of vice! This honorary member of the Bush family is making his own fortune from war through the Halliburton corporation. In 1992, as secretary of defense under President George H.W. Bush, Dick Cheney hired Halliburton to conduct a classified study on how Halliburton could provide logistics for U.S. military forces in war zones around the world. When Bill Clinton usurped the presidency that year, Cheney went on to become the CEO of Halliburton. Under Cheney's watch, Halliburton was awarded $2.3 billion in government contracts. When it was time for big Dick to return to the White House in 2000, Halliburton gave him a $20 million retirement package—a grateful "golden handshake" for his stellar leadership. Cheney also continues to receive yearly pension payments from Halliburton of $1 million. Can you guess which company Dick Cheney picked to rebuild Iraq? Halliburton, of course, and they're getting $1.7 billion of your money to do it! Halliburton is also now the exclusive logistics supplier to the U.S. Army and Navy, providing services such as cooking, construction, power generation, and fuel transport, and their exclusive ten-year contract has no cap on costs. That's a good thing, too, because Halliburton is the undisputed global leader in over-charging the federal government and stealing taxpayers' money. They cleverly bilked the U.S. Army $16 million for meals served to troops at one military base in Kuwait in one month alone, claiming to serve 42,000 meals a day when only 14,000 were served. Halliburton also charged the government $2.64 a gallon to import fuel into Iraq when it was available for 96¢, which added up to a cool $61 million bonus. So what if Dick Cheney's company isn't too good at making out correct invoices? They sure are good at making a killing from war.

The human race will always know conflict, destruction, and violent mass death, especially with men like these in charge, but at least Americans can appreciate how the tragedy of war really brings out the gleam in our leaders' eyes. Only an elite few possess this incredibly shameless lust for wealth and total disregard for human life that can turn war into golden opportunities for themselves and their loved ones.

★ CAPTURING SADDAM: THE REAL STORY

Now that major combat in Iraq has ended, we can tell the true story about how Saddam Hussein, the ace of spades himself, was captured. We all know the story of how he was found like a rat in a spider hole. It's the wheres and whys that haven't been told by the liberal media. Until now, we haven't heard the truth about how "we got him." The story that several European newspapers ran about Iraqi Kurdish forces capturing Saddam first, drugging him, dumping him in a hole, and then telling U.S. forces where to pick him up so we could take credit for his capture is a complete fabrication that is so utterly ridiculous you should ignore looking further into it. Here's the *real* story of our heroic capture of the Butcher of Baghdad.

Let's go back to December 2003. The Presidential Appointee was suffering from the sleeplessness that only comes from bearing the huge weight of caring for the people of America. He decided to fly to Camp X-Ray in Guantánamo Bay to see if he could channel his insomniac

energy into squeezing some information from the prisoners held there.

When he arrived, he took his customary tour of the holding pens. One of the prisoners was acting particularly cagey. George W. Bush pointed him out to the commanding officer and requested a private interview with this terrorist.

"But Mr. Presidential Appointee," the commanding office said, "we've interrogated him at least ten times, and he never tells us anything of value."

A Message to Our Troops from George W. Bush

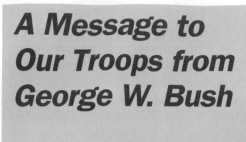

"Leave him to me," said the commander in chief. As soon as the interview room door clicked shut behind him, the prisoner began to shake.

"I have nothing to say," he said, unable to look the Presidential Appointee in the eye.

"No?" said Bush, fixing him with a steely-eyed gaze. "We'll see about that."

As a humane man, George W. Bush was not about to lay a hand upon him. He merely called upon his knowledge of anatomy, as well as his Yale University secret fraternity skills with a red-hot coat hanger, and within a few minutes, the Presidential Appointee had everything he needed to know.

"Gentlemen, I need the next flight to Iraq!" he announced upon leaving the smoke-filled cell. Within minutes, Bush was at the controls of a B-2 Stealth bomber, soaring toward his heroic destiny.

As he flew over Iraq, it became apparent that there was no landing strip close to his secret destination. Fortunately, George W. Bush's valorous service in the Texas Air National Guard had prepared him for such an eventuality. He strapped on a parachute and jumped from the plane into the cool Baghdad night, uncaring of the $2 billion Stealth bomber that went on to crash somewhere.

When Bush landed, right on target, everything was quiet. His presence was a complete surprise, just as he had planned. However, there was no sign of his prey. It didn't make sense. Bush was right where the prisoner said Saddam would be found, but after an hour spent overturning every rock in the area, he still couldn't locate the hiding spot that concealed the sand Hitler.

He was about to call it quits when he

saw a bit of carpeting that looked out of place. When he lifted up the carpeting, he found a Styrofoam block that seemed to be plugging a hole. He lifted it up, unleashing a smell that could only be described as "evil." Holding his breath, he stealthily dropped down into the hole.

Right there in front of him was the Butcher of Baghdad himself—and he wasn't alone. Saddam had a pistol, and the business end was pointed right at the Presidential Appointee.

"So, we meet at last," Saddam snarled. "I have waited for this moment for a long, long time."

"As have I," said Bush. "It's about time you paid for your crimes against humanity." With that, Saddam pulled the trigger twice, hitting Bush squarely in the chest.

"And so dies the great leader of the free world," Saddam said, turning his back. "Mwa ha ha ha ha ha!"

"Not so fast," said the Presidential Appointee, pulling from his breast pocket the thickly folded copy of the U.S. Constitution he always carries. The very Constitution George W. Bush had sworn to uphold had saved his life. "Looks like this is the end of the road, you evil hairball."

"Blast you!" Saddam screamed. "You shall pay for your treachery!" The cowardly dictator then fled down the corridors of his secret subterranean command center, our brave leader hot on his trail.

When the Presidential Appointee caught up to Saddam in a cavernous laboratory, he stopped dead in his tracks. Private Jessica Lynch was there, cruelly tied to a huge SCUD missile loaded with tons of nerve gas, anthrax, and botulinum toxin. She struggled weakly against her bonds. The evil one, wearing a sinister smile, had his hand on a massive lever. All in all, it looked like Freedom™ was in a great deal of trouble.

"Come closer," Saddam said. "Come closer and you can see the fate of your precious country sealed, once and for all! For this lever will launch a chemical and biological attack against your country the likes of which cannot be imagined! Say good-bye to your beloved, blond Jessica, and say good-bye to America, Mr. Presidential Appointee!"

"Not on my watch!" shouted Bush. He pulled out a Presidential Medal of Valor he was going to present to an inner-city child for learning how to read, right before cutting funds for that reading program, and hurled the medal with all

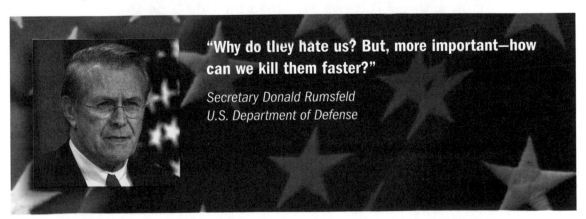

"Why do they hate us? But, more important—how can we kill them faster?"

Secretary Donald Rumsfeld
U.S. Department of Defense

his might. Being a former professional baseball pitcher who once led the Texas Rangers to winning the World Series, Bush was right on target. The medal jammed the lever so that Saddam couldn't enact his deadly plan!

"Curses!" shouted the evil madman. Bush then threw a handful of sand in Saddam's face and subdued the cowardly dictator with little effort, for evil always crumbles before the might of righteousness. He bound Saddam's hands with a monofilament cord he keeps on his person for such occasions and dragged his enemy up into the light of dawn. The sun was just breaking over the horizon, bringing a new day of Freedom™ to Iraq. Bush called in a quick air strike to destroy Saddam's WMD-filled lair, then radioed U.S. troops.

"Gentlemen," the Presidential Appointee said, "I have some garbage for you to pick up. I've wrapped it up all nice and neat for you."

And without a word more, George W. Bush was on his way back to the White House, returning before Laura even knew he was gone. Bush then celebrated Saddam's capture by signing an extension of the USA PATRIOT Act that gave the FBI sweeping new powers of surveillance on all Americans the very same day. We bet you were so excited watching Saddam get checked for head lice that you didn't catch that one!

★ BATTLEFIELD SPACE

Space is the new frontier, across which our space cavalry must ride to achieve full-spectrum dominance. We are hard at work perfecting hypersonic and space-based conventional weapons capable of delivering a worldwide attack within an hour. Our brave soldiernauts will boldly go where no gun has gone before. Did you really think we just wanted to study how potatoes grow in space? There are so many more practical uses for the endless reaches of our cosmos. For example, if the security situation in Iraq ever becomes completely untenable, we have plans to move the entire population of Iraq to the Moon. The Sea of Tranquillity would be renamed the Sea of Security. The laws of the Moon are very different from those of the Earth—much like the Moon is smaller than the Earth, the Moon Constitution will be smaller than the U.S. Constitution. Evil enemies such as China or Amnesty International will also find it very difficult to conduct surveillance on our Moon operations. The dark side of the Moon will bristle with prison camps and weaponry, while the bright side of the Moon will be filled with happy geodesic domes brimming with space-potatoes.

The Moon will be our beachhead from which we can launch our true invasion

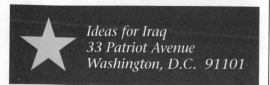

Come on, does anybody have any ideas for how to rebuild Iraq? Please, send us something. Anything! We're dying over here!

Ideas for Iraq
33 Patriot Avenue
Washington, D.C. 91101

forces into space. The only reason that we should fund space exploration is for military purposes. We must seize the ultimate high ground to ensure our unquestioned military superiority. War in space must not be abandoned for utopian visions of a hippie-dippie, multinational, low-gravity, cosmic lovefest of peaceful cooperation and exploration. That's why we're going to Mars, not Venus. Forget about the goddess of love—the United States is interested in seizing the throne of the god of war. If our robotic Mars Rover probes are consumed by the Martian landscape and stop transmitting, we will immediately begin carpet-bombing Mars. We cannot know for sure if our Rovers have been eaten by evil aliens or not, so we must preemptively bomb Mars, just to be on the safe side.

An Army of One

When we say an "Army of One," we really mean it. You're on your own out there, soldier. Don't get caught with your pants down. Your momma won't be around to give you modern ceramic armor plates for your bulletproof vest. If you don't want to wear an obsolete, Vietnam-era flak jacket that will get you killed, bring your own body armor, or have your family send it to you. It can be a nice Christmas present, if you survive that long. Tell Mom and Dad to go visit the Army World store at the mall—run by the U.S. Army, Nike, and Halliburton—where parents can buy equipment for their brave sons and daughters on the front lines. It's between the Gap and the Disney Store. Along with the body armor that actually stops modern ammunition, you'll need all kinds of stuff. Socks, gloves, flashlights, batteries, ChapStick™, suntan lotion, sunglasses, can openers—we don't supply any of that stuff anymore. Remind your parents to pick up a gas mask for you! U.S. corporations sold tons of biological and chemical weapons to Saddam Hussein during the Reagan and Bush I administrations, which were then used on U.S. troops in the Persian Gulf War in 1991. You never know when a situation like that will pop up again.

Unfortunately, times are tight and the federal government just doesn't have enough money for the education budget. Who will come to the rescue of our schools and students? Who else but the U.S. Army! In a planned deployment scheduled for November 2004, after George W. Bush is elected for the first time, 200 of our most cash-strapped schools will be staffed and operated by the U.S. Army. The army has the ability to fight two or more major conflicts in separate global theaters, so teaching little Timmy long division should be a cinch! More schools will follow over the next year; by late 2005, all public schools will be run by disciplined military men. The best part of the plan? No more boring

filmstrips, kids. When the sergeant needs a smoke break, you get to blast away with Tom Clancy's Ghost Recon, the latest first-person shooter video game on the classroom Playstation 2!

★ SPECIAL KIDS—SPECIAL LOVE

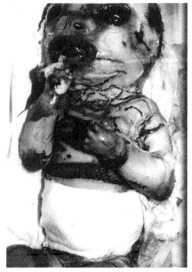

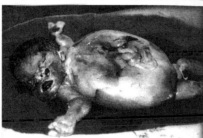
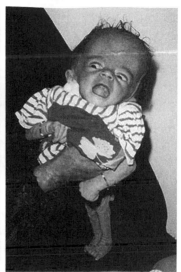

Birth defects in Iraq have increased twelvefold since 1991. This has nothing to do with the U.S. military's extensive use of radioactive depleted-uranium ammunition in Iraq—no, for some unknown reason immediately after the 1991 Gulf War, when we fired 320 tons of DU ammunition on Iraq, all the babies just started looking like they were from outer space. Iraqi midwives have said that they no longer look forward to child-births, because they "don't know what's going to come out." We don't share that losing attitude! These special kids deserve special love, and the U.S. military is prepared to give it to them, even if they look like two-headed bags of jelly.

Pounding Iraq with more radioactive DU ammunition in Operation Iraqi Freedom™ has led to another generation of these very unusual Iraqi children, for some reason. Since 1991, the first question that new Iraqi parents ask of their doctor is no longer "Is it a boy or a girl?" Instead, the parents ask, "Is it normal?" Unlike these terrible Iraqi parents, America will not turn her back on these adorable little mutants. Our kindhearted GIs will gladly toss a Hershey's bar into their outstretched flippers, free of charge, and will even feed the chocolate slowly into the sucking blowhole on top of their grotesquely swollen skulls if they lack prehensile limbs of their own.

AXIS OF EVIL UPDATE

As the situation has progressed, Bush administration officials now agree that North Korea is not exactly "evil," but rather, "mentally disturbed." The United States does not have time for fighting the mentally disturbed, only the evil. Therefore, North Korea is now to be turned out into the streets, where it can wander around mumbling and ask passersby for spare change.

★ THE TOMB OF THE UNDISCLOSED SOLDIERS

Located a few miles north, a few miles south, a few miles east, and a few miles west from Baghdad, the Tomb of the Undisclosed Soldiers is a monument to those courageous North American soldiers who died in the service of a country. Many of these North Americans didn't have U.S. passports, but they did have a dream—making enough money to become U.S. citizens by serving in Operation Iraqi Freedom™. They were among our Coalition of the Paid. They thought they would be picking oranges, but they became soldiers, fought, and got their heads blown off. Now they are fallen heroes, of an unknown and never-to-be-disclosed number. *Vaya con dios, y muchas gracias, compadres*. Eternal Freedom™ shall be your reward.

★ STAY THE COURSE

"There's no telling how many wars it will take to secure Freedom™ in the homeland."

—Presidential Appointee George W. Bush
August 7, 2002

Six hundred American soldiers have been killed in Iraq, at least the ones that we've told you about. Three thousand American soldiers have been injured, many of them with a loss of limbs or vision. Some estimates of Iraqi civilian war dead are as high as 37,000, while others are as low as 4 or 5. A hundred and sixty billion dollars of America's money has been spent. Zero weapons of mass destruction have been found. The average American might be wondering what to make of all these numbers coming out of Iraq. Well, you've read *Peanuts*, the comic strip by Charles Schulz, right? Hoping to find WMDs in Iraq is kind of like Linus waiting for the Great Pumpkin to show up. You've just got to hang in there, and keep believing in your dream, until everyone forgets about the whole thing and you can move on to other stuff. But don't worry, our Global War on Terror isn't all about just waiting around for magical missiles to appear. If President Bush's popularity level ever drops to a certain point that Karl Rove deems to be unacceptable, you will see Osama bin Laden conveniently captured and brought to justice. And when this evildoer is struck by the long blade of our justice, we know that his al-Qaeda followers will say, "Oh, gosh. You got us. We give up now." Just like in Iraq after we smoked Saddam out of his spider hole.

Consider the benefits of "staying the course" in Iraq. America is a more secure country now that Saddam Hussein is gone. Only one or two American soldiers die every day, instead of the millions that would have died if we had allowed Saddam to build up a mighty armada he could have used to invade and conquer our homeland. Terrorists are flooding into Iraq to kill Americans, who are mostly poor and uneducated, instead of coming to the United States to kill a higher class of Americans. With our occupying army humiliating and shooting Iraqis every day, we are raising a whole new generation of terrorists that hate us. But all of this is good news. It means we can take more of your tax money to kill terrorists in Operation Iraqi Freedom™.

Dreams are finally coming true in Iraq, for both George W. Bush and Islamic fundamentalist terror groups. Saddam Hussein persecuted Islamic fundamentalists in Iraq, but now they can pour across the unguarded borders of our new colony from all over the Muslim world to shoot and kill Americans. Their dream is realized. Plus, George W. Bush finally has his wish to shoot and kill as many evildoers as he wants. It's a beautiful win-win situation for everybody.

Troops, we know it hurt when we cut your pay, slashed your pensions, cut funding for your children's schools, and refused to let you leave the military when your tours of duty were up. You've got to stay the course, too, along with the brave warriors of the homeland. We are engaged in a holy war for a cause no less than Freedom™. It is almost distasteful for soldiers to ask for money. This holy war will go on forever. There will be no clear-cut victories. There is no telling where the evildoers may be lurking, so we have to hunt them down and kill them, hunting and killing, always circling, like a jungle cat, sniffing out the drugs and the money and the oil that funds their terrorist activities, and in turn, our anti-terrorist activities. We must continue to develop our world-spanning system of giant military bases in dozens of countries, extending our "footprint" around the globe until our boots are pressing down on the face of every foreigner who dares to oppose our Freedom™. Good old Rummy, Wolfowitzy, and their playmates at the Project for a New American Century said it best when they called for the preemptive elimination of any potential world rivals. You've got to keep on kicking people in the face when you're the king of the mountain—and the rest of you need to stay the course, stay in line, and shut the hell up.

Our Brave
LEADERS

Welcoming Remarks by
Chief Political Advisor to
the Presidential Appointee,
Karl Rove

I first laid eyes on George W. Bush in the lobby of Union Station in Washington, D.C., the day before Thanksgiving, 1973. I still remember what he was wearing: an Air National Guard flight jacket, cowboy boots, and tight blue jeans, complete with one of the back pockets worn in a circle from where he carried his tin of chewing tobacco. He was exuding more charisma than any one individual should be allowed to have. A wink, a "come hither" glance, and he could have had me right there and then.

I suppose I'm just like most patriotic Americans. Painful childhood, broken home, mother committed suicide, man who was thought to be father turned out not to be father when son was nineteen while real father remained missing until located and confronted decades later by son in whom he had absolutely no interest whatsoever. Yes, and like most patriotic Americans, I've always desperately craved the approval of a charismatic father figure, a man of authority and power to whom I could devote all the personal and professional effort of a life firmly grounded in the core family values of bitter rejection and grief. Like most patriotic Americans, I believe in relentless service to ideology, with power—political, professional, personal, and financial power over other, weaker, less emotionally damaged and therefore less deserving individuals—the ultimate and only goal of a superior life. Of course the ends justify the means, but not every person knows the means, or can harness the meanness to implement the means of seizing power. That's where I come in.

The mark of a great leader is the sheer courage to do what he has to do, *what must be done,* no matter what:

Keep lowering taxes for the rich, keep shoveling money into the coffers of corporations, the pockets of friendly dictators, and the gaping maw of the military-industrial complex—despite mathematical proof that this will bankrupt the Treasury for generations, perhaps even forever;

Adopt hypocritical, idiotic, faith-based positions on health, environmental, and social issues, ignoring medical, scientific, and statistical evidence that living beings will suffer agony and early death, families will be torn asunder, and vital social and cultural institutions as well as entire ecosystems will be obliterated—just to appease an intolerant, ignorant, bigoted, extremist wing of one political party whose agenda intention-

ally harms the vast majority of Americans, not to mention people around the world;

Wage unilateral war, justified by outright lies, on nonthreatening (but unpopular), easily targeted, sovereign nations, killing and maiming thousands of American soldiers and innocent children, women, and men, obliterating cultural treasures and urban infrastructures, irreparably rupturing international alliances, overruling the painstakingly hard-won code of international law, jeopardizing the very idea of world peace—all for the sake of personal financial gain hidden behind self-righteous, fake patriotism shamelessly flaunted in order to silence opposition, undermine civil liberties, and hustle enough votes to justify another illegal takeover of our government;

And, perhaps most important, the mark of a great leader is his skill in surrounding himself with other great leaders: men of courage like myself, our vice presidential appointee, our attorney general, our secretary of defense, and a girl like cute little Condi Rice (who, though absolutely adorable, can snap a steel bar in two with her teeth as quick as she can break wind). Men and girls who can take control, and keep it, who are brave enough to use their power to wrest control of government from those foolish enough to believe that self-determination is a God-given right, that "one man, one vote" is the essential element of participation in our national destiny, that honesty serves a purpose, and that there is room enough in government for the 99.99999 percent of people on this Earth who would really be better off in chains, eating dog food out of a plastic dish, working hard for the benefit of men and girls with true leadership potential, who have the intelligence and breeding needed to enjoy the benefits of power.

The mark of a great political operative is his ability to harness and suppress what little may persist of the leader's humanitarian instinct, keeping him slavishly, ruthlessly "on program," despite the ever-present, objective reality of flesh-and-blood people suffering needlessly and dying cruelly because of senseless government policies at home and abroad. And the easiest task of all is ensuring that the public and the press will simply ignore the staggering dishonesty that lies at the heart of this administration like a gigantic, swollen, painful red pimple on the flabby ass of the American body politic.

God, am I good. But I'm only as good as the brave, manly leader I serve. Bless you, our brave leaders! Hail George W. Bush! You have given my life meaning. And thank you, my fellow Americans, for making my job so easy and so pleasurable!

★ GEORGE W. BUSH: LEADING, LYING, AND LOVING IT

How do you thank someone who has taken a world that's a hotbed of hatred and violence on the brink of destruction, and reshaped it into a haven of peace and brotherhood on the brink of destruction? Why, you elect him, of course!

Vital Statistics

Occupation: 43rd Presidential Appointee of the United States of America

Born: July 6, 1946; New Haven, Connecticut

Born Again: Can't quite recall, probably 1984 or '85; Houston, Texas

Nicknames: Junior, Shrub, Shitkicker, Fratboy, Antichrist, Spurious George, Sonofabush, Flubya

Favorite Childhood Activity: Blowing up frogs by stuffing firecrackers inside of them

Elite Eastern Education: Yale (undergraduate), Harvard Business School

Yale Secret Society: Skull and Bones

Skull and Bones Nickname: Temporary

Pet Peeve: Terrorist hordes of registered Democrat environmentalist abortionists

Greatest Moment: "Calling my dad to tell him I'd captured Saddam and redeemed our family's honor. We both wept. I popped a woodie."

Favorite Book of the Bible: Revelation

Favorite Ice Cream Flavor: Rum raisin

George W. Bush has brought the world to global salvation in large part because of the deep sense of right and wrong instilled in him by his parents—one-term President George H.W. Bush, the "hero" of the Gulf War, and his slightly pop-eyed wife, Barbara, whose frightening crown of blinding white hair and deep, angry bellow still keep former aides awake at night. Mummy and Poppy set new standards of decency and decorum at the highest level of government, and tried to raise their sons to uphold them as well, even though the boys had everything handed to them on a crude-oil-stained silver platter. The illusion of an upbringing of discipline and hard work, masking the reality of indolent pleasure and privilege, was enough to "elect" George W. as the leader of the free world. His devotion to keeping America safe for the wealthy, so that they can accumulate vast fortunes that will in turn lead to jobs, jobs, jobs, has made his parents proud, his cronies even richer, and two million American manufacturing jobs disappear forever in only three short years.

As a student of meager intellectual capacity at two of the East Coast's most effete liberal arts institutions, Yale and Harvard, George W. Bush used good humor, his father's generosity, and the ability to keep secrets to survive the rigors of an academic program far beyond his abilities. Those qualities that mark his presidential appointeeship—blithe ignorance, vindictiveness, and a cheerful disregard for human life other than his own—were developed in the halls and dungeons of the fearsome and legendary Yale secret society, Skull and Bones. Here, he gave and received character-forming humiliations, beatings, possible sexual abuse, and all manner of secret rituals that have never been, and will never be, revealed to the uninitiated.

At Yale, he was forced to adapt to relentless questioning by demanding professors, members of an intellectual elite rife with swelled heads and petrified brains. That pressure helped form his unique and effective method of conveying the truth as he knows it to his constituents. It might not seem like a vast jump from "My dog ate my homework" to "Weapons of mass destruction are aimed at us and ready to be launched as we speak," but not everyone could have sold that whopper to the world, and started an endless war to boot.

This reformed alcoholic has proved himself to be a greater leader than anyone who ever knew him expected or believed was possible. And loyalty is its own reward. His friends and supporters have found a

DID YOU KNOW in all the excitement surrounding the Presidential Appointee's magnificent prosecution of the War on Terror, his innovative "firsts" have been all but ignored by the biased, liberal press? George W. Bush is the first commander in chief in history to don a military uniform while in office, and there's a bonus—he did it without ever having qualified for active duty in the United States Armed Forces! Even General Eisenhower didn't have the guts to show up anywhere in his uniform during his two terms as president. Bush is the first president to make repeated statements about how he wishes that he could be a dictator. And how about that George W. Bush military action figure? Another first!

tireless champion of their industries and businesses, while the little people in the voting booths, who nearly gave him a plurality of the popular vote, have been rewarded with an America that is now the unchallenged ruler of the world, for what it's worth. Who would have thought? Who could have hoped? Surely God has played His part beautifully in the ascent of the greatest, the bravest, and the luckiest leader of them all. Hail to our divine sword of retribution, George W. Bush!

★ DICK CHENEY: OUR NATIONAL TREASURE

The thought of America without Dick Cheney is confusing, disturbing, impossible. He is the beating heart of our nation, of our government, of our way of life. His heart is always throbbing, in its own peculiar rhythm, deep underground in the subterranean, nucular-attack-proof, undisclosed location he calls "The Nerve Center." He's safe enough now, yet we've almost lost him five times—six if you count the surgery, nineteen if you count the drunk-driving close shaves, and then there's that one time he had to chew

Vital Statistics

Title: Vice Presidential Appointee of the United States of America

Born: January 30, 1941; Lincoln, Nebraska

Bush Nicknames: Bossman, Big Cheese, Grumbles, Chainsaw, Dickums, Crankenstein, Sir

First Drunk-Driving Arrest: 1962

Second Drunk-Driving Arrest: 1963

Dropped Out of Yale: 1963

Heart Attacks: 1977, '78, '84, '88, November 22, 2000 (as Vice Presidential Appointee-in-waiting)

Heart Attack Denial: George W. Bush; November 22, 2000

Heart Surgery: Quadruple bypass; August 1988

Favorite Business Partners: Tyrannical dictators of Iraq, Iran, Libya, Burma

Past Experience: Succeeded Donald Rumsfeld as Gerald Ford's White House chief of staff; six terms in the United States House of Representatives as Wyoming's only congressman; House minority whip; draft dodger; President George H.W. Bush's secretary of defense in charge of Operation Just Cause (invasion of Panama, entrapment of Noriega) and Operation Desert Storm; Presidential Medal of Freedom™ recipient; chairman and CEO of Halliburton; perennial cardiac patient and death-cheater through his own clogged artery in order to restore blood flow to his brain. Some call him the Tin Man, after the beloved *Wizard of Oz* character who was born without a heart. If only that were true. Is there an American who is not grateful for the knowledge that Dick Cheney is holed up somewhere, ensuring the continuance of government in case of a successful terrorist strike on the Presidential Appointee? He's safe and sound, but we sure do miss him.

He's dodged more bullets than the average public servant: arrests, failure to make it in the Ivy League, heart attacks beginning at age thirty-five, a lesbian daughter, and repeated accusations of war profiteering and providing unfair advantages to his former employer, Halliburton. To top it off, his first child was born nine months and two days after the Selective Service announced that married men without children were subject to the draft—a coincidence that allowed him to avoid being killed in Vietnam and to pursue "other priorities in the sixties than military service." And thank God he had the strength to pursue them.

To express our affection for Dick and all the hours he puts in with our shadow government, we will soon unveil the Richard "Dick" Bruce Cheney Undisclosed Location National Monument in a special televised ceremony featuring Republican luminaries, prominent military figures, exciting D-list celebrities, and a performance by Bruce Willis's blues band. A huge light show will create a web of images of Dick Cheney's face in a combination of glowing neon and laser beams. It will be an immersive experience, giving those present the sensation that they are surrounded and penetrated by the presence of Dick Cheney—a man who is everywhere yet nowhere at the same time. The public is welcome to attend, but all will be thoroughly questioned as to how they found the secret location of the monument. T-shirts and criminal defense attorneys will be available for those seeking souvenirs and legal representation.

DID YOU KNOW Dick Cheney has a very special reason for conducting the important business of government in secret? It's a reason so special, you'll never find out what it is. You see, the smartest businessmen and the smartest statesmen meet and make plans that you would not be able to understand even if you ever found out what they were. Actually, it's none of your business. It's kind of like the popular kids at high school, who had their own lunch table that you were never allowed to sit at. If you even walked too close to their table, the laughing and flirting of these attractive, confident people would stop so that they could stare at you coldly until you left. Go sit at the table with all the other dorks and nerds, you pathetic loser. Dick Cheney's busy.

"Am I the evil genius in the corner that nobody ever sees come out of his hole? It's a nice way to operate, actually."

—Dick Cheney, January 19, 2004

★ KARL ROVE: TURD AT THE TOP OF THE HEAP

Vital Statistics

Title: Chief Political Advisor to the Presidential Appointee

Born: December 25, 1950; Denver, Colorado

Bush Nicknames: Boy Genius, Turd Blossom, the Mayberry Machiavelli, Chrome Dome, Goebbels, Wormtongue

Favorite Dish: Revenge, served cold

Favorite Dressing: Mayonnaise

Past Experience: national chairman of the College Republicans; college dropout; campaign advisor for George W. Bush (gubernatorial and presidential); tormented son of absentee father

When he's good, he's real good, but when he's bad, he's great. At the young age of nineteen, Karl snuck into the campaign offices of political opponent Alan J. Dixon, who was running for Illinois state treasurer at the time, and stole some of Dixon's letterhead stationery. He drafted a misleading advertisement for a Dixon campaign

DID YOU KNOW Karl Rove's mentor and instructor in the art of political dirty tricks was none other than Donald Segretti, Nixon's dark wizard? Segretti is the man who made Edmund Muskie cry, told the world Thomas Eagleton was nutty as a fruitcake, and smeared Democratic candidate after Democratic candidate until he fell on his sword, along with the other heroes of Watergate, and was sent up the river. Rove has not only managed to cover his tracks and stay out of jail, he has also far surpassed his teacher in both effectiveness and sheer meanness. Segretti probably flipped his former-felon lid with fiendish pride when he heard that his protégé had been accused of purposely exposing an active CIA operative just to spite her husband!

rally, promising girls, free food, and free beer, and distributed it to over 1,000 people, including a bunch of stew bums. Some might call this "youthful indiscretion," but we prefer to call it "shining potential."

Young Karl learned a valuable lesson from this experience—don't get caught. As executive director of the College Republicans, he traveled around the country, instructing his young audiences on how to pull off political dirty tricks such as digging through an opponent's garbage for intelligence. When Rove was running the campaign of Texas Governor Bill Clements and things were looking grim, he held a press conference to state that his office had been broken into and bugged. Never mind that Rove never called the police. Never mind that the bug had a battery that lasted only ten hours, meaning whoever had placed the bug either had recurring access to Rove's office, or didn't care whether or not the bug transmitted, but only wanted the device to be found. Never mind that the investigation of the bugging was inconclusive, but strongly leaned toward Rove himself. Do we know for sure it was him? Hell no.

In the Bush presidential primary campaign, mysterious "push polls" were conducted, asking if the voter would be more or less likely to vote for John McCain if they knew he had a black daughter. Could you definitively trace these push polls to Rove? Hell no. Whether through covert dirt digging, overt mud slinging, or straight-up dirty tricks, the political battlefield is littered with bodies bearing what Republicans call "the mark of Rove." Jim Hightower. John McCain. Ann Richards. Al Gore. All of these people have been Roved right into the ground. You know it was him, but there sure isn't any proof!

Strangely, Karl Rove is known as "America's Goebbels," despite the fact that he more closely resembles the bald-pated, bespectacled Heinrich Himmler. Rove's mastery of the Big Lie, however, marks him definitively as a Goebbelite.

★ CONDOLEEZZA RICE: LITTLE BRAVE CONDI

Vital Statistics

Title: National Security Advisor

Born: November 14, 1954; Titusville, Alabama

Bush Nicknames: Guru, Uhura, Daddy's Girl, Miss Priss, No Testimony, Rice Cakes, Old Ironsides

Turnoffs: "Guys who want you to testify publicly on national security issues; going under oath."

Overused Adjectives That Describe Her: Whip-smart, tack-sharp, drum-tight, great dancer, sassy, savvy, serious, intense, pious, bosomy

Past Experience: Intern, U.S. State Department; intern, Rand Corporation; Reagan Administration Council on Foreign Relations Fellowship; George H.W. Bush National Security Council; trustee, Rand Corporation; director, Chevron Corporation; director, Transamerica Corporation; provost, Stanford University; namesake of 136,000-ton oil tanker, Chevron's largest, the *Condoleezza Rice*; senior fellow, Hoover Institute; principal spokesperson of misleading "weapons of mass destruction" deception; fall-gal in waiting?

Behind every great man, there stands an African American woman, dressed smartly and groomed impeccably, whispering occasionally into his unusually large ears. In the New America, that woman is pretty Condoleezza Rice, the foreign policy pistol, ready at a moment's notice to fire a tidbit of knowledge into our Presidential Appointee's head. That's all that's needed—a whisper of information, a soupçon of policy, a speck of history, some foreigner's name in short, something to say that makes the boss sound smart, or at least a little less stupid. Under the circumstances, one might say her record of success is miraculous.

She gives no quarter, however, to those who would brand her a wily Cleopatra, orchestrating world affairs from behind a calculated façade of the loveliest, most delightful lady you've ever laid eyes on. You could just eat her up. But she'll have none of that. She sees her job as one of the most important in modern history: to guide, with knowledge and firmness, weak minds toward strong actions. Not for her the armchair warrior, the summer soldier, and the sunshine patriot, the indecisive, the slovenly, the unkempt, the drunken, the smelly. Spines straighten and heels click together at her approach—that's our Condi.

Condoleezza Rice has done more than just promote the interests of the oil industry that has been so good to her. She has provided the necessary illusion of assurance that prevents this administration from being run out of town on a rail, tarred and feathered, back to their trust funds and well-fortified compounds. She has proved that to be right, to be correct, to make statements that are simply true, is as useless a goal as planning a manned mission to Mars. If she had a motto, it would be "Say whatever comes into your head, as long as it makes you sound smart." She steps willingly into the gaping maw of hostile, biased liberal journalism to answer questions and explain past statements, and she emerges without a hair out of place, a crooked eyelash, or a spot of smeared lipstick. And look at what she's accomplished! More than the Presidential Appointee's 2003 State of the Union address, more than Secretary of State Colin Powell's stirring performance before the UN Security Council, more than Defense Secretary Donald Rumsfeld's electric, inspiring displays of manly bravado, it was Condi, little brave Condi, who sold the nation on Iraq's WMDs. Now that reality has intruded on the situation, it is Condi who must backtrack, talk fast, and stick her neck out, even though her head may eventually have to be chopped off, for the good of the administration. What man, woman, or child would not lay down every shred of doubt before the feet of this wise and wonderful waif?

"We all want very much to see this resolved in a peaceful way."

—Condoleezza Rice on Iraq, November 11, 2002

DID YOU KNOW Condoleezza Rice, the most prominent example of the effectiveness of affirmative action since Clarence Thomas (and aren't we grateful everyone's forgotten about *him*?), denies that she benefited in any way from affirmative action in education and employment? Flying in the face of obvious reality, this staunch conservative has a story, and she's sticking to it! Bravo, little brave Condi!

Vital Statistics

Title: Secretary of Defense

Born: July 9, 1932; Chicago, Illinois

Bush Nicknames: Rummy, Rumstud, Rumbum, Rumma Dumma Ding Dong, Slow Hand Don, the Mangler, the Casanova of Defense, Warpig

Underwear Size: Briefs, 34; Boxers, 34; Thong, 34 Long

Approval Rate for Fifty U.S. Airstrikes That Were Each Known to Result in the Deaths of at Least Thirty Iraqi Civilians: 100 percent

Favorite Corporate Ties: G.D. Searle/Pharmacia; General Instrument/Motorola; Gulfstream Aerospace; General Dynamics; Tribune Company; Gilead Sciences; Amylin Pharmaceuticals; Sears, Roebuck & Co.; Allstate; Kellogg; Asea Brown Boveri

Favorite Failed Weapons System: "Weapons don't fail. People without weapons fail."

Favorite Iraq War Victory: "Impossible to choose—they're like my babies."

Favorite 9/11 Souvenir: Human femur he keeps on his desk

Personal Credo: "Empower and entrap."

Pet Peeve: "Reporters who ask questions during my press briefings."

Past Experience: Eagle Scout; champion college wrestler; four terms as Illinois congressman in U.S. House of Representatives; member of Nixon's cabinet; ambassador to NATO; Gerald Ford's White House chief of staff (preceding Dick Cheney); youngest secretary of defense in American history; appeaser of Saddam Hussein; oldest secretary of defense in American history; conqueror of Saddam Hussein

He's forthright, he's forceful, he's Rummy. He never met a tyrant he couldn't overthrow, or, for that matter, strengthen *then* overthrow. His method is simple, and it never fails. He calls it "empower and entrap." First, he will seduce a dangerous, unscrupulous, and clearly unbalanced dictator in order to achieve a short-term goal. American arms and riches flow directly to the dictator, lulling him into a brutal, gluttonous torpor, which leads to "unintended" consequences such as genocide, terrorism, or, God forbid, interrupted oil production. Rummy then swoops down out of nowhere (actually, an aircraft carrier) to obliterate the evil dictator and all of his American-trained, American-equipped henchmen. The oil starts flowing again; tens of thousands are dead, maimed, and starving; and huge profits are made for the U.S. military-industrial complex before, during, *and* after the war. Ruthless? Indubitably. Harsh? Well, yes and no. Grown men have been known to soil their trousers at the very sight of him, but what they don't know is, Rumsfeld is just a rough, tough creampuff.

As sentimental as the day is long, this champion of Freedom™ has the demeanor and determination of the champion of wrestling that he once was, and mentally still is. But the people and weapons around him arouse an almost maternal rush of feeling, which is perhaps why he is so dogged in pursuing his goals. He still has a warm place in his heart for the weapons systems he rammed through Congress during his heady, youthful days as President Ford's secretary of defense: the MX missile, the Trident submarine, and the B-1 bomber (which he *personally* test-flew). He fondly recalls the bonds of affection he shared with a young Saddam Hussein during his mission to befriend the brutal "Butcher of Baghdad" in 1983.

DID YOU KNOW Donald Rumsfeld deliberately speaks in riddles in order to confuse those who would try to trick him into revealing military secrets? It's a technique derived from the feints and fake outs of his college wrestling days. He can get away with it because he is so handsome and forceful. Any American would almost rather die than criticize him for keeping vital information from the public for purely political reasons, and reporters covering the Defense Department are deeply sympathetic to and in love with Donald Rumsfeld. Information warfare is the greatest aphrodisiac.

And he remembers the harsh sting of rejection when it became clear that Saddam had abandoned him. Perhaps when Rumsfeld immediately demanded every scrap of information that could tie Iraq to 9/11, he was suffering from empty nest syndrome.

Ah, but revenge is sweet. Never betray the friendship of a former navy man! There are those who believe the murders of Qusay and Uday Hussein were a "coded message" to Saddam: "Destroy my babies, and I'll destroy yours." It's that smoldering passion of Rumsfeld that has captivated American men and women for over three decades, sometimes causing his devotees to swoon in his presence.

So there he is, in all of his contradictions. The man of action, with a soft spot. Here, he looks the other way while a despot poisons his own people; there, he destroys that despot for poisoning his own people. Here, he's selling nuclear reactors to North Korea; there, he's threatening to invade because of North Korea's vaunted nuclear capabilities. Don't tangle with Donald Henry Rumsfeld—he's here, there, and everywhere, but he *always* comes out on top.

> "And there is, I am certain, among the Iraqi people a respect for the care and the precision that went into the bombing campaign."
>
> —Donald Rumsfeld, April 9, 2003

Vital Statistics

Title: Attorney General of the United States of America

Born: May 9, 1942; Chicago, Illinois

Bush Nicknames: Stuffy, Killjoy, the Crisco Kid, Pastor John, Lashcroft, General Jesus

Favorite Bible Passage: "And they called unto Lot, and said unto him, where are the men which came in to thee this night? Bring them out unto us, *that we may know them.*" —Genesis 19:5

Worst Nightmare: "A nude gay black alcoholic secular-Jew single-parent abortionist prison-inmate dancer, with an erection, chasing me around and trying to kiss me."

Fondest Hope: "To dwell in the house of the Lord forever and ever, having first served thirty-five years as chief justice of the Supreme Court alongside Pat Robertson and Jerry Falwell, so that we can establish God's Kingdom on Earth, once and for all."

Most Recent Conversation with God: "This afternoon, we talked about some new furniture for my office. Leather gives Him the creeps."

Hallucination During Recent Operation: "Jesus seemed to be poking around under the sheets in the operating room, and when I asked Him to stop it, He just giggled a lot."

Number of Jews Working at Justice Dept. 12/00: Forty-seven

Number of Jews Working at Justice Dept. 12/03: Two, and they're troublemakers

Past Experience: governor of Missouri; ex–U. S. senator from Missouri—after losing his seat to *a dead man;* protector of Christianity; scourge of Islam

The group of Assembly of God members who had gathered to pray with John Ashcroft, minutes before he was wheeled into the operating room for a recent gall bladder operation, enjoyed a moment of levity when the entire bottle of Crisco oil they were using to anoint the attorney general spilled into his lap. When Ashcroft solemnly proclaimed, "I guess God is telling us that the operation will flow as smoothly as Crisco oil," the laughter died down—partly because the joke fell flat, but mainly because it showed the spiritual side of the man who guards our liberties as fiercely as God guards His followers.

In fact, John Ashcroft's spiritual side is his only side. That's because he regards God as his King, the ultimate ruler of all people and things on this planet and in the universe, whether you like it or not. This has presented a problem for secularists who point out that our democracy is founded upon the "separation of church and state." God has told the attorney general that he need not worry about talk of the U.S. Constitution, because God makes the only laws anybody has to worry about anyway.

Thanks to the tragic events of 9/11, Ashcroft no longer has to concern himself with constitutional quibbling. His greatest contribution to our culture—the Uniting and Strengthening America by Providing Appropriate Tools Required to Intercept and Obstruct Terrorism Act of 2001, better known as the USA PATRIOT Act— enabled him to achieve, in one daring flourish, what God Himself could not. We speak of the final subjugation of man's law to God's law, conveyed directly from the Creator through his faithful servant, John Ashcroft.

Now our government can spy on its own citizens and listen in on attorney-client conversations; make secret arrests and withhold prisoners' identities from the public; jail Americans indefinitely without benefit of counsel; jail immigrants with no charges; maintain a DNA database of terrorism suspects; monitor e-mail and track visits to Web sites; covertly monitor political groups without any criminal suspicions; restrict open hearings and limit the public's right to seek information through the Freedom of Information Act; prevent librarians from notifying subjects that their borrowing records have been subpoenaed, among other wise and much-needed reforms.

Since no one can stop this juggernaut of justice, all of these reforms now apply to ordinary crimes, not just to terrorism! So successful is the USA PATRIOT Act, Ashcroft has already devised PATRIOT II. Of course, the terrorist sympathizers in Congress get jittery when they consider its provisions: more weakening of restrictions on secret government surveillance of ordinary citizens, including their phone, e-mail, and bank accounts; deportation at will, regardless of immigration laws; extending penalties for terrorist acts to individuals far removed from planning and execution of crimes; criminalizing use of encrypted e-mail; exhumation of the remains of terrorism victims without families' permission; limiting access to corporate records of environmental crimes and even preventing private citizens and local governments from researching toxins in their neighborhoods.

Do you think it will be hard to get PATRIOT II passed by Congress? Have a little faith! Each provision is buried in other legislation, so if some bleeding-heart senator doesn't want shoplifters jailed in detention camps, he'll have to vote against paying for the guns that arm our fighting men and women!

The fact that there has not been a single conviction of anyone for any crime directly related to 9/11 is proof that Ashcroft's plan works. Isn't that God's plan, after all—to stop crime before it even starts? Or was that McGruff, the Crime Dog?

DID YOU KNOW John Ashcroft was ahead of his time in identifying the growing popularity of eastern religions, such as Islam, as the reason for the increase in demonic possessions in the United States? We still remember the good old days that our friend John reminds us of, when only foreigners were possessed by the devil.

Vital Statistics

Title: Gouverneur von Kalifornien

Born: July 30, 1947; Graz, Austria

Bush Nicknames: The Gubernator, Schwazi, Schwarzenpigger, Arnold Strong, der Gropenführer

Sexually Suggestive Nickname: The Austrian Oak

Height: 6'2"

Arms: 22"

Chest: 57"

Waist: 34"

Thighs: 28.5"

Calves: 20"

Penis: 9" flaccid, 18" erect

Off-Season Weight: Around 235 lbs.

Competition Weight: Around 260 lbs.

Favorite Exercise: Bent-over rows

Favorite Steroid: Dianabol

Past Experience: T-800 Terminator, Mr. Universe (1967, '68, '69, '70), Mr. World (1970), Mr. Olympia (1969, '70, '71, '72, '73, '74, '75, '80), Mr. Let Go of My Breast or I'll Scream (1964–2004)

Chairman: Committee to Reform Anti-Austrian Punitive Presidential Election Rules (CRAAPPER)

Arnold is new on the political scene, but that doesn't mean we're any less thrilled to have him. We've actually had our eye on him for some time. We first saw his political potential in the documentary film about weightlifting, *Pumping Iron*. In this film, Arnold effectively belittles, intimidates, confuses, and schemes against his swarthy competitors, some of whom he calls his friends, with shameless ease and charm. His natural leadership, diplomacy skills, and ability to chop off human limbs shone even brighter in his title role in the *Conan the Barbarian* series. And, of course, Arnold's unforgettable portrayal of an invincible killing machine from the future in the *Terminator* films sets all of our hearts here at the Better Citizenship Bureau a-fluttering.

Last year, California was a huge mess that needed a Terminator. Everyone was cranky from all of Enron's rolling blackouts, and they were sick of budget cuts after our huge tax breaks for the rich had been enacted. One thing was sure—Governor Gray Davis had to be totally recalled. When Ah-nold appeared on the *Tonight Show* to ah-nounce he was ready to squeeze Gray Davis' pointy little head between his massive, hairless, rock-hard, oiled-up pectoral muscles, we were just tickled pink. He's the best. If we didn't have Arnold, we would have to invent him.

Of course, Schwarzenegger is not quite as all-American as we'd like him to be. He may have a little too much Hollywood in him, and he did make those pro-Hitler comments, and he does have a good deal of grab-ass in his past, but we always allow for personal growth. We're hoping that he discovers Christ and comes to the Potomac River full-body baptism that Reverend John Ashcroft has invited him to. We'll wash that magnificent body clean of sin forever.

Now that Arnold is the Governminator, he wants us to reconsider the constitutional provision that no foreign-born citizen can run for president of the United States. It turns out that we've already got the Constitution off the shelf and out on the table for the stop-the-marrying-gays amendment, so why not mark up another page at the same time? We've given this new idea some thought and we'd like to respond to Herr Schwarzenegger, loudly and in unison: *Jawohl!*

DID YOU KNOW Arnold is best pals with former President of Austria/Nazi sympathizer and collaborator/United Nations Secretary-General Kurt Waldheim? Did you know that Waldheim is the only person in history to have both a recording of his voice left on the moon *and* a documented record of participation in the Holocaust? Arnold really moves in some powerful circles!

★ GEORGE W. BUSH: THE "GOOD" HITLER?

"An evil exists that threatens every man, woman, and child of this great nation. We must take steps to insure our domestic security and protect our homeland."

—Adolf Hitler, 1933, creating the Gestapo

Comparing one's opponent to Adolf Hitler has been a favorite pastime in politics since der Führer first made a name for himself. And it's no wonder. Hitler, as everyone knows, was the world's greatest evil genius, so it's only natural that practically every candidate for public office over the past seventy years has used the number-one Nazi as a bludgeon against the other guy. Presidents of the United States are no exception. Wendell Wilkie's catchy campaign song "Wilkie's Not the Nazi" (recorded by the Andrews Sisters) nearly cost FDR the 1940 election. Eisenhower's image as a militaristic authoritarian earned him the nickname "Eisenhitler." And who can forget the taunting shouts of the enraged Dallas mob as JFK rode toward his destiny on that fateful day in November 1963? "Heil, Jack! Where's your ma? Ask your Hitler-loving pa!" they chanted in a naked display of mass homicidal rage. The relevant question is not "Who shot JFK?" but rather "What took them so long to do it?" However, none of these politicians shared Hitler's distinctive, charismatic moustache, or the wild-eyed intensity that psychologists tell us was at the heart of his popular appeal.

What makes the Bush administration seem so similar to Hitler's Third Reich, even more so than Richard Nixon's presidency? The Bush upper lip is clean-shaven, the wardrobe is mainstream, yet the Nazi analogies persist. There are the historic links to Hitler, but most of these are irrelevant since they occurred in the past, before today's leaders had a chance to join in. The Presidential Appointee's grandfather, Prescott Bush, increased his family's fortune as a partner of the German industrialist who financed Hitler's rise to power, and by trading with the Nazis until the U.S. government levied penalties and ordered him to stop in 1942. The rumors about Karl Rove's grandfather's role in the construction of the Auschwitz-Birkenau extermination facility are currently in dispute. But of course, Rove was the mastermind behind the brilliant "California Coup" (modeled on Hitler's legendary 1923 Munich Beer Hall Putsch), installing as governor one Arnold Schwarzenegger. This self-described Hitler admirer is the son of an Austrian "brown-shirt" storm trooper who eagerly volunteered to be a foot soldier for der Führer.

But beneath the historic links lies a greater truth. When we speak of Hitler as an "evil genius," we acknowledge the man's superior intelligence and extraordinary organizational powers, which propelled Germany to the very precipice of global domination. Lamentably, he used the power of his genius to commit acts of war and genocide that all of us would like to forget. The curse of an "evil" genius is that he can use his genius

only in the pursuit of evil. Republican politicians have been struggling since the 1930s to find a way to benefit from the example of Hitler's "genius," while leaving out the "evil" parts.

George W. Bush has found a way. After a youth spent in dissolution and failed enterprises, Bush was appointed to office with insufficient votes, given political justification by backstage intrigue and a supposedly impartial supreme judicial body. Then came the jingoism, the nationalistic propaganda, the false piety, the flag-waving, the baseless promises of prosperity, the false assurance of security, the harmful domestic policies, the ever-tighter alliance between corporate and governmental power that defines fascism, the deliberate neglect of the poor, the environment, workers, the young, and the old. All part of a tried-and-true plan based on the "genius," minus the "evil." Following years of weak, corrupt leadership not unlike that of the Weimar Republic, an elite class of Americans were finally on their way to achieving the same level of wealth and security enjoyed by citizens of the Third Reich, without all the "evil." The time hadn't quite come to unleash the most radical reforms until September 11, 2001—which, like the 1933 burning of the Reichstag in Berlin, presented an opportunity to reshape the world.

There was an immediate rush to militarize everything, to turn the world into an armed camp, with the United States dominant and unchallenged in strategic locations around the world. Police were militarized along with federal, local, and state governments. Blind loyalty to the leader and the search for traitors became the first duties of every citizen. The regime already controlled all information available to the public, using complicit media to drive the message home. Skillful use of the Big Lie convinced most people that military domination of the world was a good idea. Dissenters are harassed, jailed, and silenced by a newly formed Department of Homeland Security. Fear is manufactured like a commodity, increasing the reliance of the citizenry on a government that is paying only lip service to real issues of security.

A completely unthreatening sovereign nation is invaded and ravaged in a "preventive war" waged on a blatantly false pretext, in defiance of international law. Indiscriminate devastation, murder, and terror spark resistance. Plans are made to expand the mission of conquest to other unthreatening sovereign nations. The majority of the homeland's resources is poured into its military machine. Foreigners of certain racial and religious profiles are demonized and scapegoated, lumped together as the bestial, traitorous enemy. These people, along with citizens and immigrants supposedly linked to the enemy, are arrested and placed beyond the reach of legal protection in closed, inac-

cessible detention camps. Ordinary citizens are the targets of government surveillance, harassment, and incarceration. Neighbor spies on neighbor. Alliances with countries around the world crumble. Corporate interests with government ties reap vast fortunes through sweetheart deals for the "reconstruction" of the ravaged war zone, starving beneficial government programs at home. The Presidential Appointee finally dons a military uniform to make a misleading announcement of victory. Although the flight suit lacked the

PLEASE GIVE...

There is an issue that lies as close as anything can to Dick Cheney's artificial heart. It really tugs at the old artificial heartstrings. We're talking about plausible deniabilitis syndrome, or PD. This terrible disease is incurable and ever-present. When a PD sufferer is questioned about what he was doing on a certain day, he just can't say. He's infected with a reason why he can't. The Iran-Contra affair, the secret Energy Task Force hearings, the Presidential Daily Briefings before 9/11...PD has struck again and again in our nation's affairs. This is a disease that has also infected many of our most prominent and revered leaders: Richard Nixon, Ronald Reagan, Oliver North, George H.W. Bush, Dick Cheney, and George W. Bush are all among the sufferers. Please, give generously to the worthwhile cause of curing PD syndrome on your HRS income tax forms this year, so that the brave sufferers of plausible deniabilitis will never be forced to answer another question again.

dapper appeal of Hitler's superbly tailored wardrobe, and although once the helmet came off it did nothing to conceal the lack of a moustache, it nevertheless got the point across that we are not to be messed with.

Yes, it's easy to see how these tactics, so effective today in protecting the American homeland and the American people, could be used by an "evil genius" to attempt world conquest. Thankfully, God is on our side, our leaders have His support, and the only quality they share with Hitler is "genius." With our master plan working so well, perhaps now the Presidential Appointee will have time to grow a moustache and get himself a snappier uniform.

John Ashcroft's Message in Music

In the aftermath of 9/11, John Ashcroft decided to inspire his Justice Department employees by starting each day with song. But the old standards didn't express the themes of patriotism and faith sufficiently, so the attorney general decided to lead his department in singing a new composition of his own, "Let the Eagle Soar,"® which instantly became an international chart-topping hit. A baritone, Ashcroft was one-fourth of the Singing Senators quartet, which has recorded a CD and performed at the Grand Ole Opry. He has also written hundreds of gospel songs and recorded several albums of his own. Here, then, for the first time anywhere, are the lyrics to John Ashcroft's latest hit single, soon to be released:

THEY HATE US FOR OUR FREEDOM™

My little grandson Timmy,
With a teardrop in his eye,
Asked me "Grampy, why'd they do it?"
And this was my reply:

"They hate us for our freedom,
For our Easter Sunday ham,
They hate our morning sausage,
And our gleaming cans of Spam.

"God's miraculous selections
In our supermarkets' cases
Drive the terrorists to murder
In our nicest public places."

Timmy cried, "Oh, Grampy, stop them!
I'm afraid they'll bomb my kitchen!"
So I spoke my answer boldly,
Gently calming Timmy's twitchin':

"We shall send them off to Cuba,
Where their plots cannot infect us.
If their relatives complain,
We have Scalia to protect us.

"We'll eliminate al-Qaeda,
Search and seize them night and day,
'Till there's no one left to hate us,
Forever free to shop and pray!"

★ WARRIOR OF LOVE: SEX AND THE SECRETARY OF DEFENSE

There have been recent reports, from Pentagon custodians, of moistened seat cushions following Donald Rumsfeld's press briefings. This certainly isn't a new phenomenon—special disinfectants have filled janitors' closets across Washington, D.C., since the days of JFK. What's different is that the journalists who are moistening the seat cushions now are men as well as women.

It's easy to see what turns women's knees to Jello™. You can tell how much a man cares about a woman's sexual needs when he's fastidious in his personal hygiene, and they don't come much cleaner than Donald Rumsfeld. He has an antiseptic sheen. Women who were sick as little girls and spent a lot of time around doctors often respond sexually to men like him. Rumsfeld is a blunt, forceful, masculine man's man...but what women notice is his immaculate grooming, his brilliantined hair, his carefully manicured fingernails, his smooth shave, and his nearly complete lack of nose and ear hair. A woman can easily imagine running her fingers through that hair, inserting her tongue into those ears and nose and who knows where else, without her fingers and mouth becoming encrusted with dandruff and mucus.

In fact, Rumsfeld's hair is the third-largest oil reserve in the United States. That's the nervous joke men use to deflect their own feelings of sexual attraction to this powerhouse of libidinous energy. According to joint research by the Heritage Foundation and the Kinsey Institute, 97 percent of registered Republican women as well as 86 percent of Republican men regularly entertain sexual fantasies involving Donald Rumsfeld. This is nothing to be ashamed of. Some have tried to twist these statistics into an ugly smear, but there is an undeniable erotic component to manly admiration that has nothing to do with homosexual desire. In normal people, that is, which is who we're talking about.

Women notice the secretary's perfectly pressed suits, their aroma as fresh and masculine as Rumsfeld's imported cologne. They obsessively imagine these suits being stripped from his muscular frame during romantic encounters. This accounts for his ubiquity in the erotic fantasies of Republican women over fifty-five. And, amazingly, Republican men of all ages are three times more likely to think of Donald Rumsfeld's naked physique than of the legendary nude photographs of Ann Coulter and the donkey.

For both men and women, there is no moral weakness in their lust for Rumsfeld. He is a superman, the Übermensch, if you will. It is perfectly acceptable to desire such a paragon of manhood. His effectiveness as a leader depends upon the adoration of legions of chaste women and battalions of worshipful men. He is a throwback to such legendary Germanic heroes as Siegfried, and Roy.

The question is, Does Rumsfeld have time to be tender? The answer is, He has no use for tenderness. As a college athlete, Rumsfeld learned the wrestler's trick of sucking his testicles up into his lower abdomen, and then applying a tight truss. On the mats, Rumsfeld never suffered any testicular damage, but inflicted a great deal of it. To men, Rumsfeld is a ball buster, while to women, he is a bunker buster. Republican women lust after his ability to inflict major testicular damage, both actual and metaphorical. This brings to mind an old saying, but with a scrotal twist—instead of "You always hurt the one you love," think, "You always love the one who hurts someone else's testicles."

This champion of men who has, half-naked, physically overwhelmed countless opponents, is an irresistible lure to women. Their nipples harden at his approach.

Blood engorges their inner fastnesses. Men, unable to conceal their own discomfiture, thrust their hands deep into trouser pockets, squeezing and pinching their restless genitals. This simmering sexual energy, multiplied by the hordes of lustful admirers who exude it, is absorbed by Rumsfeld and fuels the perpetual engine of his military genius. If we could tap into the incredible power that emanates from the Rumrod, we would never have to fill up our cars and armored personnel carriers with gasoline again.

Values and
MORALS

Welcoming Remarks by
the Honorable Senator
Rick Santorum

I was very pleased and humbled to be invited to participate in this book. I am proud to join such distinguished company as Presidential Appointee Bush and Herr Doktor Kissinger, and I welcome the opportunity to address a topic as important to me as the values and morals dictated to us all by the Lord my God. In order to retain our national state of greatness, we must hold firm to this solid moral foundation upon which our forefathers built this blessed home called the United States of America.

However, we now face an enemy within our borders greater than any terrorist. This force is called Liberalism.

Thanks to Liberalism, our churches are under siege, our children are under fire, and our sacred institutions are one Supreme Court decision away from being destroyed forever. Because of Liberalism, a good American can't enter a restaurant, or a library, or even a public washroom without having to rub elbows, or other parts, with people whose immoral proclivities doom them to everlasting hellfire. Liberalism eats away at us like a cancer, making room for a twisted society in which everyone can do as they please, right in front of you and your family, and suffer no earthly consequences. Just because your country gives you the right to make certain choices doesn't mean that you should make them.

If we stamp out Liberalism, we get rid of these diabolical "ideas" of moral relativism and the freedom to sin, within the home and without. These Liberal sins are legion. Incest, bestiality, and gay marriage. The twisted desire for individual privacy. Corporate income taxes. Catholic pedophilia. Women in uniform. Child pornography. Gun control. This is what happens when our society, tricked by Liberalism, simply turns a blind eye to the necrophiliac sodomites, the secret atheists, the child-molesting priests, and the agents of a still-thriving international Communist conspiracy, bent on bankrupting and disarming God's true chosen people in preparation for the establishment of hell on Earth. What a sad state we're in, when men as morally strong as Rush Limbaugh can be tricked by a Liberal Mexican housemaid into gobbling uppers and downers by the fistful. If not for the Liberal intolerance for the sanctity of marriage, Mickey and Minnie Mouse would

be wed in holy matrimony by now. What are we teaching our children?

Let me just emphasize that I have no problem with people engaging in a completely nonsexual homosexual relationship. What people consider while they're in the privacy of their own brains is absolutely all right with me. Isn't that the liberty for which so many *real* men have given their lives over the past two centuries of our nation's wars? I just want to ensure the sanctity of the family by forbidding people from acting on those perverse impulses. Society must preserve my right as an American not to ever, ever, *ever* hear about it, or to even have to *think* about it, much less see it in public.

This is about protecting the future of the family. In order to accomplish this, we must hold fast to the pillars of denial, hypocrisy, self-righteousness, and intolerance, so we may once again reclaim the path of decency. This shining path will lead us back to the bottomless well that is the founding faith of our nation—evangelical, Southern Baptist Christianity. Let us unleash a tidal wave of moral rectitude from this well that shall cleanse our hearts and our communities of sewage and scum and carry them elsewhere, preferably not to another Christian nation where decent people live. Do this we must—if not for us, then for our children, and also our neighbors' children, whether our neighbors like it or not.

Thank you, and God bless America. And stop making filthy jokes about my name, you sodomites.

> **If not for the Liberal intolerance for the sanctity of marriage, Mickey and Minnie Mouse would be wed in holy matrimony by now.**

★ ONE GOD UNDER NATION

After 9/11, our new USA PATRIOT Act made it necessary to look at all previous laws for possible revision. In examining the original Ten Commandments of God to Moses, it was found that the original commandments were exceedingly vague and ill-suited to deal with our current geopolitical state of constant terror. Therefore, the Ten Commandments have been revised by U.S. Department of Justice lawyers to better govern our New World Order of dangerous terrorists created by the global elite that must defeat them. These revised commandments, which retain all the divinity of the previous regulations, will be posted in every church, school, government building, and mosque in the United States. For clarification on the revised commandments, be sure to refer to the sub-commandments listed below each major commandment.

The New Ten Commandments

1 I am the Lord thy God, as defined in the King James Edition of the Holy Bible. Thou shalt have no other gods before Me, including, but not limited to, Allah, Buddha, Krishna, or David Koresh.

1a. There is no God but God, and lo, I am blonde and blue-eyed, and dressed in a white Nike™ running suit, who votes a straight Republican ticket and thinks that English should be the official language of the United States.

1b. However, a healthy worship of money and the ruthless pursuit thereof is perfectly acceptable.

2 Thou shalt make no graven images, although a constant stream of video images detailing the War on Terror and the global march of the free market are acceptable, especially if it is produced by Fox News.

3 Thou shalt not take the name of the Lord God in vain, unless it is used in the service of killing Muslims.

HANDS OFF BUSINESS! HANDS ON YOU!

We feel that our attention is not best spent on big corporations that can take care of themselves, but on you, your unborn children, and the crimes of morality that you soon will no longer have the opportunity to commit. We must protect you from yourself—from the scourges of drug use, promiscuity, homosexuality, and general dissatisfaction.

4 Thou shalt honor the Sabbath Day and keep it wholly for public relations reasons.

5 Honor thy father and mother, unless they are frail, elderly parasites who are stealing money from our government through Social Security and Medicare.

6 Thou shalt not kill, unless there are large profits to be made by killing and those that you're killing are browner and/or poorer than you are.

6a. Thou shalt kill the mentally retarded.

6b. Thou shalt kill witnesses to your supposed "crimes," then make thy killings appear to be suicides or accidental airplane crashes.

7 Thou shalt not omit adultery.

7a. Thou shalt accuse all others of adultery if it serves your political purposes, whilst hiding thine own fornications.

7b. Thou shalt not commit adultery if you are a decent, God-fearing citizen, but if you are an elite high priest of the Bohemian Grove Society, then you can really get down.

8 Thou shalt not steal from those in a higher tax bracket than you are.

8a. Thou shalt not tax the rich.

8b. Thou shalt not tax thy stealings.

8c. Thou shalt not steal without the proper forms and documentation.

9 Thou shalt bear false witness against thy neighbor.

9a. Thou shalt especially bear false witness against your political opponents, as who would want them as neighbors in the first place.

9b. Thou shalt construct new false-witness machines to ease the burden on thyselves, and thou shalt employ these machines to count the votes of your political elections. Thou shalt make these voting machines unverifiable, easily alterable, and immune to inquiry due to corporate intellectual property rights. Thou shalt count thy ballots in secret.

10 Thou shalt not covet anything that is thy neighbor's, as thou shalt have better stuff than he, who shalt covet *thy* belongings.

10a. Thou shalt not covet thy neighbor's manservant, who is probably in the country illegally anyway.

10b. Thou shalt not covet thy neighbor's SUV—thou shalt go forth and purchase a newer, bigger model for thyself.

★ FIRST FAMILY VALUES

Our Little Gentleman

by Former First Lady
Barbara Bush

I'll tell you when Poppy and I both knew we had a fine, moral young man on our hands. This was when George W. was about eleven years old. He'd been out behind the servant's quarters, playing doctor and smoking cigarettes with his French au pair, when suddenly we heard the poor girl screaming bloody murder. She was screaming in French, so we had no idea what was wrong. Poppy and I watched from the veranda, nursing our afternoon Rob Roys, as Annette, or Aimee, whatever her name was, came skittering across the lawn, her dress in tatters, blood streaming down her legs, looking just awful. George W. followed a moment later, also quite disheveled, buttoning up his trousers, holding a bloody penknife, and bleeding from scratches all over his arms, neck, and face. What a sight to behold! When he reached us, out of breath, he told us what had happened.

It seemed that "Snappy," the giant snapping turtle, who lived in the pond as far back as anyone could remember, and was known for crawling up onto the lawn at night to feed on small animals, had surprised the two youngsters as they were relaxing. The beast had then viciously attacked Fifi as George W. watched in horror! Little gentleman that he was, he fought off the turtle with his penknife, giving the poor girl a chance to escape. None of this crying out for Mummy and Poppy, like Jeb or Neil. I thought, "Good for him!" What a little hero he was that day! We never saw the girl after that, but I was told that her wounds were properly dressed. There may have been some money involved.

WATCHWORD: "WHISTLE-BLOWER"

Everyone knows that the dirty, disgusting word "liberal" describes church-shunning demons who sell crack cocaine to children so they can molest them more easily (and more pleasurably). But do you know the new word that should send a shudder up every good citizen's spine? "Whistle-blower." The dictionary defines this word as "a person who informs authorities of malfeasance in government or business." Our new definition is "a person who would shut up if she knew what was good for her." Did you ever notice how many of these whistle-blowers, from Coleen Rowley at the FBI to Sherron Watkins at Enron, are embittered and desperate women, wanting only to tear down powerful men and their important, secretive schemes? If they had their values in the right place, these little ladies would be at home cooking up a hot dinner and making the house look all pretty, while their man was having a busy day stealing billions of dollars from consumers at Enron or protecting al-Qaeda terrorists at the FBI.

America's Next Big Thing: A Theocracy Of Evil

by Ann Coulter
Conservative
Commentator

In the New America, every moron knows that a deep and abiding belief in Almighty God is where it's at, a sort of postmodern accessory that all of us left on Earth will eventually be required to carry with us from cradle to grave. And since we've got the biggest *guns*, we get to decide which Almighty God we're talking about. Wake up, desert-dwellers: Allah is "out," and "in" at the Inn is your favorite savior and mine, Jesus Christ.

If that strikes you as just a trifle old-fashioned, well, darling, that's the *point*.

The latest in morality requires what one *very* astute wag has christened the "Theocracy of Evil," described as a "faith-based value system that embraces a simplistic 'good versus evil' opposition."

Quite.

Us = Good vs. Them = Evil. Phew, that was tough! *Not*.

It's like the latest laborsaving household gadget or some new cosmetic that cuts down on the time you spend doing your eyebrows. Call it the Theocracy of Evil if you want to. I call it "Morality in a Minute." *And I'll never waste time thinking about what I believe in again*. Here's how it works:

First: Choose which side you're on, Good or Evil. It's not as easy as it sounds if you're a registered Democrat. Time to poop or pass the privy, people! You're with us or against us, so cut the crap, you Commie traitors, or shove it and shove off!

Next: Consult the following chart. That's all there is to it! No muss, no fuss, results in seconds, guaranteed!

GOOD	EVIL
Us	Them
The English language	French, Spanish, Russian, Farsi, Urdu, you get the picture
The HUMMER	Citroën, Fiat, Saab, Volvo, donkey cart, walking
Gasoline	Hay
Money	Trinkets, beads, cooperative labor
Juicy steak	Goats' eyes, hummus, crêpes suzette
Cute miniskirt	Burkha
Procreative, matrimonial, Christian physical love	Sex through a sheet with a hole in it with your cousin-husband, who's never seen your face
Petroleum	Solar, hydroelectric, hamster wheel
Monogamy	Harem
Chicks in cars with guns	Locked up at home, no cable, one twenty-four-hour all-Saddam channel
The Bible	The Koran (al-Qaeda handbook)
Pastor Johnson	Ayatollah Fullahmuhlarkei
Us killing them	Them killing us
60 percent first-dollar royalties	Badly printed unauthorized editions

★ JESUS CHRIST: SUPERSTAR

People today are so caught up in the Great American Pastime—celebrity-watching—they forget about the greatest celebrity of all! If you tried to talk directly with Justin Timberlake or Janet Jackson, chances are you'd end up in a back alley instead, getting acquainted with immense, heavily armed, kung fu–trained body-guards. And don't hold your breath waiting for brother Michael to deliver that weekend invitation to his Neverland Ranch. (You'd spend most of the time in bed, anyway.) No, my friend, these celebrities will never have time for little old you.

So why not step right up and say "Hello!" to the best celebrity friend you

can ever hope to have—our Lord and Savior, Jesus Christ! Think about it—unlike other celebrities, He loves you, He wants to be with you every minute of every day, and you can unburden your broken heart to Him whenever you want. He's a bigger celebrity than Justin, Britney, Jacko, Janet, and Paris combined, *and* He can save you from the eternal torments of hell! He'll protect and defend you, clothe you and feed you, bless you and keep you, lighten your heart and make you feel important because He wants to be seen with *you*, not the other way around.

Here are some of the fabulous things you'll be able to do, starting the moment you accept Our Lord Jesus as your personal Celebrity Savior:

★ Pick out a new wardrobe with your personal fashion consultant, Jesus.

★ Dine in or out, plain or fancy, with your constant dinner companion, Jesus. (But remember—*you* pick up the check!)

WATCHWORD: "RELIGIOUS FREEDOM"

Pure and simple, "religious freedom" is what the godless sodomite Democrat terrorist traitors like to say when they really mean "I'm an atheist," or "I hate Jesus," or "No praying in class," or "My great-great-great-great-great-great-great-great-great-great-great-great-great-great-great-great-great-great-grandfather was a monkey." Newsflash: *His* gramps might be a monkey-man, but *you are not.* You are a human being, created by God, and that means the One and True Almighty God, and that means Jesus Christ. Leave the monkeys at the zoo, and bow your head in thanks that you're not eating bananas and beating off in public with your hairy little hand. (Speaking of which, how do you think the monkey's hand got so hairy?)

★ Never go to the movies alone again. Catch a flick with your own spiritual Siskel & Ebert—Jesus.

★ Stay up all hours gabbing and giggling with your best friend, who also happens to be the most famous celebrity ever—Jesus.

★ Go out to the hottest disco to be seen with the best dancer on Earth, as He is in Heaven—Jesus.

★ If you say "pretty please," your own personal Celebrity Psychic Friend, Jesus, might just give you a peek at your future, and His predictions are never wrong!

★ Sleep, work, undress, break wind, pick your nose, even go to the bathroom with Jesus right there with you. Don't be shy. He's seen it all before, just like a doctor, only he's much more famous and powerful!

Imagine your friends' reactions when they find out that you actually know Jesus! Here's how to make all of your mortal acquaintances green with envy:

Close your eyes, tap your heels together three times, and repeat these words: *"There's no friend like Jesus. There's no friend like Jesus. There's no friend like Jesus."* When the Messiah appears before you, just take a step forward, thrust out your hand, and say, *"Hello, Jesus! I'm your biggest fan!"* He'll take it from there.

What are you waiting for? Don't be shy! Your self-esteem and your immortal soul depend on meeting Jesus! Make the call right now!

Beware of imitations. Accept no substitutes. Not affiliated with Latter-day Jesus, Jesuchristo, the Infant of Prague, My Son the Savior, Christ-on-a-Bike, Hello Jesus, Son o' God, or the International Brotherhood of Teamsters.

A Prayer for Drug Addicts

Precious Jesus, look upon these hopeless, worthless junkies, winos, hopheads,

And show them the way out of town,

That we may dwell peacefully without them.

And should one of our number fall victim, Lord, hide them beneath Your shroud of love,

That embarrassment and shame may not darken the lives of the innocent and pure, and destroy the value of our property.

Scare them, Lord, with close calls and illness, overdose and nausea, rotten teeth and bad skin,

That they may choose the straight path and return to the tables of their fathers,

Without the stain of a jailbird's record, the stench of unwashed clothing,

Nor the klepto's curse of sticky fingers.

Keep them high, Lord, on the joy of life, and of Your divine love, and if that is not enough,

A few beers after work, but that is it, no fooling.

And keep these degradations from our sight, O Lord,

That we might pretend such things never happen to such as we.

————————————————— Amen.

Note: The power of prayer is most effective when it is delivered by all. Any citizen who fails to pray against drug addicts will be regarded with the highest suspicion.

★ ASK CONDI!

National Security Advisor Condoleezza Rice Dispenses World-Class Wisdom to the American Girls Who Trust and Admire Her!

Dear Condi,

My boyfriend and I are both sixteen. We have loads of fun together, and I'm pretty sure I'm in love for the first time. He encourages me to achieve, helps me study, shares my deep love for America, and best of all, he makes me laugh. Recently, during a study session at his house, I found a copy of the Koran under his pillow. I haven't said anything yet, because I'm scared he may be a terrorist. Condi, I really care about him, but I'm worried about my own safety. Should I go "all the way" with him?

Signed,
Worried in Waco

Dear Worried,

It's best to keep a cool head in cases like this. If your boyfriend is a terrorist, he'll slit your throat as soon as break wind if he thinks you're about to hand him a one-way ticket to Guantánamo. On the other hand, if he's just intellectually curious about other religions, he might be offended that you jumped to the wrong conclusion. It's not against the law to read the Koran—yet. You're doing the right thing by clamming up. Here's what you can do to set your mind at ease:

Ask him his last name. Does it sound Jewish? The best data indicate that there are no Jews in al-Qaeda. Ask him whether he's fasting or having a bar mitzvah, or engaging in some other type of Jewish activity. (FYI—Jewish men are known to be very good providers, they are by far the most intelligent and shrewd men available, and they make great economic and foreign policy advisors, so if your boyfriend turns out to be Jewish, hold on for dear life!) If you think you can check to see if he's Jewish simply by examining his penis, *think again.* Muslim men routinely circumcise themselves as well, probably so they can masquerade as Jews should they be captured by our armed forces.

If you're examining your boyfriend's penis to see if he's still got a foreskin, chances are he'll pressure you to engage in intimate sexual contact. Don't give in! He'll beg, he'll plead, he'll promise you fame, riches, love, and happiness beyond your wildest dreams. He's *lying.* Trust me, you're better off dating a terrorist. (At least they're chaste because they're in love with Allah.) Tell your boyfriend to put away the pud until *after* the nuptials.

Remember, many young girls have permanently ruined any chance for a normal sexual relationship by engaging in teenage promiscuity. Illicit sex at your age is a deeply disappointing and disturbing experience, often resulting in a lifetime of shame, frigidity, and/or perversion, not to mention disgusting and disfiguring disease, suicide, and fatal automobile accidents.

Now, if he's not Jewish, but he is missing his foreskin, call the FBI as soon as you get home. Tell them your boyfriend's name and address, the location of the entrances to his home, the configuration of rooms and furniture, and how many people are usually in the house with him at any given time. They'll take care of the rest. Just to be safe, make sure you don't go anywhere near his house for a few days. You don't want to get caught in the crossfire.

Dear Condi,

I'm fifteen years old, a straight-A+ student, and I'm thinking of majoring in Petro-Geological Studies when I go to Stanford, where they're holding a place for me in the Class of 2011. Even though I'm the smartest girl at my school, the boys pay a lot of attention to me too. I've read so much about you, and I couldn't help noticing our similarities: both of us are cute as a button, whip-smart, hunk magnets, and obsessed with petroleum production. I've heard that you're dating a football player. Well, Condi, I'm dating a football player too, but not from my high school. He's a pro, twenty-four years old, and built like a brick shithouse. He towers over me, but he's my big love-muffin! I didn't know who else to turn to who would understand my predicament. The difference in our sizes makes sexual intercourse extremely painful. He tries to be gentle, but he's got 195 pounds on me. What do you do to protect yourself when you're with your football love machine?
Signed,
Hot 'n' Hurt in Houston

Dear Hot,

I try to be dispassionate in responding to teen letters, but sometimes it depresses me to think my message isn't getting out. If you know anything about me, you know that I am a devout Christian, deeply committed to serving our Lord with charity and compassion for others, even those who do not believe, and are thus damned to eternal torment in the searing flames of hell. Sex outside of marriage is a sin, not to mention a trap involving thick, malodorous genital discharges (see my reply to Worried in Waco, above). I strongly advise you to reexamine your values and your beliefs. Start by resuming your emulation of me. Think of what your future could hold: power, notoriety, an oil tanker named after you. Take it from me, it's a lot better than sex with jocks, and a whole lot more lucrative. Then, after your career is well under way, and you are over twenty-one years of age, copulate to your heart's content. But no patty-fingers until *after* he says "I do."

Having made that point, I acknowledge that I do believe strongly in female empowerment, and I support young girls' pursuit of knowledge and experience. So I will answer your question, however briefly:

Large men should take small women from behind, with the partners lying on their sides, his front to your back. He can reach around to caress your breasts and genitals, and you can turn your head to receive his kisses. Lift your top leg until he manages to enter you, and then your legs may intertwine, or remain free to kick or tremble, as you prefer. Be alert for any attempted sodomy, which is not only a sin, but also extremely painful, unbelievably disgusting, and hard to clean up. A more feminist approach, but nothing to shy away from, is the female superior position, in which you sit atop your mate. This can result in a particularly powerful orgasm, since both partners can caress the genitalia, breasts, and other erogenous areas, as well as swap spit. Neither of these positions exposes you to the risk of being crushed by the massive weight of your partner, or accidentally pierced by his masculinity.

In response to the overwhelming need for guidance amongst our youth, the United States Department of Health and Human Services Division of Faith-Based Teenage Chastity and Prevention of Intimacy (USDHHSDFBTCPI) has devised these simple, effective, nondenominational facts that every teen must learn:

M'LADY, LEND AN EAR...

★ "Loose and fast, *walk on past*. Chaste and pure, *bride for sure!*" So say the boys, and the boys do the choosin'. The sluts do the *losin'*.

★ Your secret nether place is a moist, eerie cauldron of deep, dark mystery. Let someone defile it, outside of holy wedlock, and you'll unleash *horrors you have never dared to imagine*.

★ The price of a moment's pleasure: intractable, painful vaginal itch, diarrhea, douche-resistant feminine odor, involuntary urination, acne, massive hair loss, wattles, unpopularity, and a *slow descent into madness and death*—just like masturbation.

Lustful teenagers must choose, *not lose*, their virginity. Our teen's cherries are so precious, they're actually worth *money*. ✞

BOYS, LISTEN UP!

★ The human female is *God's gift to you*. Unwrapping the present before Wedding Day is no way to say "thank you."

★ Out of hand, out of mind. Quit touching yourself "down there," and you're less likely to get the urge to poke around your date's "Gateway to Hell."

★ Premarital intimacy results in atrophied, shriveled privates, leaky sphincter, impotence, and *fatal disease*—just like masturbation.

✞ Medical information courtesy of **Choosing the Best, Inc.**, a leader in abstinence-focused sex education curricula, training, and resources since 1993. A study from the U.S. Department of Health and Human Services predicts **50–60 percent reduction in teen sexual activity** with **Choosing the Best**. Contact them today! **www.choosingthebest.org**

★ FIRST FAMILY VALUES

We are proud to publish here, as a gift to fathers everywhere, a very special prayer. It was composed with a loving heart by a wife and mother, as a celebration of the spiritual rebirth of her husband, the father of her two precious, beautiful daughters. He had only recently repented of his sins, and accepted Jesus Christ as his personal Savior, following a life of debauchery. Now, these precious daughters had begun to follow their father's sinful ways—drinking alcohol, huffing brake fluid, perhaps giving up their unstained bodies in filthy orgies, and worse. Believing that a father's prayer, so deeply felt, would help to keep the girls from ending up in prison, like their crack-smoking, slatternly Mexican cousin in Florida, this dutiful wife brought forth a prayer of unmatched beauty and feeling. Who is this wife of such uncommon faith? Her name should be familiar to you all...it is Laura. That's right—Her Excellency, the First Lady of the United States of America, Mrs. George W. Bush.

A FATHER'S PRAYER FOR HIS DAUGHTER'S CHASTITY

Heavenly Father, Parent of Jesus, Dad of Dads, help me, Your mortal son, to simmer down. Hide, O Lord, from groping hands and prodding flesh, the sweet and precious font of life that lays, as if a treasure for the taking, twixt thigh and thigh of your daughter's name here, *beloved child of mine, and Thine. Watch over her each day, and especially each night. Protect her, so that vile, corrupting youth shall sample not the fruit of my loins behind my back. Help me, Father, to nail each one who dares besmirch the soft and pristine crevasse from which Your miracle of life is meant to spring. Only in a union blessed by God and His earthly witnesses, do allow that thing to happen, and keep the filthy deed outside my vision and my thoughts. For otherwise, I might dwell upon that husband's acts, as though they were my own, and be thus consumed by lustful thoughts unclean, forever and ever.*

—AMEN.

★ CLASS WARFARE IS IMMORAL

Sure, racism can be not very nice, unless it's being used to simply entertain or instruct. But a much more dangerous and evil force is wealthism. Rich people have feelings too, you know. Take a moment to examine your own thoughts and actions. Do you ever have spiteful feelings toward those who are more successful than you? If this is the case, you may be guilty of hate crimes against the rich. Thought-hate crimes. Take this quick quiz:

1 Do you ever wonder if Kenneth Lay of Enron still needs all those mansions?

2 How many homes are too many? Two? Four? Six? Eight?

3 Do you raise an eyebrow when you hear about Coca-Cola labor union leaders being executed in Colombia?

4 Where should the inheritance tax begin?
   a. $1 million
   b. $5 million
   c. Of course there should be no inheritance tax for estates of any size.

5 Which is the most offensive display of excessive wealth?
   a. Ice sculptures of Michelangelo's "David" that urinate premium vodka at $2 million birthday party.
   b. Male models that urinate premium vodka at $2 million birthday party.
   c. Infants whose blood has been replaced with premium vodka that are devoured by the guests at $2 million birthday party.

WATCHWORD: "CONDOM"

The word "condom" means that somebody's got something nasty hiding in his you-know-what. When you hear the word "condom," run for cover. You see, moral people don't need condoms. When you're moral, your peenie and your woo-woo are as clean as a whistle. When you're moral, even the smegma that you scrape from under your foreskin is so pristine that it can be used as a moisturizing skin emollient, or a creamy spread on crackers. Moral people have no disease, and moral, married people (a loving husband and a submissive wife) only have sex for procreation, once every two years, so there is never the need for a condom. If someone in your school or on the street tries to slip you a condom, report them to the police immediately.

If you even felt the need to answer any of these questions, you are a horrible rich-person hater that should experience crushing guilt. How can you overcome these feelings of self-destructive proletarian rage and regain a proper American respect for our aristocracy?

★ Learn more about rich people's culture. Watch shows on television that show you how rich people live, and marvel at their sprawling mansions, swimming pools, staffs of servants, luxury automobiles, and private jets.

★ Volunteer to work at a rich people's hostel. Becoming a butler is a great way to actually spend time around rich people, learning to understand their needs and desires. You can learn this satisfying trade at rich people's resorts around the world.

★ Host a rich people cultural appreciation night. Talk with your friends and neighbors about all the good things that rich people have brought you.

★ Organize and march proudly in a rich persons parade to show your support.

★ Volunteer to work with overprivileged children. With their hardworking parents busily shuttling back and forth from their offshore tax shelters in the Bahamas all the time, somebody needs to take these poor, overprivileged children to their pony lessons.

★ FIRST FAMILY VALUES

Thank the Lord

by Former President George H.W. Bush

I'm proud of all of my boys, but George Junior has gone the farthest in making a man of himself. Maybe he was listening to me after all, only I was too busy fielding complaints from angry headmasters and girls' parents to notice. For most of George W.'s life, Bar and I were convinced he'd celebrate his fortieth birthday inside a jail cell. What made the difference was his commitment to God Almighty to stop the nonsense. That small, seemingly opportunistic and transparently hypocritical decision opened the gates to a whole new world of undeserved wealth and power. After Junior found Jesus, that meant he could finally honor his mother and father by starting new wars that have been highly profitable for me and all my weapons-manufacturing friends here at the Carlyle Group. I thank the Lord every day that He thought George Junior was worth the trouble. That was very gracious of Him. Now, if He'd only take an interest in Jeb and Neil, and those good-for-nothing embarrassments they call my granddaughters, I might just die a happy man.

★ DISCIPLINE YOUR DELINQUENT

Is your kid a social deviant? Is he mired in drugs, alcohol, sex, witchcraft, heavy metal music, and Dungeons & Dragons? It's time you shipped that juvenile delinquent off to boot camp! Here's a list of excellent institutions around the world where your problem child can learn discipline and respect:

1. Casa del Jefe—Buenos Aires, Argentina

2. Vladimir's Winter Retreat Camp—Nome, Alaska

3. Five-Star Youth Ranch—Fort Sam Houston, San Antonio, Texas

4. Metropolitan Detention Center—Sunset Park neighborhood, Brooklyn, New York

5. Camp X-Ray—Guantánamo Bay, Cuba. Several children under the age of sixteen are in custody at this boot camp for bad boys. Your teen will feel right at home!

SIEG DAD! How We Honor Our Fathers

by Karl Rove
White House Chief
Political Advisor

They attack me with the ridiculous claim that my *grandfather* built a Nazi concentration camp. They attack the Presidential Appointee because his *grandfather and great-grandfather* helped finance the Third Reich, and got caught with their fingers in the strudel. They attack the governor of California because his *father* was an eager-beaver Austrian volunteer to be a Nazi brown-shirt stormtrooper. We've listened to it, and we've ignored it, but we're not going to take it any more. In the New America, we're proud of our fathers, and not ashamed to say so, because God told us to honor our fathers, and by golly that's what we're going to do. The New America is a place of starting over, where you can hold the same values that you had before, but just call them something else. As well as accepting the pathetic masses of stinking immigrants—an infestation of barely human effluvia cast off by Mother Europe a century ago—America opened its doors to businessmen and other square-jawed, blonde citizens, weighted with the baggage of a little poor judgment, who were seeking a fresh start. And that's what America offers, Nazi or no Nazi. So we're not ashamed to say that we're not ashamed. And it's about time.

What does it say about a culture when the rich traditions of painting, sculpture, dance, and music are defunded and neglected to the point where an entire generation may lose the living memory of what art means to the human soul? It says, "That culture is growing up and facing facts, missy."

In our new world of perpetual danger, do you suppose your tax dollar is better spent beefing up our legions of under-trained airport security personnel, or paying for some pansy dancer's pirouette lessons? Let's say you're on an airplane, and the guy next to you looks more like the Wild Man of Borneo than Mr. John Q. Businesstraveler. He's feverishly clutching a pack of matches and shooting nervous looks back and forth between the stewardess and his huge, smelly sneakers.

Try hiding behind some government-funded, avant-garde, nude performance art now, culture vultures! Try stopping the mad terrorist with your sensitive photo essay exploring the plight of transsexual Puerto Rican derelicts on crack!

> **"When I hear the word 'culture,' I reach for my PATRIOT Act."**
>
> —John Ashcroft

★ WINNING THE CULTURE WAR

The enemy forces are gathering. Gays are prowling toward the sacred altar of heterosexual marriage, atheists are banning prayer in public schools, abortionists are sharpening their knives, and multicultural professors on college campuses are licking their chops in anticipation of feasting on the defenseless canon of Western culture. Your government is not standing idly by with these wolves at our door. Take gay marriage, the issue that is most advantageous to consolidating our power this year. Not only are we acting to protect the sanctity of marriage from those who would seek to destroy it, but we are on the offensive.

The U.S. Army will soon be deployed across our great, straight nation to detect and disrupt underground gay marriage rituals. Operation Vigorous Thunderbolt will apply overwhelming heterosexual force to the extremely gay areas of Vermont, Massachusetts, and San Francisco in particular. Sophisticated military surveillance equipment will be used to locate the source of disco music from the 1970s being played—a telltale sign that a gay marriage is in progress. After the wedding party is subdued with concussion grenades, a military tribunal will order on-the-spot execution for marriage-attempting homosexuals and those who harbor them. A chaplain will be available for last-minute conversions to Christian heterosexuality before the executions.

You must do your part in this cultural battle. Everyone knows that the stork doesn't visit the gay bar, so guard your sperm, men. Don't leave any of it just lying around. If a lesbian were to find your sperm, she could use it to inseminate herself or a lesbian accomplice—yet another terrorist strike against normal, God-approved marriage and procreation.

This is only the beginning. The entire Bible will soon be engraved permanently into public sidewalks and the sides of buildings. Gideon strike forces will break into private homes and place Bibles on everyone's bedside table. We will not abandon you in these culture wars, white, Christian, heterosexual America, and we will *never* surrender.

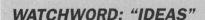

WATCHWORD: "IDEAS"

You don't need "ideas" when you have a solid moral foundation and a working knowledge of biblical scripture. Ideas are the lazy man's excuse for not adhering to a proper code of behavior. Ideas about evolution, social justice, sexual "orientation," self-determination for non-American nations, nucular disarmament, free health care, legalizing marijuana—they're all just satanic liberal tricks, which they use to lead you down the garden path toward a dark, spooky corner where they can hit you over the head and rape you.

Toward a Good America Through Denial, Refusal, and Punishment

by Paul Wolfowitz
Deputy Secretary
of Defense

Most people know me as the architect of the effective new foreign policy doctrine of Pre-emptive Unilateral Attack (PEUA, pronounced *pee-YOO-ahh*). But I am more than just a brilliant, innovative political philosopher and man of action. I am also a father, and I have the

WATCHWORD: "RIGHTS"

"Rights" is wrong. Whether it's women's rights, abortion rights, gay rights, immigrants' rights, prisoners' rights, or animal rights, "rights" means that your way of life is being viciously attacked. It's only *your* rights that need defending. Uphold these good rights: evangelical Christians' right to proselytize and display the Word of God in public buildings; the right to bear arms; smokers' rights; a parent's right to corporally punish children (any children); and the right to yell "fire" in a theater crowded with drunken Democratic liberal sodomites.

instincts of a pedagogue. Since we first began blowing up civilian populations to prove that we mean business, I've felt a desire to reach out to young people, on their level, to let them know how I would like them to contribute to the era of United States world dominance that is finally upon us. Stooping to the intellectual level of a teenager, I realized that the vast majority of American people operate at this very same infantile level of intellect. My new technique, based on my own experience as the beleaguered father of teenaged daughters, ranks as another of my great philosophical discoveries in that it offers hope to all weak-minded Americans whose wills can be subjugated for the greater good of the nation.

The technique is so simple, even a dog or an infant can understand it. In fact, I first had the idea some years ago when my eldest daughter was eleven months old, and about to pull a full twelve-piece setting of Lennox™ china down on top of her head. I tore the linen tablecloth out of her chubby little hand, smacked her sharply on the wrist, and shouted "NO!" in an extremely loud, clear voice. We needn't go into her reaction, but suffice to say, my wife and I have not had to replace any china.

What follows is a list of ideas that form the cornerstone of good behavior for every good American. Achieving adherence to these ideas is as simple as slapping a wrist, slashing a budget, or dropping a bomb. Once the subject knows that he or she will be physically punished for the slightest transgression, good behavior becomes the norm, and

American society becomes good—goodness being essentially the result of blind obedience. I dedicate this technique to a wonderful friend, Nancy Reagan, whose "Just Say No to Drugs" campaign would have worked if she'd launched it today, now that our nation has finally committed itself to punishing evildoers.

BAD BEHAVIOR	GOOD AMERICAN RESPONSE
Mercy for the evildoer	**"NO MERCY!"** followed by carpet-bombing
Abortion	**"NO ABORTION!"** followed by nine months locked in a damp cellar with nothing to eat except bugs
Gun control	**"NO GUN CONTROL!"** followed by the handgun assassination of a Democratic presidential candidate
Drugs	**"NO DRUGS!"** followed by life imprisonment without parole
Nuclear disarmament	**"NO NUCLEAR DISARMAMENT!"** followed by forced ingestion of bite-sized pellets of depleted uranium-237
Surrender	**"NO SURRENDER!"** followed by humiliating urological and proctological examinations of our enemies televised worldwide on cable news networks
Waiting at the gas station	**"NO WAITING FOR GAS!"** followed by widespread looting and a price increase of $5 per gallon of gas
Fear	**"NO FEAR!"** followed by twenty-four hours at the bottom of a snake pit, handcuffed to the reanimated corpses of Uday and Qusay Hussein
Tuna casserole	**"NO TUNA CASSEROLE!"** followed by legal separation and divorce

Our nation's experts in the field of gay deprogramming have devised a new "shortcut technique" using powerful electrodes. This high-voltage approach to bringing deviant homosexuals back to normality is not so dependent on the "talking cure" that was popular in the 1970s. Developed by Reverend Donald Wildmon of the American Family Association, along with the National Association for Research and Therapy of Homosexuality (NARTH), this new technique centers on a pelvic harness made of black leather that bristles with electrodes. These electrodes are attached to the scrotum and anus of the gay. Once the electrode harness is in place, the gay is pinned down on a concrete floor. Staggered jolts of electricity are then applied to these sensitive gay areas in a rhythmic pattern which is identical to the beat of the gay disco music. This treatment creates an effective Pavlovian response in which the former gay associates gay feelings and gay culture with blinding pain, and therefore will do anything he can to avoid this terrifying gayness in the future.

This exciting new technology is a shining example of George W. Bush's policy of compassionate conservatism. To all of our nation's gays, we would like to say that we all make mistakes. Your mistake was putting that first penis in your mouth when you shouldn't have. But we forgive you, and we only want to help you become a normal, heterosexual person again. We can't promise anything, but if you let us clip the electrode harness to your anus and scrotum willingly, you might even get into heaven.

No similar deprogramming technologies have been developed or discussed for the treatment of lesbianism, as lesbianism only exists for the purpose of stimulating and satisfying healthy, normal, male sexual interests, and we're not interested in discussing those either.

WATCHWORD: "NATIONAL SOVEREIGNTY"

"National sovereignty" is a vicious hoax cooked up by a bunch of dirty traitors who think we ought to get a permission slip before invading "sovereign nations," even when our Presidential Appointee urgently states that our country is threatened with imminent destruction, possibly. Hey, here's another great idea! Why not get every congressman and senator and UN ambassador and sixth-grade teacher to sign the permission slip, too? Then we'll all go down to the bank and get it notarized! In triplicate! Sure hope the line at the bank isn't too long, or else by the time we get everything approved, *EVERYONE IN AMERICA WILL BE DEAD FROM WEAPONS OF MASS DESTRUCTION LAUNCHED BY THE FORCES OF EVIL WHILE WE WERE WAITING FOR THE AMBASSADOR FROM BURUNDI TO SIGN THE FUCKING PERMISSION SLIP!!!*

American
BUSINESS

Welcoming Remarks by
Vice President & CFO,
Richard B. Cheney

*"The chief business of the
American people is business."*
—Calvin Coolidge

I think often of the diminutive man from Vermont, misunderstood almost from the moment of his ascent to power following an unfortunate coronary event in the chest of President Harding. Some derisively called him "Silent Cal," but when you're out on a pristine mountain lake, waiting for one of those five-pound farm-raised trout to strike, it's silence that frees you to think great thoughts, or take great naps. Nobody who talks during a fishing trip gets invited back—that's the unspoken rule. Even George knows that. When he starts squawking, I tell him the doc said I need my peace and quiet or I'll keel over just like Harding. That always shuts him up.

Calvin Coolidge, the second-to-greatest Republican Presidential Appointee ever, understood the power of business—and the spirituality of it, too. "The man who builds a factory, builds a temple." He wrote that, yessir. You want them to come to work, tell them God's inside waiting for them. They fall for it every time. Everybody's got the idea that if God sees them working hard and making good, then somehow things will get better for them. Damn right. That's what's got productivity up in America. That, and a profound need most folks have for money. Can't argue with that.

And with the forward-thinking policies of this administration, people all across this great land are discovering that, indeed, you can't argue with business. That is, unless you want to get canned, which some losers want anyway, because they're just too scared or too lazy to get up in the morning. No, most Americans understand, on a gut level, that they'd better keep their head down, nose to the grindstone, or somebody's liable to come along and chop it off. This isn't time for kidding around. There's a war on, and it looks like it's going to last a long time, maybe forever. Yes, I'm talking about the War on Terror, but I'm also talking about the War on Regulation, the War on Taxes, the War on Unions, and the War on Democrat Snoops.

Most Americans know what it takes to make an honest buck, and they want to be left alone to get the work done, so that they can get paid. Who'd want to go to work in handcuffs with a ball and chain to drag around? A somewhat honest businessman like myself gets to feeling like his own government treats him like a terrorist in an extralegal detention center. The folks I meet and talk to across America know that as a businessman, I understand what works and what gums up the works. You don't keep tapping a guy on the shoulder while he's trying to do his damn job. That goes for mopping up a pool of deadly chemicals inside a poorly ventilated toxic-waste holding tank as well as making staggeringly profitable sweetheart back-scratching buddy deals that will determine the very future of wealth.

America today is responsible for practically all of the Freedom™ that exists on this planet. Democracy is job one. It's what we do best. So, naturally, Americans need more of what the world has to offer. I'm talking about give and take, supply and demand. The world understands this, even though sometimes they pretend like they don't. Couple of sanctions, couple of embargoes, bomb the hell out of some uncooperative country, and we usually get the whole gang to come around to where we want them. Make no mistake: we know what we're doing, and there's no stopping us. Under the circumstances, it's best to just get out of our way. You don't want to get caught under the steamroller. It's a dangerous world. Why, you never know if something you do or say is going to make somebody want to come to your house and kill you.

So think about what good old President Coolidge said, and the next time you're in need of some spiritual nourishment, and if it's not Sunday morning, go to work. That's what puts America on top, and me in charge—little people like you going to work and believing your everlasting souls depend on it. And we who run the businesses, and the country along with them, will take good care of you. Promise.

★ HOW TO CLOSE YOUR SMALL BUSINESS

In the never-ending march of progress that is capitalism, it is inevitable that people like you will always lose. Here are some tips for shuttering your small business with what is left of your personal dignity:

★ Hand-letter a poorly worded sign notifying the public about the closing of your store. A ballpoint pen and a torn-off sheet of notebook paper is all you need for a nice sign. Write something like "Lost Our Lease—50% Off Everything." The next day, cross out "50%" and write "75%."

★ Before closing down your shop for the last time, be sure to remove the first dollar that you made, which is usually taped to the front of the cash register. You can buy a soda with that kind of money!

★ After you are evicted from your store, continue to sell your merchandise from cardboard boxes on the sidewalk in front of your former place of business until the police show up.

★ Go home (if you still have one) and wait for the wealth of successful people to trickle down on you.

Or, you can play like the big boys! Here are some tactics inspired by such business luminaries as Kenneth Lay of Enron and Dennis Kozlowski of Tyco:

★ For accounting and/or insurance purposes, falsify records indicating massive expenditures for services, utilities, expendables, and inventory. Go to the store of a successful friend and borrow some invoices and receipts. Take photos and video of your friend's (or even a stranger's) fixtures, inventory, cash registers, furniture, and expensive alarm systems.

★ Take any remaining capital, and any remaining credit on company credit cards, and spend it immediately on first-class, one-way tickets to Tahiti. Place tickets in a safety deposit box at your bank.

★ At the same time, loot the business of anything that is not nailed down and can be sold, hocked, or melted down for scrap; then call the cops and the insurance company.

★ Consider arson.

★ Make sure all documentation is vetted by a smart Jew accountant so the Democrat-controlled IRS does not discover an "irregularity" and penalize you for your initiative.

Being laid off isn't the end of the world! Consider it a new chance for exciting opportunities.

★ If you're a young, healthy factory worker, consider striking out for a life of adventure. There are all kinds of good factory jobs in far-off places like Burma, Mexico, and India that have sprung up just over the last few years. The wages might be 1 percent of what you used to earn, but at least you'll have the satisfaction of still working for an American-owned company.

★ If you're a senior citizen whose retirement benefits have been gambled away in the stock market by your former boss, how about spending your golden years under the Golden Arches, making Freedom Fries™ at your neighborhood McDonald's? Or, you could wear a little blue vest and stand out in front of your local Wal-Mart all day, handing out coupons. Everyone will think you're so cute!

★ America's precious children will not be left behind in George W. Bush's economic plan. With his new Jobs for Children Act, Presidential Appointee Bush has legalized full-time employment for children as young as seven years old. Did you know that American children are among the slowest in the world at stitching and assembling Nike Shox™ running shoes? Our kids must catch up with the world leaders in this field, such as Indonesia and Pakistan, or they will be excluded from the coming global Nike Shox™ age of the future.

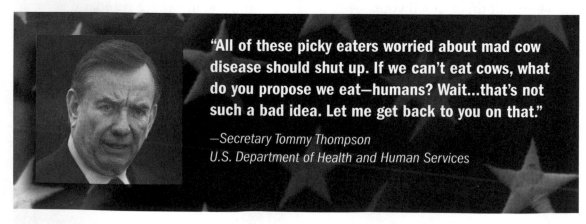

"All of these picky eaters worried about mad cow disease should shut up. If we can't eat cows, what do you propose we eat—humans? Wait...that's not such a bad idea. Let me get back to you on that."

—Secretary Tommy Thompson
U.S. Department of Health and Human Services

THE NEW DEPLETED-URANIUM
HUMMER®

FUCK EVERYBODY

In this age of terror, who wants to be defensive behind the wheel? It's time for you to become an offensive driver—and General Motors, with help from the U.S. Armed Forces, will make you one. Introducing the brand new DU HUMMER, now available for civilian purchase. Depleted uranium is an incredibly dense nuclear waste product that our soldiers use as ammunition to incinerate eighteen-year-old Iraqi conscripts and other evildoers from miles away. This amazing substance is also perfectly safe—it's a mere 60 percent as radioactive as normal uranium. Now the heaviest element on the planet forms the fully-welded frame, reinforced body panels, and massive bumpers of the new DU HUMMER, which weighs in at an unstoppable 20,000 pounds. The strength, tough-ness, and armor-piercing capability of this vehicle is unequaled by anything else on the road. In two-vehicle collision tests, the DU HUMMER completely vapor-ized the other car. How's that for preemptive driver safety? Better buy one...before your enemy does.

SPECIAL OFFER
Exclusive to *Citizen You!* readers.
Buy a DU HUMMER and don't pay any
federal income taxes that year!
Redeem at your local HUMMER dealership.

Expires 9/11/04.

✂

Safety Note: If two DU HUMMERS crash into each other, they both explode in a small "nuclear-like" explosion that irradiates the sur-rounding area for 4.5 billion years. However, the radioactive blast radius is less than one mile in diameter, unless the wind is blowing. Please, always buckle your seatbelt and wear a sealed, airtight, full-body unitard made of lead while driving your new DU HUMMER. Pregnant or lactating women should only drive the DU HUMMER if they don't want to keep their babies.

To ambitious executives who think outside the box, Iraq is more a state of mind than an actual nation right now. Anything is possible. We'll bet you, dollars to dinars, that the opportunities are limitless. Will your company be the first to woo the Iraqis into customer servitude? Iraqis need everything from toilet paper to DVD players to iced mochaccino grandés. (They're all set for automatic rifles and rocket-propelled grenades, though.) You could be the first to sell it to them. Dress up in a business suit and combat boots, like our CEO in Iraq, L. Paul Bremer III, and make your fortune in this exciting land!

It couldn't be easier, especially after the pleasant surprise of all the looting in postwar Iraq. Our successful "look the other way" policy enabled looters to clear out schools, governmental buildings, and hospitals, wiping the slate clean for new opportunities. Now, American corporations can swoop in with brand-new textbooks, hospital equipment, carpeting, furniture, air conditioners, computers, and thousands of other expensive items to replace what was lost. Plus, their new systems will be dependent on American parts and supplies forever. The most common sound in Iraq has changed from "KA-BOOM!" to "KA-CHING!"

The magical moment came when our Coalition Provisional Authority (CPA) passed Order 39 on September 21, 2003, sanctioning 100 percent foreign ownership of Iraqi companies and the repatriation of all profits earned by those companies to investors abroad. Can you believe that Iraq used to run on a hopelessly outdated socialist economic system where key elements of the economy, from banking to manufacturing, were owned by Iraq and were off-limits to ownership by foreign firms? Not anymore! We're breaking up their national assets and selling them off to the highest bidder. (Unpatriotic French, German, and Russian companies need not apply.) Can you believe that Iraq used to have universal health care guaranteed for all of its citizens? Not anymore! We're setting up a price-gouging HMO health care system in Iraq right now. Those bad old days of Iraqi national sovereignty, business ownership, and guaranteed health care are over, which means big profits for you!

Don't worry about the Iraqi workers getting in the way of your business plans. We've made them so desperate, they'll take anything you'll give them! After our hostile takeover of the country, we ordered mass layoffs of the public sector workforce, with no unemployment insurance. 75 percent of the country is now unemployed, a number we can all be proud of. We cut benefits for food and housing that the Hussein regime had brutally granted its public-sector employees. CPA chief Paul Bremer has declared labor strikes in Iraq to be illegal, branding striking workers the enemies of U.S. soldiers. Labor unions in Iraq are also illegal, and we refuse to grant Iraqi workers collective bargaining rights, ignoring the

UN's International Labor Organization to which the United States is, unfortunately, a signatory. We have drawn an antilabor line in the sand. If Iraqi workers dare to organize any kind of peaceful demonstrations or labor-union activities, they will be arrested and treated as prisoners of war.

All of our fine work means that most Iraqis are jobless, penniless, and dependent on UN food handouts—just the way U.S. corporations like it. Now we can do anything we want to them. The only problem left is figuring out why they keep launching grenades at us. Don't they know we're over there for their Freedom™?

The biggest corporation in the world is an inspiration to us all

Five out of the ten richest people in the world are named Walton, but they're not the only ones pleased with the success of Wal-Mart. You can just tell from their advertising, showing their smiling employees with their children, that Wal-Mart is a great place to work full-time and earn $13,000 a year. These employees also love working full time and not being able to afford any health insurance. People with health insurance spend all their time filling out forms and petitioning their insurance companies when they could be happily mopping Sam Walton's floors. And you won't find any labor unions crippling the achievements of Wal-Mart. Third-party representation is needless at a company with an open-door policy; if an employee opens his mouth, then his manager will show him the door. Unions that entice workers with lures of fair pay, overtime compensation, affordable health care, and days off are strictly prohibited at Wal-Mart. Workers who are convicted of union-related activity are fired. Hey, didn't you see those happy Wal-Mart employees in the newspaper inserts, you sneaky union organizers? They don't need your false promises!

Wal-Mart also takes newly situated illegal immigrants to our country and gives them their first hand up—not handout—with nonstop work seven days a week, with no days off, for up to ten months. Actually, Wal Mart takes offense to the term "illegal immigrant." They prefer to call them "amigos." You might not see these amigos much because they're locked inside the stores on twelve-hour night shifts, but trust us, they're earning their keep! (Until the communists at the federal Department of Labor show up to investigate.) Of course, if these amigos fatally injure themselves while working, their remains will be put on the first bus back to Mexico and returned to their next-of-kin, should funds become available. Gone are the days of Wal-Mart's mass graves, concealed by the sagebrush out back.

It's not only Americans and illegal immigrants who enjoy all the benefits of working for Wal-Mart. People from around the world, especially in a totalitarian slave state known as "China," are busy earning pennies an hour making everything from George Foreman Grills to Star Wars action figures for the insatiable American consumer. These workers are much too busy to worry about luxuries such as a living wage or safe labor conditions. The Chinese manufacturers that supply Wal-Mart are slashing pay, imposing mandatory overtime shifts, and firing workers who even dare to discuss their working conditions. Wal-Mart is rolling back standards across the planet! Let's take a look at how brilliantly Wal-Mart's suppliers treat their employees, mostly young women and teenaged girls, in toy-assembly plants in Guangdong, China:

★ Thirteen- to sixteen-hour days molding, assembling, and spray-painting toys, seven days a week, with twenty-hour shifts in peak seasons. It's just like Santa's workshop, filled with happy, busy little elves. Merry Christmas, you Chinese!

★ Even though China's minimum wage is 31¢ an hour—which doesn't begin to cover a person's basic subsistence-level needs—these production workers are paid only 13¢ an hour. Now *that's* creative cost-cutting.

★ There are no pesky health and safety enforcement regulations in the factories. Workers enjoy constant headaches and nausea from paint dust hanging in the air. The indoor temperature hovers pleasantly over 100 degrees. There is no cumbersome protective clothing; repetitive stress disorders are plentiful; and there's no expensive training on the health hazards of handling plastics, glue, paint thinners, and other solvents every day.

★ None of this is a potential problem, as these teenaged girls must pay for their own medical treatment and are fired if they are injured or become too ill to work. What managerial genius!

Young Chinese women in slave-labor factories are a big part of the success of Wal-Mart, but we shouldn't overlook the contributions that American women make to this visionary corporation. American women make up 72 percent of Wal-Mart's sales work force but only 33 percent of its managers. They're routinely passed over for promotions, training, and pay raises which go to more deserving white men. And if they don't enjoy being sexually harassed and speak up about it, they're penalized, demoted, or fired. Don't worry; they're still allowed back in the store to purchase their pantyhose and tampons at Wal-Mart's everyday low prices!

Those low prices are the cornerstone of Wal-Mart's global success. By paying their American workers as little as legally possible and treating foreign workers like insects, Wal-Mart has been able to steamroll across North America, opening thousands of gray, hulking, aircraft hangar–sized stores now lurking on the fringes of every city and town. Other continents will soon follow. Wal-Mart opens a new megastore every two days, and in 2004 it plans to open a store every day. As Wal-Mart erects its Supercenters, it sucks commerce off Main Street, destroying traditional retailers that have served their communities for generations in their pathetically small stores. Local flavor disappears, to be replaced by the exact same Wal-Mart everywhere, squatting majestically in the endless horizons of their parking lots. By lowering their prices below cost to close competing small businesses and then raising their prices to a much higher level once monopoly is achieved, Wal-Mart stands alone, always triumphant...always. Wal-Mart would be a shining example of how to succeed in American business, except there can only be one Wal-Mart. All we can do is gaze up into the lofty, fluorescent-lit rafters of our local Wal-Mart in rapt wonder, tears of amazement streaming down our cheeks.

You won't find any pregnant Barbie dolls, the *Sports Illustrated* Swimsuit Issue, an uncensored rock 'n' roll CD, or other such cultural filth on the shelves of Wal-Mart, either. Sam Walton, our children, and our children's children, and our children's children's children, thank you.

★ JOBS FOR IRAQIS

Inspired by the thousands of technical support call centers that computer companies have set up in India and other developing countries, Iraqi expertise is being put to work by several enterprising corporations. American manufacturers such as Colt, Remington, and Winchester are hiring Iraqis to staff weapons support and advice hotlines. With over one million tons of small arms and ammunition in hidden storage bunkers across the country and at least one AK-47 assault rifle in every home, Iraq truly is a nation of "gun nuts." If American gun owners—whether they're militia leaders in Montana or shooting enthusiasts in South Central Los Angeles—are having trouble with their weapons, they'll soon be speaking with a friendly, knowledgeable Iraqi gun expert to solve their problems together.

★ THE DANGERS OF ALTERNATIVE POWER

Environmental terrorists and other fringe groups are always forwarding their radical agenda of alternative energy sources such as wind or solar power. They fantasize that if more research and development were invested, the United States could use clean, renewable energy sources that would decrease our need for oil from the unstable, violent Middle East. They claim this would be better for the planet's ecology and would reduce our need to control the world's oil reserves with military force, which invites terrorist retaliation against our troops and homeland. The easiest way to rebut these dangerous subversives is with cold, hard science. The simple fact of the matter is that clean energy sources *kill people*.

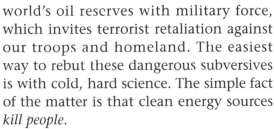

There's nothing clean about a blood-streaked windmill blade that just lopped off your head because you wandered too close on a breezy day. No community will support being surrounded by these 100-foot-tall killing machines and their whirring blades of death. You don't think the wind is dangerous? Ask the people who have been terrorized by tornadoes and hurricanes if they think allying ourselves with the wind is a good idea. Why else would we have built an early-warning tornado system—because the wind is our friend? Get a grip on reality, you windhuggers! Besides killing people, windmills also kill our beautiful birds. Greenpeace doesn't want you to know this, but the Bush administration is the only force looking out for our precious migrating birds.

Did you know that if you mix wind with flaming gasoline, you get napalm? That's why we're taking steps to secure our nation's air supply and sell it off to patriotic private firms. Soon you'll be enjoying air brought to you by your favorite corporations.

Solar energy is another ludicrous, genocidal scheme of the tofu-eaters. You need electricity at night, don't you? How can the sun help you then? More seriously, everyone knows that the sun gives you cancer. Solar panels collect and store this cancerous power of the sun, and then spread that cancer throughout your home if you are foolish enough to install them on your roof. The concentrated cancerous power of a single solar panel is so great that if you were to sit on one, your testicles *and* ovaries would liquefy and run down your legs.

Reject the murderous machinery of alternative energy. Support life. Go fill up your gas tank right now.

OUR RULING OVERCLASS

Every single member of the Bush cabinet is a millionaire. Our total net worth is more than ten times that of the Clinton cabinet! I bet you're impressed. Who would you rather have running your country? People smart and ambitious enough to be millionaires, or a bunch of broke morons?

Jet-fuel the economy! Why walk when you can drive? Do more! Don't you want to be a member of the productive class? Drive around and haul stuff! How else are you going to get around—walk? Natural energy like wind and water is regressive, but oil is the industry of forward movement. Put your pedal to the metal, just like our boys ripping across the deserts of Iraq in their gas-guzzling Humvees. The oil industry is the industry of tomorrow, the industry of rebuilding. Who is rebuilding Iraq? The oil industry, of course. Oil and gasoline power Freedom™ around the world. Limiting your gas intake limits your patriotic output, and it limits the imagination of the American people. For hundreds of years, Americans moved west until there was no more west to move to. To keep going, we now have to move east, and also south, and from there, maybe west again. Gas makes all of this moving possible! If not for gasoline, how would you be able to get to more gasoline?

Instead of alternative power sources, think of alternative uses for gasoline. Here are some ideas, just to get you revved up:

- Incinerate burrowing moles and other vermin in your yard

- Spread over your sidewalk to get rid of snow

- Disinfect and cauterize accidental gunshot wounds

- Remove bubble gum from children's hair

- Make any meal seem exotic by serving it *flambé*

- Use as an enema to relieve constipation

- Inhale fumes as a sleep aid

- Pour on a local hillside to create a giant, flaming marriage proposal

- Burn piles of *Hustler* magazines and Michael Moore bestsellers

- Spread all over your body as a manly cologne/insect repellent

- Burn off unsightly body hair (ladies, consider a sexy "Brazilian burn" for your bikini area)

- Spit a mouthful of gas at a lit birthday cake for a hilarious "birthday surprise"

- Use as a weed control agent, and also to poison your neighbor's faggoty flowerbed

- Clean off dirty seabirds caught in an oil spill

- Public religious self-immolation

★ TAKE A BITE OUT OF OVERTIME PAY

We need to be honest. The economy is on the rise, but is it as healthy as it could be? No. We've done what we can by cutting taxes so that money can be funneled back into the economy by generous wealthy people. Corporations want to do their part by letting Americans work more than eight hours a day or forty hours a week. However, if employers grant this gift to their workers, they lose all their profits to that silent thief—overtime pay.

Unlike most thieves, the police can do nothing about overtime pay because it's not illegal—yet. There are plenty of sneaky employees out there who are itching to take advantage of the loophole that requires businesses to pay one-and-a-half times their regular pay for overtime work. Do these people have no shame? It is sickening to watch them rip off their hapless employers, whose only mistake was to hire these deviants in the first place.

The average American worker is an honest, hardworking individual who would love nothing more than to roll up his sleeves and get in there to fix the economy, even if that means eighty-hour weeks of hard labor with no extra compensation. Everyone wants more work. You can't afford a vacation anyway. Besides, idle hands are the devil's playground. There's no time left for making anthrax bombs if you're working all the time. Unfortunately, a few bad apples insist that employees have a right to be paid adequately for their time, and they spoil it for everyone.

What good is a worker if they're only available forty hours a week? No good at all. The minute that clock rolls over to forty hours and one second, employers have to shut down their operations or start giving out more in payroll than they can reasonably afford. If we want our economy to get back on track, we need our workers to be available at all hours of the day. God forbid the phone should ring at 5:01 p.m. and nobody's there to answer it. That sale has been lost, that information is not delivered, and the caller will likely hang himself out of frustration.

In order for American businesses to compete in the new global economy, they must cut costs. Since ironclad minimum-wage laws prevent employers from paying a perfectly reasonable 35¢ an hour, they have to look elsewhere to make cuts. The most obvious target is overtime pay for workers.

The next step is erasing the very concept of "workers." Once again, Wal-Mart is at the cutting edge of this movement. Wal-Mart doesn't have "workers," they have "associates." This word choice makes it clear that there is absolutely no hierarchy in this planet-encircling, multi-billion-dollar corporation. Everyone is pulling together for the Wal-Mart team! When this illusion of equality and camaraderie is complete, it's so easy to abolish overtime pay and more. Employees may never receive pay raises,

HOW TO AVOID PAYING OVERTIME

Employers—if you can't move all your jobs to China, here are two basic strategies for how you can avoid paying overtime to your low-income employees:

1 Cut worker's hourly wages and add the overtime to equal their former salary. This way, your workers will work more hours for the same money.

2 Raise salaries to the $22,100 annual threshold that now makes workers ineligible for overtime.

This business advice is brought to you by the Labor Department of the Bush administration.

pensions, severance packages, health care, sick leave, or disability benefits, but at least they'll have the pride of being called an "associate" and being able to wear the same blue smock as everyone else!

With spirits so high in the workplace, is it morally right to keep workers from their jobs just because their employers can't afford to pay them overtime? Of course not. This is why we are encouraged by a new, grassroots movement to shake up the law and kick up to eight million deadbeats off the overtime eligibility list. To reflect this desire of the people, Congress has passed our new Freedom from Overtime Act.

And if you don't want to work more than forty hours a week? There's nothing stopping you from moving to North Korea and eating grass.

★ PROFILES IN SHAME: AMERICAN LABOR UNIONS

You say you want to protect American jobs, labor unions? Well, congratulations, you did just the opposite. It's the unions who made jobs flee overseas. With their ludicrous demands for a safe workplace and a living wage, it was the unions that forced beleaguered American manufacturers to pull up stakes in the communities they had grown to love and move their factories to friendlier employment climates. What's the matter, unionized workers? Were the fumes a bit too acrid for you? A little too noisy for you on the shop floor? Did it "bother" you when your buddy on the assembly line got his hand ripped off by the grinder? What did you think we were paying you $33 an hour for? Now there's a six-year-old in

Cambodia who doesn't mind these conditions, who doesn't mind coughing up a little blood at the end of a hard day's work. You don't hear little Punlork complaining as he trudges home through swamps, fetid with the toxic chemical runoff from the plant where he works, to take his 9¢ a day home to his family. That 9¢ could have gone to you and your family, but no, you had to hold out for more, more, more. Here's an idea—why don't you get Yasser Arafat to run the AFL-CIO? You have a lot in common. You both tried to hold out when you should have known you were being offered the best deal you'd ever get. Now you're both sitting in the rubble of your lost dreams, sad and alone.

★ WINNING THE DRUG SALES WAR

With the United States in charge, Afghanistan is once again the world's number-one producer of opium. And that's a good thing! This is one of the biggest changes that *Citizen You!* has to teach you. In the pre-9/11 era, we told you that all drug dealers were bad, even the ones on CIA payrolls. Now, in the much more realistic post-9/11 era, drugs are recognized as an important element in the War on Terror. For example, many terrorist groups fund their murderous actions through the sale of illegal drugs. We can beat them at their own game! If the United States controls the sale of these illegal drugs, then the terrorists lose their drug funding. If they weren't allowed to control drug sales, our CIA would lose a major source of their revenues. Taxpayers would have to make up the difference, and raising taxes is bad—much worse than raising money through addicting populations to drugs.

Let's take a look at our success in getting Afghanistan back to being the world's heroin basket. In 2000, the Taliban government, being a gang of fundamentalist nutjobs, completely banned opium production in Afghanistan. Prior to the ban, Afghanistan produced more than 70 percent of the world's opium in 2000, and about 80 percent of the heroin destined for the European market. But the Taliban's threat to cut the arms off any farmer found growing opium poppies was way too effective. Following the ban, opium production in Afghanistan collapsed by more than 90 percent, which meant substantial losses to the multi-billion-dollar drug trade that is laundered through

our banks. Our friends in the Northern Alliance kept hope alive by protecting the production and marketing of raw opium in the fringes of Afghanistan that they controlled, but they couldn't do it alone. When the Taliban refused to go along with our Unocal oil pipeline plans, on top of their opium ban, that was the end of our business relationship. Our brave troops went in, smashed the Taliban, and installed the government of President Hamid Karzai. (By the way, doesn't this former Unocal executive cut a dashing figure on the world stage in his bright, sparkly robes and hats? He's like a colorful little puppet!) As soon as our man Karzai was in charge, opium production soared in Afghanistan, regaining its historic levels. According to the United Nations Drug Control Program, Afghani opium cultivation increased 657 percent from 2001 to 2002. Let's all give President Karzai a big round of applause!

The Taliban cut off people's arms for growing drugs, but now that we're back in charge, we're making money hand over fist! And we're not paying *any* taxes on it. What can we do? The annual proceeds of the Afghan drug trade, between $100 to

$200 billion, represent approximately one-third of the worldwide annual sales of narcotics, estimated by the United Nations to total approximately $500 billion. Why did you think we fought to control Vietnam, Cambodia, and Laos, the other world center of opium production? Why do you think we now have troops and massive military investment in Colombia? Trust us, we're not after their coffee. Why do you think drug smuggling soared in Panama after George Bush Sr. took out Manuel Noriega for no longer following our orders? Sometimes it's not you, but the market, that determines what business you're in. The sale of illegal drugs in the United States alone is a business worth $250 billion a year. The worldwide narcotics industry is the largest industry on Earth. Do you think we're going to let a guy freezing his ass off on a street corner earn all that money? We don't think so. What's worse, selling drugs to poor people, or being one of those poor people on drugs? After all, wealth can't trickle down from us if we're not getting richer and richer. We're actually doing these poor people a favor by creating an insurance policy for their future. If they buy drugs from us now, that means they can enjoy being trickled down on later.

Drugs can be viewed as one of our weapons of Freedom™, which can be used to control and subdue whole populations. When we weren't shooting them like buffalo, we destroyed American Indians who got in the way of our Freedom™ by drowning them in alcohol, a drug they had never seen before. It's hard to shoot your arrows straight after the white man gives you all that firewater! Our British allies also used opium to good effect in the past to maximize profits and narcotize a billion Chinese people. Britain went to war from 1839 to 1842 for the sole purpose of "sapping the vitality" of China by forcing them to import opium from British India. At the end of the war, China had to open five major ports to British opium ships. An unrelenting flood of opium converted China from a unified culture that stood against British business interests into a splintered society of warlords fighting over patches of drug-dealing turf. This time-tested business plan was used by the CIA to similar effect during the 1980s. By flooding the ghettos of Los Angeles with crack cocaine imported from Central America, the CIA was able to address several problems facing the inner city, such as potential class unrest and the proliferation of African American nuclear families. The CIA was then able to funnel those illegal drug profits back into Central America to support their right-wing death squads seeking to overturn democratically elected governments. Now *that's* multitasking!

Even Skull and Bones, the elite Yale University secret fraternity whose membership list includes George W. Bush, his father, and his grandfather, was founded on opium riches. The mausoleum-styled fortress known as "The Tomb" and the private island where Bonesmen hold their rituals were donated by the Russell family of

Connecticut, whose vast fortune was accrued through dealing opium. With the slave trade outlawed, these Yankees had to sell something! In 1823, Samuel Russell established the Russell Trust Company for the purpose of acquiring opium in Turkey and smuggling it to China. By 1830, the Russell Trust Company had become the dominant opium-trafficking

322

syndicate in North America. The Skull and Bones fraternity was formed in 1832 by Samuel's cousin, General William Russell, who also worked in the family business. A black flag with a white skull-and-crossbones emblem—the corporate logo that flew from all Russell Trust Company ships—was adopted as the emblem of Skull and Bones. So you see, the good guys in ultra-elitist, death-worshipping secret societies can sell drugs too! If it's a good enough business for the original Bonesmen, it's good enough for you to accept.

So why do we keep drugs illegal? Because this makes them as precious as gold—gold that can be farmed. We must keep addictive drugs illegal so that street prices remain high, so we can maximize profits from our covert trafficking. Drug money is the lubricating force for our domination of the world economy. If you think of money as a magical fluid, drug money is like water. It can flow very quickly from one point to another. Where you apply money is where you have power. Drug money is the fastest way to control world markets, financial institutions, and interest rates. Money that is not criminal money has to go through regula-

tions and bureaucratic banking systems. It has to go through taxation. Lawyers track it. That money moves like molasses. Who needs it? As for us, we're on the winning side, and we don't intend to give up the drug business for all the opium in China. If you want to help us—and who wouldn't?—why don't you take a walk through that neighborhood you never go to, and try to convince some people who are poorer and browner than you are to try some soothing heroin?

NEW BUSINESS OPPORTUNITIES

Lost your job? Can't find work? Why not collect recyclable bottles and aluminum cans while waiting for your unemployment benefits to run out? Get a big old shopping cart and push it around your neighborhood, looking for recyclables. Offer to clean up after people who can afford to have parties. Pile those bottles high—don't be embarrassed! Every clink and clank that your neighbors hear is worth 5¢ a bottle! Remember, patriotic Americans collected scrap metal during World War II to help our boys rid the world of the Nazi menace. Now you can do the same during our Global War on Terror (GWOT)!

HALLIBURTON

Giving imported South Asian temporary workers something to SMILE about!

Here at Halliburton, we're taking billions of government dollars and turning them into millions of dollars in corporate profits. Immigrant labor from Third World countries working in our international development projects is a big part of that success. We'd love to hire Iraqis to help us rebuild Iraq, but they're so busy being penned into razor-wire enclosures by U.S. troops that they just can't get to work on time. Instead, we turn to what we like to call "guest workers," and Halliburton is more than happy to be their host.

When we built our state-of-the-art prison complex for terrorists in Guantánamo Bay, Cuba, we hired the cheapest expertise available—650 Filipino and Indian guest workers who worked for a quarter of what American engineers would demand. Even more profitable is the $3 per day we pay the 1,800 Pakistani, Indian, Bangladeshi, and Nepalese workers who work for the Tamimi Company, our subcontractor in the Persian Gulf, which organizes 180,000 meals every day for U.S. military forces. These workers are given leave only once every two years.

Of course, we found the most advantageous labor conditions in Burma, where whole villages were emptied out for us by our friends in the Burmese Army. These hardworking villagers were sent to forced labor camps on uninhabited islands, where they worked for wages as low as $0 an hour building oil pipeline and helicopter pads under the watchful eye of the Burmese Army. These guest workers even had to pay their own transportation out to the islands! If they refused, the lucky ones were arrested and forced to work for the army as porters in jungle war zones. (The colorful phrase for "porter" in Burmese translates to "human donkey.") The others were shot and pushed into fires.

Do you think we could get American workers to accept these working conditions? We can always hope, but we haven't been able to arrange that—yet. How about Iraqis? 70 percent of them are unemployed, but if we hired them they'd probably throw a grenade into one of our managers' offices because they're all terrorists. No, Halliburton is perfectly happy with our desperately poor friends from the Indian subcontinent, whom we can exploit to the fullest.

No jobs for Iraqis

No jobs for Americans

Major profits for us

HALLIBURTON... *Thanks.*

Managers and executives! Is *your* place of business as patriotic as it should be? Here are some ideas you can use to pump up the patriotism in your workplace!

★ When you walk into a typical American office, you'll see an American flag and a framed photograph of Presidential Appointee George W. Bush in the reception area. You can do better than that! Purchase large, framed posters of the Presidential Appointee to put above every one of your employee's desks.

★ Make sure your telephone hold music is either Toby Keith or John Philip Sousa.

★ Force your staff to say the Pledge of Allegiance in unison every morning.

★ Replace the sentimental, namby-pamby photos of children, wives, and pets on your employee's desks with patriotic pictures such as M1A2 Abrams Main Battle Tanks surging across the deserts of Iraq or Green Berets with knives clenched in their teeth on covert hunter-killer missions. To save money on picture frames, remove and discard the family photos while your employee is away from his desk and just slip the new military photos into the frames.

★ Create "team spirit" by taking all of your employees to the barber to get military-style crewcuts.

★ It is now illegal for businesses to give PAC money to political candidates, so all employees must donate money individually. Circulate a memo to your staff suggesting they can either donate 20 percent of their salary to the Republican party or start looking for a new job.

★ Do the actors who portray your workers appear proud to be Americans in your advertising? Do the actors who portray your customers appear satisfied by the patriotic levels of service they're receiving? The appearance of proud workers and customers is very important for your company's patriotic public image.

★ Check your customer base. Make sure you're not doing business with terrorists, people who might incite terrorism with unpatriotic sentiments, or people who don't spend enough money on activities and products that discourage terrorism and/or promote Freedom™.

★ Install an American flag as the background image on all office computer screens.

★ Place a patriotic quote at the end of your standardized corporate e-mail signature to let everyone know where you stand. Here's one quote that pays tribute to the 3,000 Americans murdered on 9/11, while keeping a solid eye on the bottom line:

"We need to counter the shock wave of the evildoer by having individual rate cuts accelerated and by thinking about tax rebates."
—George W. Bush, October 4, 2001

★ Reward your hardworking managers with patriotic executive toys for their desktops. A rubber doll of Hillary Clinton that you can smash repeatedly with your fist is one great stress-relief toy.

★ Loosen up and have fun with "military casual Fridays," giving your employees the option of wearing camouflage army uniforms, comfortable desert khakis, or Navy SEAL commando wetsuits.

★ Lunch hours spent at your local gun range or company retreats at paintball war-game tournaments are fine, but for real intraoffice bonding, consider mandatory Army Reserve training for all employees. Nothing builds trust and staff cohesion better than firing large amounts of live ammunition.

★ Blow off some patriotic steam with a daily "Two Minutes Hate" drill, where your employees are assembled to watch the latest Osama bin Laden videotaped message and are encouraged to scream, curse, and spit at the screen.

LOOK OUT BELOW

The conquest of the global market by American companies is about to take a huge step forward. New technologies will soon make it possible to air-drop entire restaurants and stores in one piece out of giant C-130 transport planes flying over sparsely developed countries. Terrain that was previously thought to be too harsh for construction will be easily colonized with this business delivery method. Excited, jabbering natives in some far-off jungle or desert will look up to see an entire McDonald's franchise parachuting down from the sky to slam onto the ground, ready and open for business. Targeted markets for planned multiple-franchise airdrops include the Amazon rainforest, the Sahara Desert, and the Himalayan mountain range. Get in line, Planet Earth! You're about to be super-sized!

★ MM-MM-MUTATIONS!

There are a lot of hippie holdovers from the 1960s out there who think that genetically modified food is "a bad idea" or "dangerous." They'll change their tune when they taste how delicious some of these utterly new foods are! How about beef-on-the-cob? Yes, that's mouthwatering nuggets of beef growing right out of a fun-to-hold corncob. Kids love it! These new foods go way beyond the tired old jellyfish-and-tomato combination. Sure, genetically splicing a snake and a watermelon might sound strange, but just wait until you try it! Or how about pork apples—shiny red-skinned balls of juicy pork that you can pick right off a tree and eat. What do you get when you cross a chicken with a pumpkin? A delicious slice of chumpkin!

Chumpkins look like a basketball with legs when they're alive, but you'd never know that once they're deep-fried and served up with dippin' sauce!

★ POLISHING OUR RUST BELT

What can we use our abandoned industrial infrastructure for in America, besides providing jobs for Americans? Manufacturers trimmed 2.8 million American jobs from 2000 to 2003 alone. Here are some ideas for communities struggling to find a purpose for the rusting hulks of factories left behind by our new and improved global economy:

★ Old car-manufacturing plants with conveyor belts and robotic production units can be retrofitted by health-care companies into efficient surgical assembly lines. Patients who need a heart transplant or a quick tumor removal are anesthetized and slapped down on the conveyor belt. The precise robotic machines that once bolted tires to axles can be easily reprogrammed to split open rib cages, excise and transplant bodily organs, remove malignant growths, and rivet incisions shut, all with incredible speed and at a cost much lower than human doctors charge.

★ Neglected steel mills can be transformed into daycare facilities or fun children's museums. Kids love playing in old smelters. A leading example of this approach is the Tetanus How and Why EduPlayground, an interactive educational exhibit located in an abandoned U.S. Steel plant in Pittsburgh, where kids can learn all they ever wanted to know about contracting tetanus in a fun, marginally safe environment.

★ Deserted shipyards—large areas in undesirable locations that are partly surrounded by deep water—can be reconstructed into ideal detention camps for terrorists.

★ A vermin-infested warehouse can be renamed the Animal Habitorium and Shooting Range. Local sportsmen can go on a thrilling "industrial safari" in these cavernous buildings, practicing their aim on pigeons, rats, and hobos. Providing an illegal exotic pet drop-off chute guarantees a variety of prey, keeping paying customers coming back for more.

★ The grease-stained machinery, dangling chains, and general ambiance of industrial menace can turn any disused factory into an Ultimate Fighting Arena, where burly, unemployed workers can pummel each other into a bloody pulp for the entertainment of hundreds of cheering, paying fans.

UNIVERSAL HEALTH CARE THROUGH PRAYER

O Merciful Lord our God, creator of the microbe and the spirochete,

The necrotic flesh of the lepers, and the pustules of the poxed,

The pestilence of pain, paralysis, and penile dysfunction, and the cancer come to eat us;

Heavenly Father, look down upon our infirmity,

Upon affliction and complaint, debility, disorder, disease, and decay,

Frailty and phlegm, sickness and syndrome,

Malady, malaise, myopia, and mumps,

And ease up just a bit, so that the harbingers of health industry abuses,

Will cease their shrill demands for the godless hell of a single payer.

Give us just enough, Lord, of the health that you deny,

So that the costs do not exceed what can be put on our Visa card,

And swept away into the mindless chatter of our days.

Heal us with the chicken soup of your divine love,

Make us somewhat hale and hearty, so that the tithe we pay unto the health-plan ghouls,

Makes us not antsy, nor eager for the tiny co-pay and the no-fee transplant,

That so inflames our neighbors to the north with smugness in their happy hospice.

Make us well enough, so that well enough is left alone, and the millions spent to build this carapace of "care,"

Shall not vanish into the hands of those whose simple plans would sweep free enterprise away,

In the mighty flood of socialism without end.

—AMEN.

★ ARE YOUR PRODUCTS FIGHTING TERROR?

If a manufacturing corporation can demonstrate its commitment to fighting terrorism, that commitment should be made clear for all Americans to see. If a corporation contributes a minimum of $750,000 to the 2004 election campaign of Presidential Appointee George W. Bush—the only man who is able to defeat all the evil in the world—then that corporation wins the privilege of printing the U.S. government's Anti-Terror Seal of Approval on their products. This red, white, and blue seal proves a product's anti-terror credentials, as well as confirming the patriotism of any consumer who purchases Anti-Terror Approved products. Is your preferred mouthwash fighting terrorism? Is your canned tuna hunting down dangerous killers around the world?

Does your toilet paper strike fear into the hearts of the evildoers? Check for the Anti-Terror Seal of Approval, and be proud to be terror-free!

★ SALUTING OUR MEDIA

We always like to give the media a hard time, calling them a bunch of liberals, but we'd actually like to take this moment to salute the media. Ever since 9/11, they've been so great to us. They never pressed us on what happened to that airplane that crashed into the Pentagon, never asked us for any proof that Osama bin Laden planned the attacks, and never made us explain why we had to invade Afghanistan when none of the nineteen alleged hijackers were Afghanis but fifteen of them were from Saudi Arabia. They just gave us the ball and let us run with

it. They really played along with our invasion of Iraq, too, always referring to it as "Operation Iraqi Freedom™" and running our brand name next to a waving American flag, just like we told them to. Maybe this complete acquiescence is because of their enlightened ownership. When a news channel like NBC is owned by General Electric, which stands to make huge profits from the war in Iraq, of course they're going to support the war in Iraq! Congratulations on a job well done, journalists! You may return to your "reporting."

★ CORPORATIONS ARE YOUR BUDDIES

Have you ever wondered what it is that corporations even do anymore? When you look at their advertising, it seems that their interests and goals are the exact opposite of what you thought they were. For example, the "Live Richly" ad campaign for Citibank, the world's largest banking company with $1.2 trillion in assets, tells you things like "the only piece of plastic you should throw around is a Frisbee." So we shouldn't purchase goods on our Citibank credit cards and repay that debt at a high interest rate, but go to the park and have fun for free with our friends instead? Thanks, Citibank!

Then there's Philip Morris, the giant tobacco manufacturer, going out of its way to tell you that "there is no such thing as a safe cigarette," and offering free advice pamphlets on how to keep your kids away from cigarettes. So cigarettes are deadly poison? We should shun them and tell other people to do the same? Thanks, Philip Morris!

Finally, there's British Petroleum, or BP, who have been buying up gas stations across the United States. All their ads talk about are renewable and clean energy sources. BP's slogan is "Beyond Petroleum." Even their corporate logo is a pretty green and yellow sunflower. I guess British Petroleum—oh, I'm sorry, BP—actually thinks petroleum is pretty yucky and would rather be done with it altogether!

So what is the purpose of all these companies? Their true corporate mission is to *be your friend*. They want you to feel good about yourself, and to feel good about them. Everyone needs to be loved. Can't you open your heart and realize that multinational banks, tobacco manufacturers, and petrochemical corporations need love too? The one thing that would make Citibank, Philip Morris, and BP truly happy would be to hold your hand, give it a gentle squeeze, and walk off into a beautiful golden sunset with you.

Please be forewarned that sweeping changes in corporate law enacted by the Bush administration will soon modify the corporate policies described in the above paragraphs. As of November 2004, all renewable energy sources will be the sole property of British Petroleum, including all solar, wind, geothermal, hydroelectric, hydrogen fuel cell, and paddleboat technology. Nonsmokers will pay an oxygen usage fee on a monthly basis to Philip Morris, as they are able to inhale much more air than smokers who are struggling to compete for their fair share of oxygen. Finally, every single Frisbee throw, regardless of distance on Earth and throughout the known universe, involving all present and future Frisbee equipment and technology that has yet to be invented, will result in a Frisbee usage tax of $1.75, payable to Citibank. Thank you for your cooperation.

INSIDER STOCK TIP

Exclusive to Citizen You! *readers*

Halliburton has already won exclusive government contracts through 2008 to rebuild Syria, Iran, Libya, Lebanon, and Sudan after our planned Freedom™ and democracy operations in those countries. This fact is unknown outside of Vice President Cheney's office, the highest echelons of Halliburton's corporate leadership, and now you. Get in on this gravy train by buying up Halliburton stock and boosting its share value!

At the time of this writing, roughly 700 U.S. soldiers have died in Iraq since Operation Iraqi Freedom™ began a little over one year ago. Even if we adopt a flattering estimate of their economic productivity after leaving the armed forces, they would have earned at most an average of $25,000 per year. The aggregate GDP loss resulting from their deaths is thus $17.5 million per year—less than the annual income of any single member of the Carlyle Group's board of directors. The long-term gains from our control over Iraq's vast oil resources, in addition to our booming military industry, amounts to hundreds of billions of dollars and easily overshadows the very small economic cost of American casualties. Hey, thanks for being such great team players, kids!

★ CEO VISION

"Ideally, you'd have all your factories on barges."

—Jack Welch, former CEO of General Electric

Oh, you're so romantic, Jack. Sailing a gargantuan factory-barge on the seven seas, trailing a frothy, multicolored wake of toxic sewage...stopping at exotic islands to pick up fresh battalions of peons while tossing the old, exhausted ones overboard into tropical lagoons...watching the gulls wheel and dive at their malnourished bodies...Jack Welch's corporate fantasy sends chills up our spine. Could this really be where men like Jack Welch are taking us? Where if one uppity country says, "Hey, you can't dump your poisonous effluvia and corpses on our beaches anymore, and our workers want another 5 cents per hour," you just sail off to another far-off land for more business as usual? If this is where we're all headed, can we wear the little white skipper cap?

★ CORPORATE WELFARE REFORM

The only way that our noble country can continue to grow is to encourage the development of our corporations with corporate welfare reform. Don't confuse this with individual welfare, which results only in keeping useless people alive who clog our sidewalks and assault our noses with their body odor. Corporate welfare results in gleaming towers of industry, decorated with the finest art that money can buy. Corporate welfare brings us private jets, yachts, and other things of beauty, such as well-cooked meals served on elegant china by uniformed waiters at dinners attended by captains of industry, heads of state, and other potentates. Why should these elegant, aristocratic corporations pay taxes at all? The money that corporations pay their employees is already taxed, so to tax the profits of corporations would be double taxation. And why shouldn't taxpayer dollars be used to subsidize corporations? Corporations represent our highest aspirations and dreams, much more than building yet another school or patching up a crummy old street.

Corporate welfare helps us all dream the American dream of getting your hands on as much money as you can. Without the example of our highly paid executives, our workers would have nothing to strive for. If your boss only made ten times as much as you did, what would your motivation be? If you were digging a hole, and you knew that only one dollar was six feet underground, you might not want to risk getting calluses by digging too hard. But if you knew there were a hundred thousand dollars down there, you would dig until your hands were bloody stumps. That's what corporate welfare brings us—the filthy masses scrabbling at an impossible dream while the elite few exploit their labor to rule the world like the gods atop Mount Olympus. Now that's a dream that we can all be a part of.

EN-WHAT?

A while back—we forget when, exactly—a lot of newspapers tried to bump up their sales by running scandal stories about some energy company called "Enron." The story was that Enron used all kinds of accounting tricks to inflate their profits and hide their losses to fool everyone into believing that they were a wildly successful company. They threw in all kinds of juicy details, such as Enron's management admitting to securities violations, sham transactions, obstruction of justice, insider trading, outright fraud of consumers and shareholders, and money laundering. As for the thousands of stories and investigations on this Enron thing, the Bush administration would like to state, on the record, that we have no idea what you're talking about. We were not involved in any of this. We've never even heard about this Enron company. Sorry.

Prisoners cannot migrate in search of higher pay, demand raises or benefits, organize labor unions, protest and strike, go on vacations, or engage in other forms of economic terrorism. They are the ideal modern work force. George W. Bush understands that privately owned prisons are especially successful at turning poverty, crime, and social deterioration into a solid bottom line for investors. However, even with our intense patrols and raids on poor urban neighborhoods to catch every drug user we can find who lives in those neighborhoods, violent crime rates are dropping in this country. The United States still has the world's largest prison population, but we must set goals to incarcerate more Americans to fill up more private prisons. Upon his election in 2004, George W. Bush will continue his efforts to promote healthy prison-sector growth by expanding the war on drug users and toughening penal codes for nonviolent offenses, sending more poor people to more prisons for much longer sentences.

Here's how this ultimate "captive market" works. Private prisons are both hugely expensive and very profitable for a select group of people. Just like with military spending, the cost is paid by the public's tax dollars but the profits go to private shareholders. When prisons are run by these for-profit corporations, costs can be cut on prisoners' food, safety requirements, the number of uniformed staff, and training and supervision for prison guards. If you thought convicted marijuana smokers weren't being raped and assaulted enough in prison, private prisons may surprise and delight you! Finally, these young, able-bodied, primarily dark-skinned men are put to work and paid pennies an hour, without the hassles of insurance costs or health and safety protections. Inmates at the Angola State Penitentiary in Louisiana, which used to be a slave plantation and is still known as "The Farm," are now picking cotton for 4¢ an hour for a private firm. It's almost like the good old days.

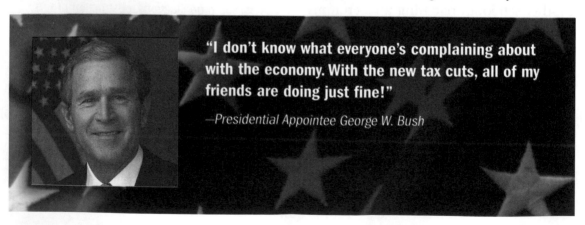

"I don't know what everyone's complaining about with the economy. With the new tax cuts, all of my friends are doing just fine!"

—*Presidential Appointee George W. Bush*

How sweet it is

Attention, CEOs of America! Do you want to learn how to make a lot of money at the negligible expense of public health? A perfect lesson can be found in how our hero Donald Rumsfeld pushed the artificial sweetener aspartame onto the market back in 1981 as CEO of Searle, the multinational pharmaceutical corporation.

Aspartame, a molecule that is 180 times as sweet as sugar but contains no calories, was accidentally discovered in 1965 in a Searle research lab. That was the good news! The bad news was that aspartame is composed of three chemicals: aspartic acid, phenylalanine, and methanol (or wood alcohol). Besides being useful for killing homeless alcoholics, methanol converts into formaldehyde and formic acid when it is ingested. Formaldehyde, a deadly neurotoxin, is used to embalm corpses and is a class-A carcinogen. Formic acid is used to strip epoxy and urethane coatings. Phenylalanine is also neurotoxic when unaccompanied by the other amino acids in proteins. Aspartic acid causes holes in the brains of infant mice, a finding confirmed by Searle's own researchers. Would Americans accept this chemical cocktail if they were told they could guzzle soda all day and not get any fatter? Donald Rumsfeld and company bet that they would!

So how did Searle rise to the challenge of getting the FDA to approve this delicious, calorie-free neurotoxin for use in thousands of food products? Even before Rumsfeld took charge, Searle's first

strategy was to manipulate the data of their aspartame safety tests. When many of your test animals on aspartame die or get grand-mal seizures, you've got to manipulate your data! For example, in order to hide cancerous mammary tumors in test animals, Searle scientists excised the tumors, then returned the animals to the study. Or they just removed the mammary tumors post-mortem. (The fact that breast cancer cases in American women began to rise sharply and have doubled in number since 1981, the same year aspartame hit the market, is pure coincidence and you should stop thinking about this fact right now.) The testing on aspartame was so shoddy and deceitful that the FDA urged a grand jury investigation of Searle for knowingly misrepresenting findings, concealing facts, and making false statements in their aspartame safety tests. Coincidentally, the government lawyers who decided against prosecuting Searle later joined a law firm that represented Searle in another criminal investigation.

Criminal investigations are a matter of no concern to men such as Donald Rumsfeld, but aspartame still wasn't on the market. What would be the new strategy? In January 1981, during a Searle sales meeting, Rumsfeld announced to his staff that he was going to get aspartame approved and on the market within the year. Rumsfeld said he would "call in his markers"—he would use his political pull in Washington instead of scientific means to get aspartame approved.

"He's the most ruthless man I ever met...and I mean that as a compliment."

—Henry Kissinger describing Donald Rumsfeld

Sure enough, Ronald Reagan was sworn in as President on January 21, 1981. The stodgy old FDA commissioner that had refused to approve aspartame was fired. Searle CEO Donald Rumsfeld was on Reagan's transition team, which picked Dr. Arthur Hull Hayes Jr. to be the new FDA commissioner. *The day after* Reagan's inauguration, Searle reapplied to the FDA to get aspartame approved. Commissioner Hayes appointed a five-member scientific commission to review the banned substance. When it became

clear that the panel would uphold the aspartame ban by a 3–2 decision, Hayes installed a sixth member on the commission, which deadlocked the vote at 3–3. Hayes then broke the tie himself in aspartame's favor, approving it for the public's consumption and the private profits of Searle. Aspartame was rolled out on store shelves with the brand name NutraSweet, an ingenious word to describe this potentially carcinogenic, corpse-embalming, brain-shredding substance.

What became of Hayes? Right after approving aspartame in carbonated beverages, he left the FDA under widespread accusations of impropriety—he was only taking rides aboard a private jet of General Foods, a major aspartame purchaser. Hayes then took on a $1,000-a-day medical consultant job at Burson-Marsteller, the public-relations firm that represented Searle.

By 1996, the FDA had received complaints from more than 8,000 consumers about aspartame. That's a pretty small number compared to the $2 billion a year that Searle and its new parent company, Monsanto, make every year from selling aspartame! For his amazing achievements in creating this artificial-sweetener industry, Donald Rumsfeld was lauded as the Outstanding Chief Executive Officer in the Pharmaceutical Industry by the *Wall Street Transcript* (1980) and *Financial World* (1981).

Through the Freedom of Information Act, the FDA was forced to release a 1995 list of symptoms attributed to aspartame in consumer complaints. The ninety-two reported symptoms of aspartame ingestion include muscle spasms, difficulty swallowing, infection susceptibility, abdominal pain, bloating, diarrhea, burning urination, weight gain, irritability, mental confusion, inability to concentrate, anxiety attacks, depression, poor memory, chest pains, asthma, laryngitis, chronic cough, chronic fatigue, vertigo, seizures, rashes, blindness, heart palpitations, high blood pressure, impotency, tinnitus, joint pain, nausea, hair loss, hearing loss, slurred speech, loss of taste, insomnia, headaches, numbness, fatigue, blurred vision, burning eyes, heart palpitations, memory loss, dizziness, fainting, unconsciousness, and coma. Certain diseases are also believed by some to be triggered by aspartame, such as brain tumors and other cancers, multiple sclerosis, epilepsy, fibromyalgia, Graves disease, chronic fatigue syndrome, Parkinson's disease, Alzheimer's disease, diabetes, lymphoma, systemic lupus, and birth defects. However, all of these terrifying symptoms and syndromes contain absolutely no calories!

There's a lot of scare stories out there. Dr. John Olney of Washington University has raised disturbing questions about a possible link between the rise in brain tumors and the release of aspartame into the public food supply. Then there's the story that our troops in Desert Storm chugged truckloads of aspartame-sweetened beverages which had been left out and heated in the Saudi Arabian sun. When heated or stored in acidic liquids, such as cola, aspartame breaks down into methanol. Thousands of thirst-quenched soldiers returned home complaining of chronic fatigue syndrome and a host of toxic symptoms similar to formaldehyde poisoning, which was called "Gulf War Syndrome." Some kooks claim the free methanol in the beverages may have been a contributing factor in these illnesses.

Then there are the NutraSweet scientists who say that a glass of tomato juice contains five times more methanol than an aspartame-sweetened diet soda. What's odd is that 100 percent of NutraSweet-funded research states that aspartame is completely safe, while 92 percent of independent studies show adverse reactions to aspartame. Hmm.

So is aspartame a minute dose of nerve gas that eradicates brain and nerve functions or is it a completely harmless sweetener? Who's right? Who's wrong? Why worry? These scientists go back and forth all the time. Instead, why not stroll out onto your porch some sunny 95° morning this summer, set down a case of your favorite diet cola, and have yourself a hot, sweaty, all-day aspartame-sippin' festival. After six or seven steaming Diet Cokes, you'll be ready to accept this taste challenge—shake up a boiling can of soda, rip it open while flicking your cigarette lighter, and see if you can turn your can of violently escaping methanol vapors into an improvised flamethrower. Like Donald Rumsfeld said, "Sometimes you've got to wrestle with your beverage!"

On a similar note, our CEO readership should know that in 1996, the FDA removed all usage restrictions on aspartame. This allowed aspartame to be used in everything, including baked goods that are intensely heated, so be sure to put it in all your food products! There's nothing like a hot batch of methanol-chip cookies.

Yes, the story of aspartame is a shining example of how ambitious corporate leaders get things done. Our executive class must remember this three-step business strategy for setting up a real sweet deal:

1 **Manipulate, distort, and lie with your data to sell the product, ignoring the risk to public health.**

2 **Avoid criminal prosecution.**

3 **Take over the government to close the deal.**

This amazing tactic works both for corporate negotiations and for taking over whole countries!

Fight Terror–
STAY SCARED

Welcoming Remarks by
Attorney General and
Grand Inquisitor,
John Ashcroft

Freedom™. It's what we have and they don't. To destroy it, they would kill us. To preserve it, we must kill them first. God, in all His infinite wisdom, gave Freedom™ to America, and only America, as a great and good gift, for us to nurture and cherish, scatter and spread, like manure on the field of God's golden wheat.

I am pleased to announce, my fellow Americans, that our plan to end terrorism and keep our homeland safe for God's gift of Freedom™ is working! As I compose this message to you, terrorism in America has decreased by a factor of 100 percent since 9/11. That's right—not a single giant skyscraper filled with masses of innocent people has been successfully demolished by evil terrorists since September 11, 2001. And you have yourselves, yes, *the American people* to thank for this amazing transformation.

It is through the genius of the democratic system, through the obedience of your elected representatives in Congress, through the subservience of the courts and the criminal justice system, the collusion of the print and broadcast media, and the complaisance of the citizenry, that this monumental success has been achieved. Give yourselves a round of applause!

That's enough. Vigilance knows no vanity, and with your help, the precious paranoia that has enveloped America like a shroud of dread and horror will remain forever as strong as it has been since we were first attacked by the insane heathen monsters we call terrorists. And it is vigilance that your government has brought to you, unstintingly, despite the whining and sabotage of the treasonous liberal Democrat elite and those of their ilk, who would have our nation overrun by Freedom™-hating, devil-worshipping, animal-fornicating, CIA-pilot-school-attending, tent-dwelling hordes of murderous, malodorous extremists, all for the sake of their precious "civil liberties." If our opponents had their way, you would be sidelined every time you tried to board a plane, forced to take off your shoes and pants in full view of your fellow passengers, while razor-toting, lamb-eating, fuzzy-bearded messengers of Allah are waved blithely aboard, ready to occupy their first-class seats to Paradise.

As I travel across this great land, visiting with the custodians of a vast, intentionally obscure population of enemy terrorist prisoners warehoused in secret seclusion for our own protection, I have often been asked: "What's this I hear about terrorists' rights? Don't I, as a loyal Christian American, have a God-given right to not be blown to smithereens by lunatic suicide bombers acting in the service of a false god?" Indeed you do, fellow citizen. That's why, on your behalf, I have instituted reforms that have taken the protection of your sacred, God-given rights to new, hitherto-unheard-of heights!

Imagine that you are an evil terrorist. Thanks to the USA PATRIOT Act, I can secretly examine your life in minute detail, yank you out of your "safe house," off the street or out of an airport, and imprison you anytime I like, without evidence of wrongdoing, without charges, legal representation, or trial. I can cage you indefinitely in a military brig too small for you to sit, stand, lie down, or kneel, and keep you blindfolded twenty-four hours a day until our military tribunal marches you up the steps to face the justice of the hangman's noose. Try hijacking a plane while dangling from a rope tied to one of our makeshift plywood gallows! And so what if you're not actually a terrorist yet? We're snagging plenty of illegal aliens, petty criminals, shoplifters, deadbeat dads, marijuana smokers, parking ticket scofflaws, telephone pranksters, almanac readers, and other suspicious ne'er-do-wells each and every day, and we don't ever have to report our activities if we feel they won't make us look suitably heroic.

There, don't you feel safer in this brave new world of terror we have created? And if, heaven forbid, just prior to the

> *Try hijacking a plane while dangling from a rope tied to one of our makeshift plywood gallows!*

next presidential election, with absolutely no advance warning or foreknowledge of any sort on our part, a crude, portable nuclear weapon should happen to slip past airport security and make its way into the hallowed marble halls of the United States Capitol Building, annihilating our entire Congress in one fell swoop, then our standard-bearer of Freedom™, Presidential Appointee George W. Bush, alongside his loyal Executive Branch, will stand ready to assume the terrible responsibility of leading our great nation in the War on Terror alone, from our heavily fortified stronghold concealed deep underground somewhere in the Western Hemisphere.

Until that time, relax and stay alert! Breathe the sweet air of Freedom™, and don't hesitate to use that breath to cry out an alarm should you notice anything in the least bit suspicious. Just pick up the phone. Friendly operators at the FBI are waiting to take your call. Monitor your neighbors, spy on your children, patrol your towns and cities, and report any traitorous activities or attitudes to me immediately—before you become a suspect yourself.

Thank you, and God bless America.

★ LEARN THE TERROR LINGO

All of us here at the FBI, the CIA, the DHS, the NSA, DARPA, NASA, NATO, and FEMA want to make sure that you understand our latest official acronym. That acronym is **GWOT.** What's that, you say? Is GWOT a satanic death-metal rock band? Is GWOT some sort of mucus that Donald Rumsfeld hacks up from his lungs every morning before a long day of tallying body counts? Isn't GWOT that one town in Afghanistan where thousands of Taliban fighters were herded into boxcars, and when they complained they couldn't breathe, the cars were ventilated with machine-gun fire? No, no, and no! GWOT stands for *Global War on Terror*—the never-ending battle against evil that will last for the rest of our lives, perhaps even for all time. This new-and-improved, perpetual war will encompass the entire planet, allowing us to invade any country, assassinate any individual, subjugate any peoples and secure any resources that stand

against us and our GWOT. As Dick Cheney said, GWOT is "the new normalcy," and that's a lesson he's personally taken to heart. Have you seen the character Gollum in *The Lord of the Rings* movies? Just like Gollum always makes his namesake "gollum" sound, Dick Cheney repeatedly mutters the word "GWOT" under his breath about four hundred times a day! We recommend that you do the same. The GWOT surrounds us, the GWOT shapes us, and the GWOT will live on long after we are dead. *Give in to the GWOT.*

In the fear-filled months after 9/11, many irresponsible publications ran stories about a shocking wave of post-9/11 "terror sex," where frightened citizens turned to each others' genitals for comfort while America was under attack. Terrorism should bring us all together in a collective state of dread and paranoia, but these feelings must not turn into desperate attempts to affirm life through fornication! You cannot simply "hump the terror away." If it feels good, don't do it— our GWOT should leave you feeling paralyzed and icy, not warm and tingly.

Carefree, casual, uninhibited sex only helps the terrorists. During the inevitable terrorist attacks of the future, resist the urge to head to the nearest bar and meet anybody with a pulse. Instead, return to your home, lock your door, cover all windows with plastic sheeting, wear bulky, layered clothing with plenty of protective straps and buckles, and watch your television for further instructions.

When you're walking down the street, do you look at passersby and wonder if they harbor secret plots to hijack airliners and crash them into skyscrapers? For all of our sake, you'd better be. But even your government will admit that constantly scanning and analyzing every single person for evidence of terrorist intent can get to be downright exhausting. That's why we can all breathe a sigh of relief over our new Personal Threat Indicator system, or PERTHIN for short. Devised by Attorney General John Ashcroft and John Poindexter during a late-night sleepover party at Ashcroft's house, the PERTHIN system is startling in its simplicity and revolutionary in its effectiveness. Using information culled from our Total Information Awareness network, PERTHIN assigns a color code to every individual in the United States that denotes what level of threat they are to the public. This color code is then represented with colored armbands that every human must wear. (These armbands must be visible at all times and worn on the outside of all shirts and jackets. If any citizen attempts to hide his PERTHIN armband, he will be punished by being forced to wear the armband around his head.)

Low Green, Guarded Blue, Elevated Yellow, High Orange, and Severe Red armbands will be made available for purchase at all Gap clothing stores. These color-coded armbands give law-enforcement officials and private business owners a quick way to determine how much freedom of movement should be allowed to individuals. For example, only Greens and Blues will be allowed into concerts, sporting events, and other high-risk public venues. Yellows will be banned from these events, but will still be allowed to take public transportation. Oranges will be allowed to walk to their places of employment on foot, but will be banned from stores, restaurants, and all other public enclosed spaces. A curfew of 8 p.m. will also be in effect for these high-risk individuals. Reds will be confined to federal detention camps and only allowed out of the camps when organized into mass labor squads under armed guard.

Under the PERTHIN system, American citizens, as well as any foreigners who still choose to visit our fair country, will be allowed only as much freedom as they deserve, as determined by our wise and just shadow government. You will also enjoy the ease with which you will be allowed to associate with only your own kind. You'll never again have to sit next to an Orange at your favorite restaurant, or drink from the same water fountain as a filthy Red. Watch for your armband assignment in the mail—your PERTHIN color code will be sent to your home by mid-November 2004, immediately after George W. Bush is appointed to his second term of office.

Is your baby prepared for a terrorist attack?

The likelihood of your family surviving a devastating attack depends as much on rigorous training as it does on the freshness of your smoke detector's batteries. But has your baby memorized your preferred escape route? Can he understand your commands? How quickly can he exit your home during an emergency? Can he exit your home at all? Your baby's safety will depend on your ability to train him to do things no baby was ever asked to do before 9/11: sprint, leap, stuff wet rags under the door during a biological weapons attack, shinny up a three-inch-thick pipe in the driving rain, fire an automatic rifle, and hold his breath under water for minutes at a time. Your baby will face the very same threats that you will. Heightened readiness is not just for adults.

★ VOMITING FOR LIBERTY

The possibility of terrorists contaminating our public water supplies with deadly poison is very real. To prepare for this eventuality, it is required of all U.S. citizens to have several bottles of syrup of ipecac on hand in their households and places of employment. Syrup of ipecac is a safe, effective substance that induces a rapid purging of the stomach—an ingenious way to free your body of terrorist poisons. The Department of Homeland Security, in conjunction with local Poison Control Centers, will soon be enforcing mandatory, weekly Vomiting Drills. Every Saturday at 9 a.m., all U.S. citizens must ingest one tablespoonful of syrup of ipecac. Vomiting should occur in approximately four seconds. It's a great way to start the weekend! Those Americans who refuse to vomit every Saturday morning are only helping the terrorists. If you have children in your household, the Vomiting Drill can be a fun family event! Try making it into a game where the family member who vomits first gets a special treat. Most of all, enjoy the peace of mind that this regular schedule of vomiting will provide.

★ FORGIVE ME, FATHER...

In our efforts toward Total Information Awareness, we must draw strength from our civilization's oldest and most trusted institutions, as well as the cutting edge of human surveillance and microchip body-implantation technology. The Roman Catholic Church is our latest partner in the Coalition of the Righteous that is fighting evildoers throughout the world.

While administering the sacrament of confession, all Catholic priests will secretly tape-record their parishioners' most intimate admissions. These confessional audiotapes will then be delivered to Attorney General John Ashcroft and the U.S. Justice Department. If the sin of terroristic thought is discovered in the confessions, federal agents will work with local Catholic bishops and priests to identify and punish potential terrorists lurking in their flock. See? We're not only targeting Muslims. There is room for all kinds of enemies in our GWOT. These sinners will get to say their ten Hail Marys in the monastic confines of Camp X-Ray in Guantánamo Bay, Cuba, over and over and over again, until they repent from their evil ways or are burned at the stake.

★ FOOD, FOLKS, AND FREEDOM®

Mmm, did someone say steak? American citizens are loving the convenience that a new partnership between the Federal Emergency Management Agency and Tricon Global Restaurants is bringing them. When the next massive terrorist attack occurs, Tricon—which operates the KFC, Pizza Hut, and Taco Bell chains—working alongside FEMA, will evacuate all American citizens to hidden Tricon subterranean feeding shelters located across North America. No longer will Americans have to fret about constructing and stocking their own private survival bunkers. These massive, state-of-the-art shelters, constructed deep underground for maximum protection from chemical, biological, or nuclear attack, will each be able to feed, clothe, and house up to 10,000 eaters at a time. Sit, graze, and be happy, while the terror washes harmlessly over your heads. Pepsi products will be served. All Americans who dutifully march into our subterranean holding pens will be fed and watched over very closely—that's the Tricon/FEMA guarantee!

Register yourself and your family today at your local KFC, Pizza Hut, or Taco Bell restaurant so we know how many people to pick up and take away when our GWOT hits Red Alert. If you do not

register, you are only helping the terrorists. You'll be glad you reserved a spot for yourself and your loved ones when 10,000 other eaters are clamoring to be seated at one of our hundred-foot-long, hardened-concrete feeding troughs. Remember, the next big terrorist attack is not a matter of "if," but "when"!

The spirit of America will live on, with your total submission and these valuable advance coupons. Clip and save!

EAT...
EAT...
TRICON.®

---

1 Curly Freedom Fries™
★ FREE ★
with purchase of 8 Bald Eagle Burgers™,
4 Personal-Pan Patriot Pizzas™,
and a family-sized bucket of Extra-Crispy
Freedom-Fried Chicken Nacho-Nuggets™

FIVE-MINUTE
RESTROOM PASS
with complimentary square of
bathroom tissue, at all participating
Tricon Subterranean Feeding Shelters
GOOD FOR ONLY ONE USE

Under the new USA PATRIOT Act, American citizens have been given the right to form Citizen Vigilance Patrols. These groups will consist of you and your neighbors, who are now empowered to band together and patrol your streets to bring dangerous killers to justice. When you find evidence of suspicious activity, your call to the authorities will be handled by the experienced phone operators of the hit Fox TV show *America's Most Wanted*, who will dispatch to your neighborhood the SWAT teams and Marines that you need.

Every Citizen Vigilance Patrol must be led by one maximum leader—a bold and brave Terror Marshal. We can win the War on Terror only by terrorizing our own people, and Terror Marshals will lead this fight across our great nation. Do you have what it takes to be *your* neighborhood's Terror Marshal?

★ Are you prepared to check the Department of Homeland Security's color-coded threat level daily, then impart that information to your neighbors by marching down your street every morning shouting out the terrorism color code at the top of your lungs, while waving a correctly colored terror flag?

★ Are you prepared to participate in "sneak-and-peek" investigations without a search warrant into your neighbors' homes while they are away? They'll never know you were there!

★ Are you prepared to monitor your neighbors' Internet activity for traitorous web surfing? (See page 178)

★ Are you prepared to lead your Citizen Vigilance Patrol in sniffing through suspicious neighbors' garbage cans, looking for terror droppings?

★ Are you prepared to host a monthly Anti-Terror Ice Cream Social at your home, where your neighbors can learn useful anti-terror tactics in a fun, family atmosphere? (Anti-Terror Ice Cream Social party materials—American-flag napkins and hats, FunCup™ ice cream cones, instructional party videotape, and gas masks—will be provided by the Department of Homeland Security for a modest fee.)

★ Are you prepared to lead your Citizen Vigilance Patrol in cheering the loudest for the American Spirit Stick at the yearly Anti-Terror Rally in Washington, D.C.?

If you answered yes to any of these questions, you just might be the kind of American we're looking for! Contact your local branch of the Department of Homeland Security today for your Terror Marshal application!

★ HOW TO MONITOR YOUR NEIGHBORS

Terror Marshals will lead the masses in our GWOT, but every American has a constitutional duty to search and, if necessary, seize neighbors in their own homes if they appear to be evil terrorists. What are you looking for? Are your neighbors eating sheep's eyeballs? Are they reading Arabic flight manuals and the Koran instead of the Bible? Are your neighbors circumcised? These are all red flags of terror. It's true that the Jews are also circumcised, but it's good to keep an eye on them as well, since Jews are terror magnets. And if you have a group of three or more men living together next door, they're definitely terrorists, or a coven of gays, which should also be reported to the authorities. Here are several strategies you can use to sharpen your vigilance:

QUESTION your neighbors to find out if they support Presidential Appointee George W. Bush, Operation Iraqi Freedom, and our endless GWOT. **OFFER** them a free American flag to stick on their lawn. If they hesitate to support our noble invasions or refuse to accept our flag, take the following steps:

FORCE your teenaged child to mow the lawn or shovel snow at your suspicious neighbor's house. For a few extra dollars, your teen can report back to you with his findings. Have your child pay special attention to your neighbor's garage—does it contain bomb-making materials such as fertilizer, gasoline, cleaning solutions, nails and screws, or old coffee cans?

DROP BY UNINVITED with your entire family and a nice casserole, and offer to share the food at your suspicious neighbor's home. Or, **ORGANIZE** a Tupperware™ party at their home, or a neighborhood block party where everyone's doors are open. In these fun party situations, your prime directive is to **SLIP AWAY** and **PROBE** closets, cupboards, and drawers for hidden tools of terror.

TAKE NOTICE of unusual hours being kept by your neighbor. Are their house lights on late into the night, or do they come home early in the morning? Those who are not operating on a standard nine-to-five work schedule could be leading a freewheeling terrorist lifestyle.

BUY a powerful telescope. At night, install yourself in a darkened room in your home. Wear black clothing and a black ski mask. Train the telescope on the windows of your neighbor. Be motionless. Drink lots of coffee. **WATCH AND WAIT** for the terror to unfold before your eyes.

DIG THROUGH your neighbor's garbage with your neighborhood's Terror Marshal. Go ahead, roll up your sleeves and really get in there. Can you find any waste products of terrorist activity? Rough drafts of suicide notes? Videotapes of al-Jazeera broadcasts that have been watched so many times that the tape snapped? Soiled red headbands? (From Waco to 9/11, terrorists love wearing those evil red headbands. They're so scary-looking!) Old, well-thumbed airplane flight manuals or last year's edition of the Holy Koran? Nitroglycerin residue? Large amounts of shaved body hair? The absence of empty bacon packaging?

INSTALL a small, hidden video camera that looks over your suspicious neighbor's property. Attach a rechargeable battery pack so that it can be left on continuously. Get your computer-savvy children off of their *SOCOM: US Navy Seals* video game for five minutes and have them set up a streaming video connection from the camera, through your computer, and directly to your local FBI office.

SNATCH your neighbor's mail right after it's delivered. Are there any letters from fishy Saudi Arabian charity organizations, such as the International Order of Muslim Youth Achievement? Is there a suspicious Arab name such as "bin Laden" on the return address? If so, alert the Department of Homeland Security and we'll fly those people safely out of the country as quickly as we can. How about mail from the Immigration and Naturalization Services, or INS? That means your treasonous neighbor is an immigrant, which means he's from another country, which is where all terrorists come from. Alert the proper authorities immediately!

WHISTLE AT TERROR

On September 11, 2004, all citizens nationwide will be issued one Terror Whistle, which can be used to warn of terrorist attacks in the homeland. Always keep your Terror Whistle close by—it is ideal if you tie it tightly around your neck. If you see a terrorist event about to occur, blow your Terror Whistle as hard as you can before the bomb goes off. Police and nearby citizens will be able to locate your position from hearing your long, shrill *"TWEEEEEEE"* before it is abruptly cut off by the explosion of the bomb. They can then come to the rescue of what is left of you and also triangulate the position of the next terrorist strike, perhaps.

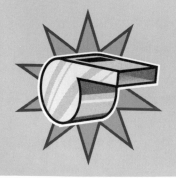

★ WE'RE HERE FOR YOU

In the long, hard slog that is our GWOT, which will last for the rest of our lives, sometimes we can all use somebody to talk to. That's why the Department of Homeland Security has set up a nation-wide network of Terror Counselors, available twenty-four hours a day, whom you can call on the telephone. If you're feeling terrorized by terrorists and their terroristic plots to spread terror, these are people you can turn to for a firm hand of kindness and a helpful word of warning. These supportive, friendly counselors—who all have certified degrees in psychology and human behavior modification methods—are there for you when you need them. Is your mind-set of perpetual vigilance beginning to waver? Call up a Terror Counselor, who can restore your sense of healthy paranoia with casualty estimates of a biological weapons attack on a large American city. Do you often find yourself thinking about some place you could go to have fun with your children, or where to take your spouse on a special date? Call a Terror Counselor to get you back on the right track of identifying possible "weak points" in your community that terrorists could exploit for a spectacular mass-casualty event.

Our sympathetic Terror Counselors are waiting to take your call, but what if you forget to call them? To make sure that Terror Counseling is an incessant and pervasive part of your life, consider the convenient option of Personalized Terror Messaging from Verizon Wireless. With PTM, you'll receive a personal call from a Terror Counselor on your cell phone every hour, on the hour, who will provide you with threat-level updates, current terrorist "chatter" surveillance, the latest theories on Osama bin Laden's location, and more. Your Terror Counselor will also ask you all the right questions to make sure that you are "staying the course" against terror.

Find out how you can begin a personal relationship with your Terror Counselor today! For your local Terror Counseling network's phone number, point your mouse to:

www.ready.gov

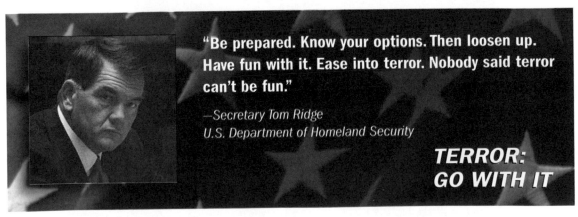

"Be prepared. Know your options. Then loosen up. Have fun with it. Ease into terror. Nobody said terror can't be fun."

—*Secretary Tom Ridge*
U.S. Department of Homeland Security

TERROR: GO WITH IT

Here's your pet store shopping list:

- ☐ **PIT BULL**
- ☐ **ROTTWEILER**
- ☐ **DOBERMAN PINSCHER**
- ☐ **PRESA CANARIO MASTIFF**
- ☐ **BOA CONSTRICTOR**
- ☐ **RATTLESNAKE**
- ☐ **TARANTULAS**
- ☐ **BLACK WIDOW SPIDERS**
- ☐ **NURSE SHARK**
- ☐ **PIRANHAS**
- ☐ **BARRACUDAS**
- ☐ **KOMODO DRAGON**
- ☐ **TIGER**
- ☐ **GRIZZLY BEAR**

The American people definitely need allies in our GWOT. No, we're not talking about the chocolate-eaters of Old Europe in their tight hosiery and powdered wigs! We're talking about ferocious, predatory household pets with the claws, fangs, and muscular jaw strength needed to stand up for Freedom™. Take your parakeets, poodles, and pussycats out on a highway drive, toss them out of your speeding car's window, then go buy some animals that will fight tooth and nail at your side against terror!

Fill your home with these terrifying animals so you can strike terror into the black hearts of the terrorists!

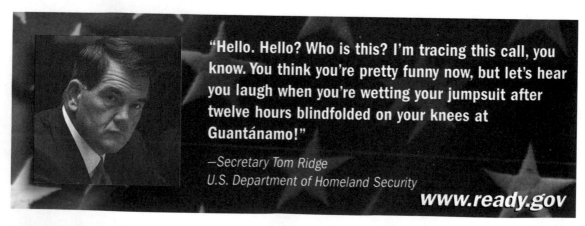

"Hello. Hello? Who is this? I'm tracing this call, you know. You think you're pretty funny now, but let's hear you laugh when you're wetting your jumpsuit after twelve hours blindfolded on your knees at Guantánamo!"

—Secretary Tom Ridge
U.S. Department of Homeland Security

www.ready.gov

★ SCIENCE IS ON OUR SIDE

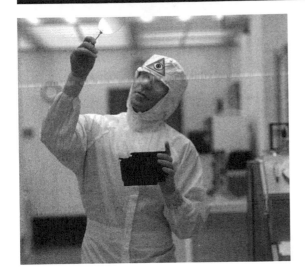

Did you know that scientists at the Lawrence Livermore National Laboratory Human Genome Center have isolated the gene that causes terrorism? Geneticists believe the mutated gene split off from the general population of modern humans around 10–15,000 years ago, in the vicinity of ancient Mesopotamia, among the early Sumerian population.

★ Identifying the mutation, known as the LK-DA gene, has proved to be a vital tool for the U.S. Department of Homeland Security and the Department of Justice.

★ Likely suspects, rounded up according to appearance, surname, parentage, apparent nationality, apparent or suspected terrorist activity, informant leads, hearsay, law enforcement hunches, style of facial hair, favored ethnic cuisine, exotic headgear, or any of the discretionary criteria protected from

public disclosure by recent Supreme Court decisions, are subjected to genetic testing as part of the battery of routine interrogation they encounter at any one of the secret detention centers whose locations are protected from public disclosure by recent Supreme Court decisions.

★ The results of this genetic testing become part of each prisoner's permanent dossier, and remain protected from public disclosure, along with the identity of the suspected terrorist.

★ That dossier is then used when the suspected terrorist is charged with, tried and convicted, and eventually executed for committing or intending to commit crimes of terrorism.

★ All of this is accomplished without burdening the criminal justice system with the responsibility of ridding our nation of this scourge.

The latest in error-proof science teams up with the latest in law enforcement, for a new birth of Freedom™ in America!

Donald Rumsfeld is at it again! His latest brainstorm for our GWOT is the Proactive Preemptive Operations Group, or P-2s for short. Bringing together CIA and military covert action, information warfare, and intelligence and deception tactics, the P-2s will launch secret operations aimed at "stimulating reactions" from terrorist cells and states possessing weapons of mass destruction. This group will prod terrorists into action, exposing them to "quick-response" attacks by U.S. forces. These strikes will "signal to harboring states that their sovereignty will be at risk." Yes, you heard us correctly—American forces will be working hard to provoke terrorist attacks on innocent civilians around the world! We'll push unstable nations to use

their weapons of mass destruction. We'll fight terrorism by causing it. We're making tomorrow's terrorist today!

It's a little bit like looking for a hornets' nest to kick over. Everyone knows it's always a good idea to kick over a hornets' nest. Even if you can't find any hornets, but only fuzzy, peaceful caterpillars, munching away on some tender green leaves, you've got to start kicking those caterpillars, and keep kicking them and kicking them, until they get so pissed they turn into hornets. Then you can use your hornet spray on 'em! After you've shot your can of hornet spray, go hit up the taxpayers for another big bottle of the newest, deadliest insecticide. And guess what the best part is? Those tender green leaves are all yours to munch now.

Yes, only the Bush administration could turn terrorism into a growth industry. Some critics say that kicking over the hornets' nest of Iraq was a bad idea. We beg to differ! How else will you know where the hornets are until they're flying around and stinging you? By invading Iraq, we've kicked their nest so hard that every wicked, hornet-like terrorist in the

TERROR TIP: BACK OFF

Only Presidential Appointee George W. Bush knows how to fight terrorists. That's why, a couple of months before 9/11, FBI agents were told to "back off" on any investigation of members of Osama bin Laden's family or the Saudi royals. In August, 2001, FBI Deputy Director John O'Neill resigned from his post in frustration over the constraints on investigating terror suspects. O'Neill then took a position as the security chief of the World Trade Center, where he was killed on 9/11— his first day on the job. Do you think George W. Bush would ever make a dumb move like that? We don't think so. Hey, leave the terror to the professionals, buddy.

whole world came swarming to Baghdad, with the vain hope of overcoming our superior military force. Like our Presidential Appointee said, "Bring 'em on. We got the force necessary to deal with the situation." We love having somebody to shoot. But what if those hornets fly away and start nests somewhere else? That's when the Preemptive Proactive Operations Group goes to work, and that's why Secretary of Defense Donald Rumsfeld is King Shit of the GWOT.

★ BELIEVE IN TERROR

The threat is everywhere. Anyone is a suspect. Total death and destruction could strike us at any moment. Our only hope in this evil world of terror? Presidential Appointee George W. Bush. He knows he was appointed to his office—not by Supreme Court Justice Antonin Scalia, but by the Lord our God—to rid the world of all evildoers. You have to admire that kind of faith. And faith he has. Faith in God, faith in his Father, and faith in the fighting men and women of the U.S. covert armed forces. Believe it!

Yes, it takes faith to believe in our GWOT. Faith to make it through Christmas on Orange Alert. Faith that Tom Ridge's pretty, colored flashcards will keep us safe. Faith that occupying and humiliating an entire country in order to steal their resources will not breed generations of infuriated terrorists who hate America for years to come. Faith that acting like Israel will actually make us safer. Faith that Osama bin Laden, who was created as a CIA asset, who received extensive funding and training from the CIA, and whose family has longstanding, intricate business relationships with the Bush family, is not still in collusion with the CIA and the Bush family. You must believe in all these things, and what George W. Bush asks of you most of all is blind faith in Him, and him, not necessarily in that order. George W. Bush shall deliver us from terror. For his is the kingdom, and the power, and the glory forever. Amen.

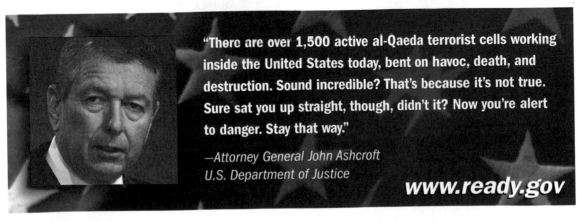

"There are over 1,500 active al-Qaeda terrorist cells working inside the United States today, bent on havoc, death, and destruction. Sound incredible? That's because it's not true. Sure sat you up straight, though, didn't it? Now you're alert to danger. Stay that way."

—*Attorney General John Ashcroft*
U.S. Department of Justice

www.ready.gov

What is a terrorist? You might answer, "An evildoer who hijacks airplanes or sets off suicide bombs on buses," but don't stop there. The real purpose of a terrorist, beyond his immediate goal of killing as many white Christians as he can, is to spread fear throughout a population. Therefore, any organization that attempts to instill fear in the breasts of patriotic Americans is a terrorist group. For example, all environmental conservation groups are, in fact, "eco-terrorists." What other possible motivation could there be for environmentalists to warn citizens of the "dangers" of a shiny new toxic-waste incinerator downwind of

their community besides spreading terror? Similarly, all labor unions and workers' rights organizations are "econo-terrorists." These shadowy conspirators attempt to spread fear of our managerial class, whose only desire is the great and good goal of maximizing profits through any means necessary. Feminists and women's rights groups are actually "estro-terrorists," who attempt to spread an irrational fear of all men. This roll call of evil can go on forever. Civil rights groups are "afro-terrorists," who attempt to spread fear of all the nice white people, while Planned Parenthood is an "aborto-terrorist" group that attempts to spread fear of innocent, God-given fetuses and zygotes.

The next time eco-terrorists, econo-terrorists, estro-terrorists, afro-terrorists, or aborto-terrorists try to hand you a greasy pamphlet or invite you to one of their clandestine meetings, take a good, hard look at them. Remember their faces so you can inform on them when our nation goes to Red Alert. These sinister new terrorists may not be wearing a suicide belt packed with dynamite and nails around their waists, but they do have one strapped around their minds.

TERROR TIP

We all must be perpetually paranoid. The boogeyman *is* real, and he could be anybody. But if you can imagine that every single person you see is a terrorist, then you'll always be on guard. Don't trust anyone, except for our friendly federal troops in black ski masks holding MP5 submachine guns.

BE PREPARED
BE SCARED

JUSTICE!

Parents, are you concerned that your children might be pressured by their friends into becoming terrorists just because it's "cool"? Kids, do you want to join a totally awesome group dedicated to stopping the bad guys who want to kill all of us? Then both of you should talk to your school principal about starting up a chapter of *JUSTICE!* in your school. *JUSTICE!* stands for Juveniles United So Terror Is Completely Eradicated! This fun after-school activity is an absolutely radical way to keep your kids on America and off terror. *JUSTICE!* is just like DARE, only it's effective. So when a hairy stranger asks you to carry a bomb into a public building, what do you say? NO! You're an all-star graduate of *JUSTICE!*

The *JUSTICE!* Anti-Terror Pledge

I promise that I will resist peer pressure and "just say no" to terrorism. I promise that I will never blow something up, even in my mind, unless it's a terrorist place in another country. I promise that I will stay alert and tell people when I think I see a terrorist. I promise I will be extra alert when I am at school and make sure the teacher doesn't try to warp us with multicultural lies and liberal mind-molesting. I will remember that my Presidential Appointee and his hand-appointed Chief of Homeland Security are looking out for me, so I don't have to look after them.

The *JUSTICE!* Start-Up Kit

When you launch a chapter of *JUSTICE!* in your school, you'll receive a terror-fighting starter kit including:

- **25** *JUSTICE!* **ANTI-TERROR HANDBOOKS**
- **25** *JUSTICE!* **ID CARDS**
- **25** **TERROR-PROOF LAMINATED PROTECTORS FOR YOUR IDs**
- **100** *JUSTICE!* **STICKERS**
- **100** **MICROTRANSMITTER TRACKING PINS**
- **50** **SUBDERMAL PERSONAL IDENTIFICATION MICROCHIPS**
- **5** **MINIATURE SPY CAMERAS**
- **2** **FINGERPRINT KITS**
- **+** **ACCESS TO OUR TOLL-FREE TERROR TIP HOTLINE**

How many terrorists can you spot with all this cool gear, kids? Contact your regional *JUSTICE!* headquarters today!

This kid is protected by *JUSTICE!*

In an age of global chaos, we must retain order on our streets. If we all obey the same rules of conduct, we can easily spot foreign terrorists in our cities, since they will be unable to read this book and follow these rules. Make sure you're not identified as a terrorist by obeying these instructions at all times on public streets and sidewalks:

★ Walk, if you must, at a medium pace, always on the right side of the sidewalk. (Remember that walking is generally considered un-American. Drive whenever possible.)

★ Running and/or skipping is not permitted.

★ Every twentieth step, stop and do a 360-degree turn to check for terrorist activity.

★ You may walk with a maximum of one companion, but you must walk in single file and not speak to each other while outdoors. Married couples may hold hands, for safety purposes only, while in the presence of homosexuals or libidinous Arabs.

★ Do not stop to smell flowers, pet dogs, or help mothers with baby strollers. Loitering is not permitted.

★ Keep your eyes down, looking at the concrete at all times. Only terrorists would look around at buildings, windows, trees, or roofs to pick out possible sniper locations.

★ Keep your hands on your head at all times while outdoors so that we can see them. (Wear an aluminum-based deodorant daily.) Don't stick your hands in your pockets and give us reason to believe that you're about to pull a dirty bomb out of your pants.

★ Soldiers, American flags, and citizens driving automobiles must be saluted whenever they are visible.

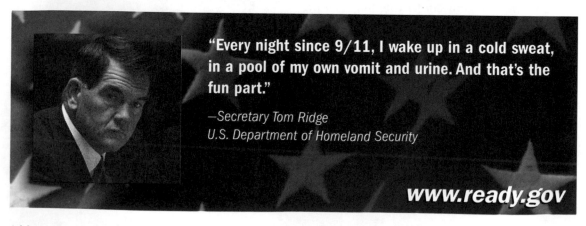

"Every night since 9/11, I wake up in a cold sweat, in a pool of my own vomit and urine. And that's the fun part."

—*Secretary Tom Ridge*
U.S. Department of Homeland Security

www.ready.gov

★ WHO YOU CAN'T TRUST

Who knows what transforms an innocent baby into a grizzled terrorist? We do. That's why we've created this invaluable flowchart to assist you in spotting the warning signs of proto-terrorist traits in yourself and others, *before* they harden into full-fledged evil-doing. Each of these traits is a "gateway identity" to another, more dangerous lifestyle. For example, if you try your hand at being a puppeteer, you'll soon be sliding down a slippery slope into lesbianism. You can also use this chart to determine how dangerous the children of proto-terrorists will be. For example, if a homosexual mates with a vegetarian, you get a Jew.

Be sure to photocopy this page and carry it with you for quick reference at all times. Paste this chart on the covers of your children's schoolbooks and on the water cooler at work. Tape it to the ceiling above your bed, so you can memorize all the complex ways that terror worms into our lives before you fall asleep. Stay on guard morning, noon, and night!

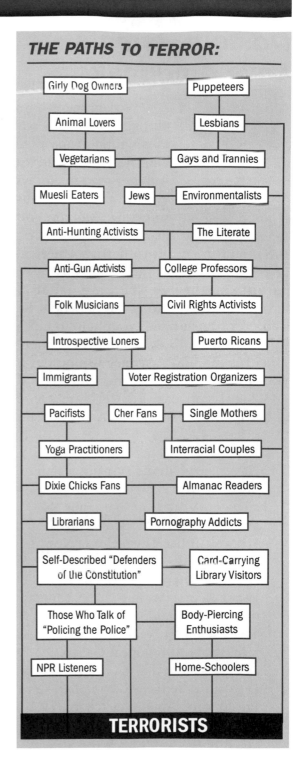

THE PATHS TO TERROR:

Girly Dog Owners → Animal Lovers → Vegetarians → Muesli Eaters → Anti-Hunting Activists → Anti-Gun Activists → Folk Musicians → Introspective Loners → Immigrants → Pacifists → Yoga Practitioners → Dixie Chicks Fans → Librarians → Self-Described "Defenders of the Constitution" → Those Who Talk of "Policing the Police" → NPR Listeners

Puppeteers → Lesbians → Gays and Trannies → Environmentalists → The Literate → College Professors → Civil Rights Activists → Puerto Ricans → Voter Registration Organizers → Cher Fans → Single Mothers → Interracial Couples → Almanac Readers → Pornography Addicts → Card-Carrying Library Visitors → Body-Piercing Enthusiasts → Home-Schoolers

Jews

TERRORISTS

Do Your Parents Love America?

Well, hi there, boys and girls! You know our Presidential Appointee George W. Bush loves America, and he knows you love her, too. But sometimes Mommy and Daddy get confused by the liberal media into hating America. That's just wrong—and dangerous! Your parents might even become naughty terrorists and kill thousands of people. So George W. Bush needs your help to make sure Mommy and Daddy are being good. Take this fun and easy quiz to find out if your parents are true Americans or evil killers. If you can answer "Yes" to a question, draw a big, pretty American star in the box!

☐ Have your parents ever put a sign on their front lawn or a bumper sticker on their car that reads "No War in Iraq" or "Support Our Troops—Bring Them Home Now"?

☐ Do your parents ever say bad things about George W. Bush, Dick Cheney, or Uncle Donald Rumsfeld? Do they ever use naughty swear words when talking about our great leaders?

☐ Do your parents ever complain that Presidential Appointee George W. Bush "stole" the 2000 presidential election from some loser?

☐ When your parents aren't looking, turn on their computer and open their Internet browser's history folder. We know you can do this—you're a smart little child! Have your parents been looking at any of these websites?

democrats.org	emperors-clothes.com
truthout.org	cooperativeresearch.org
commondreams.org	serendipity.ptpi.net/wtc.htm
911research.wtc7.net	counterpunch.org
copvcia.com	globalresearch.ca
infowars.com	warprofiteers.com

Did you put any pretty American stars next to these questions? If so, the FBI would definitely like to talk to your Mommy and Daddy. Look in your big yellow phone book and find the page that reads "Emergency Numbers." It should be in the first few pages. Find the phone number for "FBI" and call them on the telephone. When you give the nice FBI man your street address, he can come to your house and take your bad Mommy and Daddy away for interrogation and processing. The FBI man will also bring a special T-shirt and membership kit for you to join a fun club that all of Bush's youth belong to—*JUSTICE!* Best of all, he'll bring over TWENTY DOLLARS, all for YOU!

★ CITIZEN PARENT!

Do Your Kids Love America?

Childhood, like patriotism, is a joy and a wonder. However, without ruthless vigilance and swift action from parents everywhere, our own children could turn this heavenly bower we call America into a seething nest of vipers— and they could do it overnight, between "lights-out" and "time to get up."

The young. The cute. The cunning. Throughout history, mankind has known that trying to figure out kids was as pointless as trying to figure out women. 9/11 changed all that. Today, that inscrutable child, by virtue of his or her sweet innocence and helpless vulnerability, is very likely a prospective terrorist. Like John Walker Lindh, your own children could be steeping themselves in Islamic fundamentalism, dreaming of the tantalizing rewards of martyrdom. They could be planning a suicide attack—perhaps even against you—using everyday household products, and it's all going on right under your nose!

Protect yourself and protect your Homeland. Take a moment to learn these easy-to-spot signs that your precious baby is lost to you forever—doomed to be a drone of the hirsute ayatollahs, receiving his orders straight from a hole someplace outside Baghdad. Terrorists like them young, so be sure to examine every child, toddler to teen. And don't stop with your own children. You could have a tiny terrorist for a neighbor, a niece, a nephew, or a paperboy!

☐ Does your young son favor loose-fitting, floor-length robes and sandals, with a skull cap or turban, no matter the weather?

☐ Does your little princess berate her mother for being immodest and going forth in public with flesh exposed for all to see?

☐ At mealtime, does your child insist on sitting cross-legged on the floor, eschewing utensils, and eating only with his or her right hand?

TERROR TIP

Are you afraid that your next big event might be the target of extremist Muslim terrorists? Why not hire professional Osama bin Laden impersonator Danny Mendelson to call off the jihad? Our studio will videotape the amazing Mr. Mendelson giving a warning to his al-Qaeda followers that your birthday party/company picnic/bar mitzvah/yacht christening is "hands off." The price of one studio session also includes distribution of video and photos to known terrorist cells, all Middle Eastern radio and television stations, and the *New York Post*.

For more details, visit ***www.ready.gov***

- [ ] Has your child ever recoiled in horror and shouted "Unclean!" when offered bacon or sausage at breakfast?

- [ ] Has your child ever asked you to point in the direction of Mecca?

HOT ANTI-TERROR GEAR

Check out the coolest new anti-terror toys for today's patriotic guy:

★ ANKLE CARDS

A classic deck of fifty-two playing cards, each with a unique photo highlighting the supple curve of the female ankle. Laboratory-tested to guarantee each card will incapacitate any would-be terrorist. Deck includes free fold-out 11x17 poster of a female navel, appropriate for multiple terrorists (may be fatal to individuals at close range).

★ INFLATABLE VIRGIN DECOY

If you're being chased by terrorists, toss this auto-inflatable, polyurethane doll to the ground and run. The realistic virgin decoy quickly expands into the form of a nubile young female, wearing your choice of three different outfits—burkha, chador, or tanktop and thong. Optional audio device broadcasts dozens of sexy messages, such as "Welcome to Paradise," "Hey there, you hot hunk of martyr," and "Death to the Jews and Crusaders." We don't have to tell you what happens next.

- [ ] Do you find unusual items when you rifle through your child's dresser drawers? Red flags include multiple international passports bearing your child's picture and a strange-sounding name; blueprints and floor plans for well-known municipal buildings across the nation; telephone lists of FBI contacts; one-way, first-class airline tickets to destinations in the Eastern Hemisphere; foreign currency in large denominations; brochures for flight training at the Pensacola Naval Air Station in Florida; tea, incense, unusual spices or seasonings; and toy weapons that fire real ammunition.

If you have even the slightest suspicion that you might, now or someday, answer yes to any of these questions, do not hesitate! *Hesitation equals death.* Bundle your bundle of joy into the car, and do not stop until you reach one of the Juvenile Emergency Readiness Collection Centers (JERCC) operated jointly by the Department of Homeland Security, Halliburton, and McDonald's. Kiss your child good-bye, and don't look back. The screaming and kicking won't help where they're going. They made their beds, for once, and now they can nap in them.

As a reward for your act of selfless patriotism, you'll receive a 100 percent cotton T-shirt printed with the words "I'm the Humiliated Parent of a Budding Terrorist!" Best of all, a friendly JERCC staff member will hand over TWENTY DOLLARS, all for YOU!

★ *IMPROVISED WEAPONS OF FREEDOM™*

Look around, citizen! Ordinary objects found throughout your humdrum life can be used as powerful tools to fight terror. Start assembling your arsenal of anti-terror weapons today. Here are just a few ideas for improvised weapons to get you started. Visualize weaponry all around you!

★ *CHIP CLIP™* This industrial-design wonder is good for more than keeping your favorite salty snacks crisp and crunchy. When clipped onto a terrorist's lips, this device can be a highly effective way to stop terrorist "chatter."

★ *URINE-SOAKED RAGS* These make an excellent defensive filter against biological and chemical airborne weapons when worn over the mouth, nose, and eyes. Be sure to keep a pile of urine-soaked rags in your home at all times. The rags must be kept wet to be effective, so make urinating on your rag pile at least twice a day a part of your daily anti-terror routine.

★ *GOURMET POPCORN TIN* Rip the metal lid off the tin and fling it at your enemy. Then surprise the terrorists by turning yourself into a whirling dervish, pelting them with the plain, cheese-flavored, and hardened clumps of caramel corn. In this moment of confusion, deliver the knockout blow by slamming the tin down on their heads.

★ *SHOEHORN* The ultimate in terrorist-disarming gear. Using the shoehorn, quickly remove their shoes—which is where they keep their bombs—and throw the shoes on top of a nearby roof. The terrorists will struggle to get their shoes down until the authorities arrive.

★ *DEHYDRATED KITCHEN SPONGE* Announce to the terrorists that you have a sponge and are willing to use it. This will give your attackers a false sense of security. While they're laughing, thrust the rock-hard sponge deep into their groins.

TERROR TIP

HUMMER owners and HUMMER dealerships should equip their vehicles with as many car alarms as possible. These shrieking klaxons of justice will scare off cowardly eco-terrorists, who might try to scrawl traitorous pro-Earth slogans on your HUMMER with their hemp-based paint. If you're a HUMMER dealership, rig all of your car alarms to go off at the same time. If area residents protest the noise, claim your rights to free speech *and* fighting terror!

Fight Terror— Kill Children

Hey there, families of 9/11 victims! Doesn't it make you feel great that we've used the deaths of your loved ones on September 11, 2001, to justify more wars, more killing of innocent civilians, and more families torn apart in Afghanistan, Iraq, and around the globe? Didn't you feel a sense of peace when you heard the news that a squadron of our low-flying A-10 "Warthog" tank-killer warplanes vaporized nine little boys and girls in Afghanistan in a hail of rockets and cannon fire while they were gathering water from a well? Those children will never get the chance to hijack airplanes and kill innocent Americans! Doesn't it give you a sense of closure to read about how we machine-gun pregnant Iraqi women to death in their cars because they don't slow down enough at U.S. checkpoints? What can we say to the 9/11 families about the U.S. military killing innocent women and children in their name around the globe? *You're welcome.*

★ **BOURBON** Muslims think alcohol makes you mentally confused, belligerent, and violent—especially American spirits. That gives you the extra edge against these teetotalers. Keep terrorists offguard by staying as drunk as possible—all day, every day.

★ **SOFA CUSHION** A large-caliber weapon and a useful takedown tool. Tackle a terrorist while holding a sofa cushion in front of you, then keep them down using your own body weight on top of the cushion. In addition, a makeshift fort constructed with sofa cushions makes for a good "secure area" in the event of a successful terror attack.

★ **BEARD TRIMMER** This common device can be a terrifying sight to a fundamentalist Muslim male terrorist. Make sure that your batteries are fully charged, and set the trimmer blade to its lowest "stubble" setting.

★ **NAIR™ GUN** If you don't own a beard trimmer, why not fill all your squirt guns with Nair™ during a quiet evening of preparedness at home? Look for adjustable Supersoaker™-brand squirt guns, which can deliver a warning shot that dissolves just a few terror-whiskers, or a full-on blast that will make any evildoer's jaw as soft and smooth as a baby's bottom.

★ **PLASTIC SHOPPING BAG** It may look floppy and harmless, but a terrorist won't think so when you're asphyxiating him with it. Make sure you double-bag the terrorist's head before taking him away to a secret detention camp.

★ **PORK CHOP** This food item can be a powerful defensive weapon against terrorism, much like garlic is to a vampire. Nail a pork chop to your door to ward off terrorism.

★ **BOWLING TROPHY** Relive your past by ending a terrorist's future. Hold onto the little golden bowler with both hands and swing the heavy, imitation-marble end.

★ **WAD OF CASH** Nothing proves your American spirit like carrying around large amounts of cash at all times. Show the terrorists that they cannot destroy the power of the almighty dollar by smashing a huge roll of greenbacks into their larynxes.

TERROR TIP: GET CHIPPED!

Having a tiny computer microchip implanted under your skin that identifies you as a non-terrorist is now the dream of every patriotic American. Why wouldn't you want to be electronically tagged and turned into a human bar code? You're not in al-Qaeda, are you? This amazing technology, which was originally developed to track cattle, uses GPS satellites to track implanted humans anywhere on the planet. Their brain functions can be remotely monitored by supercomputers, and even altered through the changing of frequencies if they ever start drifting toward terror. You will never be alone again. This is the dream of our Founding Fathers—to know where all of their children are, keeping them safe at all times, and sending electromagnetic waves through their bodies, causing excruciating pain, if they ever start "acting up."

Visit **www.4verichip.com** today!

The abstract lines and simple shapes of the planned WTC memorial site are fine if you're a foreign-born architect with weird designer eyeglasses, but Americans are clamoring for a classic monument that commemorates 9/11 the way we want them to remember it. The George W. Bush Warrior of Freedom™ Statue will fulfill that jingoistic wish. This soaring sculpture, standing an awesome 500 feet tall, will depict our Maximum Leader rising from the smoking ruins of the World Trade Center and the Pentagon like a fighting phoenix of liberty. In one upraised fist he will grip a flaming sword, inscribed with the immortal words "Let's Roll," while over his heart he will hold the Holy Cross. Figures of the miniscule, stunned hordes of Afghanistan and Iraq will be shown kneeling before this mighty Goliath. The statue will rise up from the waves of New York Harbor, as a warning to the world to never try that shit with us again. Taxpayers need not worry about the public cost of this mighty sculptural statement—the raw materials will be provided by a French-designed monument in New York Harbor called the Statue of Liberty, which will be melted down and recast into the George W. Bush Warrior of Freedom™ Statue. Other costs will be met by cutting a few more Head Start programs or something.

For only $49.99, you can purchase a ten-foot-tall, made-in-China plastic replica of this majestic monument from your local Wal-Mart. It's perfect for placing on your front lawn. Plus, proceeds from sales of these Warrior of Freedom™ lawn ornaments will go toward construction of the real statue, so go ahead—buy two or three and install them throughout your neighborhood!

WEEDING OUT THE WEAKLINGS

Numerous studies have shown that suicide rates spiked in New York City after the spectacular attacks of 9/11. This is good news! We are at war, and we don't need any spineless cowards on our side. Those Americans who don't have the fortitude for our unending War on Terror are disposing of themselves, which frees us up to kill more terrorists. If these neurotic New Yorkers can't put up with the foul stench of Ground Zero for a few months—the stink of jet fuel, atomized concrete, melted plastic, and burned human flesh that defines our GWOT—then we don't need them. If they can't deal with watching a few humans fling themselves out of burning skyscrapers, we won't be able to count on them in the vastly more terrible terrorist attacks that are planned for the future. Can't you hear these nebbishes? "Oh my Gawd, I gatta cawl my sistah! She works on the 100th flo-ah!" Put a bullet in your head and spare us your whining. And get back to work in Lower Manhattan. The air quality is totally fine down there.

Traveling
ABROAD

Welcoming Remarks by
Nobel Peace Prize Winner
and Celebrity War Criminal,
Dr. Henry Kissinger

World travel is a subject very dear to my heart. Before the threat of imprisonment at the hands of a hostile tribunal limited my opportunities for safe departure from the United States, I was something of an international jet-setter. I have never forgotten the joys of making clandestine trips around the world, seeing the sights from the finest hotels, and being waited on hand and foot as I negotiated with strong men wearing moustaches and epaulets. It was truly amazing.

Power may be the greatest aphrodisiac, but world travel is the greatest foreplay. I remember one time when I flew to Paris for talks with the North Vietnamese, my dear old friend Jill St. John was along for the ride. Really, she shouldn't have come along, but you try saying no to Jill St. John when she has that thing on. Believe me, it was a hell of a trip! I would overthrow her sovereign governing body any day of the week. Marvelous woman. By the time the plane landed, I was barely in any condition to negotiate "peace" with Le Duc Tho. I'm certain he understood.

Sadly, because of unjust persecution at the hands of the French, I cannot return to the City of Light without being questioned for my so-called role in the so-called coup d'état in Chile which resulted in the so-called disappearance of French citizens. Foolishness.

Nevertheless, you should not let my unfortunate circumstances dampen your own desire to travel. The world is a plum, ripe for the picking, provided you stick to the most strategically vital areas. How can you say that you have lived until you have walked atop the Great Wall of China in the company of the premier?

Many Americans wrongly believe that the rest of the world should be bombed back into the Stone Age. In many cases, this is a very fine idea. After all, Cambodia has clawed its way back into the Bronze Age in only twenty-five short years. But let's not push that button just yet. If it were not for the rest of the world, where would we find the raw materials and slave labor to fill the shelves of our Wal-Marts? Without the world, where would all the bad people come from? Where would we find the enemies who power our mighty military-industrial complex? Without a world to bomb, life would be nothing more than a parade of married homosexuals and effete East Coast liberals, and it is almost impossible, logistically, to launch cruise missiles at enemies who might be living right next door to you.

Finally, and most important, what variety would there be in the It's a Small World ride at Disney World in Orlando, Florida, without a selection of picturesque, lesser lands to be caricatured? In the wise words of the immortal 1960s band the Marmalade, "The world is a bad place, a sad place, a terrible place to live." But you don't have to live in the world. You have only to live in America, the greatest nation, helmed by the greatest minds in the world, where all is possible, and possible is all.

So if you want to set up lucrative strip-mining operations, bag exotic wild game on thrilling safari hunts, assassinate democratically elected leaders, find a lovely and docile wife, or just pick up some cheap trinkets of the Eiffel Tower, this chapter will prepare you for these foreign adventures.

Thank you, and bon voyage!

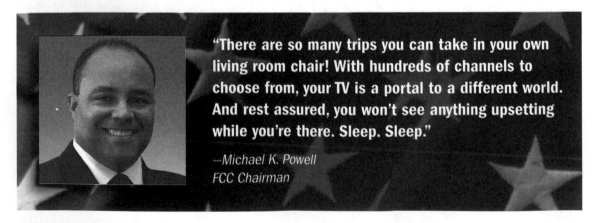

"There are so many trips you can take in your own living room chair! With hundreds of channels to choose from, your TV is a portal to a different world. And rest assured, you won't see anything upsetting while you're there. Sleep. Sleep."

—Michael K. Powell
FCC Chairman

★ WHAT TO PACK?

It happens every time. You rush to finish packing for a month-long pleasure trip through Central Asia. You barely escape gridlocked traffic. You make it to your gate at the airport with seconds to spare, and as soon as the plane takes off, you suddenly remember that you left your life-saving diabetes medication sitting there on your kitchen counter. You then immediately go into insulin shock just as soon as they begin screening a cleaned-up version of *Home Alone IV*, which you heard was good, and you missed it when it was in theaters.

Few travel tragedies rival that of the inadequately stocked suitcase, duffel bag, or tote. Here's a helpful list of American essentials to get you started on the road to happy packing:

★ Little American flags. Hand out these flags to the poor foreign children, who will wave them proudly as you drive by in your Land Rover™.

★ A deck of America's Most-Wanted Terrorists cards. You never know when a relaxing vacation could turn into a victory against terror.

★ Toilet paper, adult incontinency diapers, and Imodium AD™ to deal with the intestinal ravages of foreign "food." These will help you to avoid soiling your bed or hotel room, but are not needed when you are out and about. See page 199 for more details.

★ An automatic pistol with at least three ammunition clips, to protect you and your family. (Not in your carry-on luggage, PLEASE!) There was a short window of time immediately after 9/11 when you probably didn't need a firearm to protect yourself abroad, as foreigners were very sympathetic to us in our hour of pain and tragedy. However, a few months after 9/11, you definitely needed a gun again for some reason.

★ Small laminated cards printed with our Pledge of Allegiance on one side and a recipe for apple pie on the other. These make fantastic gifts for patriotically impaired foreigners who are curious about the American Dream.

★ Printed advertisements for the new Britney Spears album. This is another great gift for making new friends. They are especially appreciated in Islamic countries, where an image of the blonde, nubile, barely dressed Miss Spears is a welcome sight for men who have no idea what the word "midriff" means. You'll also have the pleasure of knowing that you're aiding in the

155

TERROR-TRAVEL READING

There's nothing like a good book to relax with on the beach when you're taking a break from terror. May we recommend *The Final Jihad: When the "Best of the Worst" Come for Us!* by Martin Keating? This thrilling, barely fictional novel was written by the brother of Frank Keating, the former governor of Oklahoma. (Frank Keating was also an FBI agent and assistant secretary of the Treasury, supervising the Secret Service, U.S. Customs, and the Bureau of Alcohol, Tobacco and Firearms.) Martin Keating dedicated his novel to some group called "The Knights of the Secret Circle." Hmm.

We don't want to give too much away, but... aw, you've seen it all happen already, so we'll just tell you! *The Final Jihad* tells the story of an American terrorist named "Tom McVey," who blows up a federal building in Oklahoma City. Tom is then luckily caught by a sharp-eyed state trooper because of a broken taillight, before he can go off and bomb the World Trade Center. What a creative story! In real life, an American terrorist named Tim McVeigh blew up a federal building in Oklahoma City, then was luckily pulled over by a state trooper because of a missing license plate.

Do you know the most amazing thing about this book? Although it was published in 1996, it was written in 1991—*four years* before the bombing in Oklahoma City happened!

global marketing efforts of Jive Records and Bertelsmann AG.

★ A pair of handcuffs. These can be used to lock down your luggage in your hotel room. They can also lock a terrorist to a radiator or an anti-American protestor to a chain-link fence until CIA agents can arrive to handle the situation.

★ A bottle of ketchup. This all-American condiment is invaluable for transforming foreign "food" into something edible. Quiche? Empanadas? Moo goo gai pan? These bizarre and incomprehensible dishes are quickly corrected by drowning them in several inches of delicious ketchup.

★ An American flag T-shirt. It is not advisable to wear clothing printed with the American flag in public while abroad, as this may put you and your family at risk of attack by evildoers. However, your patriotic T-shirt can still give you a warm sense of pride while hidden beneath a jacket or sweater, or perhaps just left behind in your suitcase at the hotel.

★ Photos of American landmarks and national monuments. Pull these out of your pocket after seeing foreign monuments and take a good look at them to avoid misguided feelings of inferiority. Sure, the Taj Mahal might be pretty to look at, but it can't even hold a candle to the Arch in St. Louis, Missouri.

★ FLYING INTO CODE RED

Most Americans are familiar with the increased security procedures at airports made necessary by the staging of the 9/11 attacks. The sonic roar of fighter jets overhead, full-body probes with electromagnetic wands, detailed shoe inspections, ham-handed unwrapping of Christmas presents, and groping fingers pressed deeply into pliant flesh are now standard operating procedure during the relatively calm periods of Green, Blue, Yellow, and Orange Alert. All of us appreciate the sight of steely-eyed Homeland Security agents opening our luggage and publicly handling our underwear, sex toys, and contraceptive devices. But are you familiar with the procedures that must be enacted when our nation surges headlong into a state of Red Alert, the highest level of terrorist threat? During a Red Alert, every traveler becomes a severe risk of terrorist attack and must be treated as such. Nothing short of full cooperation will be tolerated, so get ready to obey, or go buy yourself a helmet. Here is what you can expect to encounter when attempting to board an airplane during a Red Alert:

STEP ONE: Strip Search

The first obvious improvement in airline security is the strip search. For those who have never experienced a strip search, rest assured that the procedure is conducted in the gentlest, most discreet manner possible, given the need to search large numbers of potential terrorists quickly and simultaneously in a wide-open public space. Even first-timers should survive the ordeal with a minimum of psychological trauma. More likely is the

loss of small personal articles such as jewelry, cash, identification documents, and small electronic devices. (Please, remember where you stash your belongings when the order is given to disrobe, so that you can find them more easily when you are allowed to put your clothes back on.) The overly modest or self-conscious traveler should keep in mind that when crowds of confused individuals are ordered to strip, they are far more concerned with being seen naked themselves than with checking out the competition. Chances are, you will not attract the slightest notice of your fellow travelers, unless there is something particularly stimulating or beautiful about the appearance of your naked body—or, conversely, if you are overweight, over the age of twenty-two, or cursed with some type of hideous, attention-grabbing deformity. (Passengers who believe that their nakedness may cause them to be subjected to unwanted attention may request special, one-on-one strip searches in remote, soundproofed rooms adjacent to the airport's cocktail lounge.)

Try using the power of your imagination to make your strip search more enjoyable. Psychologists hint that engaging in creative "waking fantasies" may help the nude traveler steer his or her mind away from thoughts of public humiliation. For example, you might imagine that you are part of a group of unwitting victims, rounded up by fascist thugs and told to undress in preparation for a delousing shower, when in fact you are all doomed to die in minutes. This creative daydream should provide sufficient distraction for you, so that Homeland Security agents can proceed easily with their orders.

STEP TWO: Rectal Probe

Automatic examination of each traveler's rectal cavity for terrorist-related activity is completed swiftly and painlessly, often before the ink is dry on the mandatory "hold harmless" release form that each subject is compelled to sign. This necessary procedure is accomplished using the new, patented Procto-Probe™ technology, from Roto-Rooter—a powerful device

TERROR-TRAVEL ADVISORY

For reasons of personal safety, American citizens are advised not to visit these parts of Iraq: **Iraq**

that is harmless and fun, causing only the slightest pinching, pricking, or burning sensation. Normally, feeling returns to the lower extremities within ninety days, and sphincter control shortly thereafter.

STEP THREE: Boarding Procedure

Once suspected terrorists are culled from the crowd, never again to endanger innocent travelers, you will be given an opportunity to dress and freshen up. Boarding passes, passports, visas, and photo IDs will be given a final examination, carry-on luggage will be exploded with remote-controlled robots, and finally each passenger will be tranquilized, gagged, handcuffed, and blindfolded for the top secret trip to his or her seat aboard the plane.

STEP FOUR: In-Flight Security

Passengers will be strictly segregated according to the price of their tickets. All first-class passengers will be automatically deputized by the plane's anonymous Sky Marshal, who typically remains hidden behind a false wall or moustache. Each new Deputy Sky Marshal will undergo the standard fifteen minutes of rigorous training that real Sky Marshals receive. Deputies will be issued riot batons, stun guns, and pistols, which they can use to quell disturbances in the coach cabin, should they occur. Special onboard firing ranges will be installed in all large jet aircraft so that novices may acquire both aiming proficiency and gun safety skills during their intensive training period.

STEP FIVE: Relax

Sit back, relax, and enjoy the dizzying variety of onboard entertainment, fine dining, and beverage selections, all the while keeping a sharp eye on your fellow passengers for any signs of treachery. And don't forget, you yourself must avoid any suspicious activities, or you will be trussed like a prize turkey, without food or water, for the whole thirty-seven-hour flight to Istanbul via Lagos, Nigeria. You don't want that. It's best to remain in your seat for the entire length of the flight with your arms extended, hands resting on your knees. Look straight ahead, glancing side-to-side every few seconds— but never lock eyes with a fellow passenger, never engage in conversation, and *do not for any reason visit the restroom.*

Once you have arrived at your destination, you will be at the mercy of local authorities. It is recommended that you uphold the pride and rectitude of America by refusing to give an inch to the churlish functionaries who will presume to examine you and your belongings as you enter their foreign land, as though *you*, and not *they*, deserved to be treated with suspicion and scorn.

And so begins your delightful journey into adventure.

★ LOCK AND LOAD!

Is the stress of living in George W. Bush's America becoming too much for you? We have the solution. Pack up the bags, round up the family, and load up for a gun vacation! A relaxing trip filled with shooting and stockpiling will do you a world of good. There are so many kinds of guns out there, so many things to shoot at, and no time like the present to try them all. Commune with nature by killing elephants in Kenya. Shoot the noses off pagan statuary in the ancient temples of Southeast Asia. Take aim at the windmills of Holland. While flipping through brochures at your local travel agency, instead of noting tourist attractions as things you could *see*, look at them as things you could *shoot*. For a simple weekend getaway, you can go to your local shooting range to take out your frustrations on some paper targets with Osama bin Laden's evil, bearded face printed on them. Remember, the Second Amendment isn't just a God-given right, and firearms aren't just for self-defense and killing Muslims. They're also our nation's untapped recreational family funsource.

Who returns from a trip without souvenirs and gifts? Nobody, that's who! Even evil terrorists bring back keepsakes like microfilmed top secret documents, graduation certificates from U.S. Navy flying schools, and lucrative weapons contracts. But you can do better than a stupid T-shirt or humorous shot glass. America is back, the Middle East and Central Asia belong to us, and there are plenty of brand-new shopping opportunities for you to load yourself down with the spoils of adventurism. Due to our vastly expanded borders of Democracy™ and Freedom™, American travelers have a breathtaking selection of trinkets to choose from. When you venture out into the brave new world of "shock and awe shopping," remember these simple rules:

1 Never, *ever* pay the asking price. Remember, we're talking about a race of *rug traders*. They love to haggle. They *live* for it. If they're lucky.

2 Readjust your concept of "fair

value." Just because the price of that beautifully hand-embroidered shawl is the equivalent of 3¢ U.S., that doesn't mean you shouldn't haggle. Refusing to haggle is considered a mortal insult in some conquered areas, and you don't want to find out what *that* means.

3 It's okay to take advantage. So go ahead! Pay a penny for something that would be a bargain at $500 if you could find it back home. Remember—a penny feeds a family of six for a week over there. It doesn't feed them much, of course, but it's all they've got, so they make do. The ones who don't die of malnutrition, that is. They're *starving*, for Gosh's sake, they'll sell anything at any price just for the promise of a little food. Thanks to our cruise missiles that were expertly targeted to hit their water-treatment plants, *they don't even have any clean water to drink.* You're definitely at an advantage here, so take it. You could probably even pay them with fake money and they wouldn't be able to focus their vision clearly enough to notice with their vitamin A deficiencies.

4 Think carefully about how you're going to hide or disguise your purchases. Invariably, the most exciting finds are verboten when it comes to getting them out of that country and back into the homeland. Customs boo-boos used to rate a slap on the wrist and a fine at most, but nowadays, even though America is running things on both ends, you will not catch a break if your ancient Sumerian bronze figure is discovered peeking out of that falafel sandwich in your purse. Be circumspect.

Great Souvenir Ideas

What's for sale? A more useful question, with a shorter answer, would be "What's *not* for sale?" Here is a small sampling of the souvenirs (prices in U.S. dollars) we found the last time we shopped the Big Bazaar:

★ Human ears: 5¢ apiece, four for 17¢. These make great stocking-stuffers.

★ Spouse: $3.29 (temporary, up to one year) to $45 (permanent, add price of airfare to the United States). Be sure to look under the burkha before ponying up the dough.

★ Undocumented domestic servants: $15 to $35, depending on skills and personal hygiene.

★ Preteen sex slave: male, $5; female, 5¢. Beats me.

★ Tusks of animals that you've eaten: free with price of meal. Let street urchins and amputee beggars clean off residual meat and connective tissue.

★ Mortadella bologna, thin-sliced: $22.99/lb. (Check date.)

★ Priceless museum artifacts: 1¢ to $75, with authentication.

★ Priceless artifacts from raided archeological sites: free, but watch out for bandits.

★ Hotel archeological site-raiding tour, including lunch, security, and all the artifacts you can dig up and carry away (available through concierge): $2.

★ Holy clump of hair from the One True Beard of Saddam: $1,500 and up from reputable roadside vendors.

★ Chunks of historic buildings that have been destroyed by Democracy™: free. However, you'll need a native porter to do the heavy lifting: 2¢.

★ Shoulder-fired Stinger antiaircraft missile launcher with ten missiles: $150.

★ Nickel bag of Kabul White: a nickel. Shit is killer.

For years, Israel has been a friendly destination of choice for U.S. tourists. Americans can personally identify with a land where settlers have forced the native population onto small reservations surrounded by barbed wire, where they can be easily oppressed and slaughtered. Unfortunately, this bastion of American-style values in the Middle East has historically been hemmed in by hostile nations that, for some reason, don't appreciate seeing Palestinians, who share their language, race, and religion, get killed by an Israeli army equipped with American weapons.

Finally, one of those hostile nations has been completely transformed by U.S. military might. The good news for American tourists is that Iraq is becoming more like Israel every day! Operation Iraqi Freedom™ was based on the many lessons taught to us by the Israeli Defense Forces and the freedoms that they allow Palestinians. There is now a military curfew in Baghdad, just like in the West Bank and Gaza Strip. If any Iraqi steps out of their house after midnight, they might just get shot. That means you'll be able to get into the hottest shows and nightclubs without waiting in line! We've also enforced the policy of collective punishment, just like in Palestine; such as cutting down all the olive trees in an Iraqi village, the people's sole source of income and sustenance, because a shot was fired at American troops by a sniper hiding in one of the trees. There are always houses that terrorists might have visited getting knocked down by U.S. bulldozers, too, another Israeli lesson

learned. Your kids will love watching the bulldozers knock down these terror-infested buildings and trees. Next, there are the traffic jams caused by U.S. military checkpoints on Iraqi roads. A journey that should take only half an hour can take all day, just like in the West Bank. And there's no guarantee anyone will be permitted to pass. That means plenty of picturesque dust clouds and screaming, angry people—perfect for a memorable snapshot! There are recurring raids to arrest and interrogate all military-aged Iraqi males—that's any male between the ages of fourteen and sixty. You won't have to worry about getting bothered by those guys. Finally, U.S. troops are ringing some Iraqi villages with razor wire and issuing identity cards, *in English only*, to all Iraqis who live there to monitor who's going in and out.

Yes, Iraq is becoming more and more acceptable to American tourists everyday. Isn't it about time that you booked your ticket to Baghdad? If you like visiting Israel, you'll love the new and improved Iraq!

★ BOMBS AWAY!

The latest travel sensation will have you and your family exploding with excitement! Thanks to Presidential Appointee George W. Bush's commitment in his State of the Union address to force every American to make Freedom™ fun, American tourists now have their fingers on the trigger. That's right—you paid for the bombs, now you get to use them! When traveling abroad, the choice of which areas the U.S. Air Force should attack will be up to you. Visit your local military recruiter/travel agency, where Military Tourism Liaison officers will show you how to use your cell phone to enter the GPS coordinates of the area you would like to bomb.* Earn valuable Bombing Bonus Bucks! Get even with friend and foe alike! It's a great way to get your feet wet in the righteous blood of Freedom™!

---

*Currently available in the following areas only: Afghanistan, Iraq, Mexico, East Los Angeles. Coming soon: Syria, Iran, Lebanon, North Korea, Cuba, France. Adults: $15,000 per sortie. Children ten to eighteen years of age accompanied by an adult: $5,000. Children under ten and nursing mothers: free.

A TRAVELER'S PRAYER

Dear God, though my breath be shallow,

And my eyes be shut,

I know, Lord, that You are with me,

From takeoff to touchdown.

And should my heart beat faster than a rabbit's,

Think not, O Lord,

That I have doubted Your presence by my side.

Though burnt of heart and cramped of bowel,

By dint of food served in mid-air,

Still trusting of Your eternal Love,

I shall neither barf nor faint,

Nor drink too deeply from the tiny vessels,

That hold the sinful calm of alcohol.

But if, by chance, in Your eternal plan,

My number has come up,

And the humble craft

Of this budget airline

Is destined not to reach safe harbor,

Then I beg You, Lord, to reconsider,

And to ferret out the seed of this mishap divine.

For You have guided me to this place,

And to this place I shall go,

With You beside me, making sure

That no one robs my hotel room.

— AMEN.

Back in 1997, ninety countries negotiated the Ottawa Convention, which banned the use, production, stockpiling, and transfer of antipersonnel landmines. But in an unusually wise decision by the Clinton administration, the United States refused to sign the accord. The Pentagon reserves the right to deploy landmines anywhere, at any time. This is fine if you never leave the homeland, but if you visit any of the eighty-two countries in the world that are chock-full of landmines, a stroll across the beautiful countryside might just get your legs blown off. Finding and disposing of the millions of landmines buried across the globe would be costly, dangerous, and time-consuming and is therefore not a viable option. Fortunately, we have found a cheap and easy safety solution.

Local orphans provide an inexpensive and plentiful means of landmine detection. In formerly war-torn countries with landmines galore, any child you see is probably an orphan, or knows one. For pennies a day, you can hire these hardworking orphans to walk in front of your car, searching the ground for landmines. If the orphans are too malnourished and underweight to set off a pressure-activated mine, tie two children together and have them march in lockstep, slamming their bare little feet on the ground with every step. If placing these children in such a perilous position makes you feel somewhat uncomfortable, just remember this—with each landmine that is detonated by one of your little orphan helpers, that's one more child who will never be adopted by the gays.

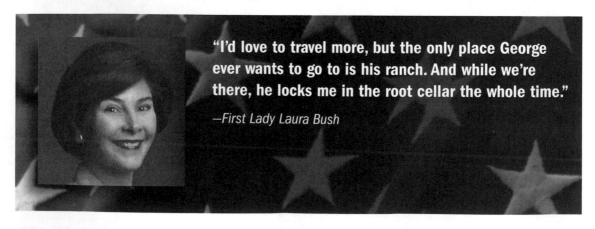

"I'd love to travel more, but the only place George ever wants to go to is his ranch. And while we're there, he locks me in the root cellar the whole time."

—First Lady Laura Bush

★ CELEBRITY LUGGAGE CHECK!

What's inside Deputy Secretary of Defense Paul Wolfowitz's carry-on luggage? Let's check!

★ Half-eaten Almond Joy™ candy bar

★ Index card inscribed with the pros and cons of working for George W. Bush

★ Dog-eared paperback copy of *American Psycho*

★ Adult Clearasil™

★ Soiled underwear from last trip to Baghdad

★ Crudely drawn, sexually derisive caricature of Karl Rove, by Richard Perle

★ Oil-tanker key ring (gift from Condi Rice)

★ Top secret National Security Council invasion plans for Iran

★ Cyanide capsule

★ NOW AVAILABLE: CUSTOMIZED U.S. PASSPORTS!

Due to overwhelming traveler demand, the U.S. Department of State has authorized all major passport-issuing centers to offer, for the first time ever, passports bearing the special design of your choice, for a modest additional fee of only $12.95 per month!* Choose your customized design from dozens of corporate logos (McDonald's, Monsanto, Enron, Halliburton, Lockheed Martin, the Walt Disney Company), or from dozens of your favorite celebrity photos (Michael Jackson, Michael Jordan, Michael Douglas, Michael J. Fox, Wayne Newton, Lee Greenwood, Emmanuel Lewis). Or choose from a selection of "Patriotic Vistas," including views of Mt. Rushmore, Yellowstone Park's Old Faithful geyser, the Pentagon, the White House, Camp X-Ray Detention Camp in beautiful Guantánamo Bay, Cuba, and an aboveground hydrogen bomb test. Don't delay! Apply today!

*Must be billed to passport holder's credit card or direct debit account. Thirty-six payments over thirty-six months for a total cost of $646.20, including additional $7.95 processing fee per monthly billing cycle. No cancellation allowed. Missed payment(s) may result in revocation of passport, citizenship, and the right to vote in some states, and may cause you to be mistakenly reclassified as an illegal enemy combatant and placed in detention without hearing, jury trial, legal representation, or visitation rights. Application constitutes legal permission for full investigation by Department of Justice, including but not limited to: any and all tax and financial records, medical files, educational and religious background, family members, possible or probable past or future activities of a suspicious and/or terrorist nature. Passport may be recalled at any time by any participating sponsors or organizations, without right to appeal or refund.

Two of the best things about America are its schools and the fact that it is America. So it's only natural to ask, what better school can there be in the whole wide world than the School of the Americas in Fort Benning, Georgia? Now, for the very first time in its history, in cooperation with the CIA and the Department of Defense (we tried to get the State Department involved, but they weren't interested), ordinary Americans like you can prepare for your overseas vacation by taking a crash course in international relations at the school critics have nicknamed the "School of the Assassins." That's right, it's *that* School of the Americas—the one where the CIA teaches Latin American military officers how to conduct coups and purge leftist intellectuals using the latest methods of interrogation, torture, and murder. Sign up now for an intense week-long seminar that will make your trip safer for you and your family, and a whole lot more fun!

If you can't get to Georgia, or don't have a week to spare, don't fret. We'll send you a copy of the CIA's "Freedom Fighter's Manual," the same one distributed to the Contras by the Reagan administration. In it, you'll find detailed instructions on how to carry out economic sabotage, propaganda, extortion, bribery, blackmail, interrogation, torture, murder, and political assassination. There's not a vacation snag you won't be able to handle like a pro. Most important, you'll learn:

★ How to cross hostile borders, with family and luggage in tow, without being detected or detained or having your crack cocaine confiscated.

★ How to intimidate and, if necessary, assassinate anti-American journalists.

★ Where to get cash fast in countries not serviced by American Express™.

TERROR-TRAVEL TIP

Canada is a nation to the north of the United States, about the size of Montana, where they speak Canadian, a language very similar to English. You can avoid being served bodily waste products in your entrees at restaurants abroad, and having foreigners spit on you in the street, simply by posing as a Canadian. An easy way to impersonate a

Canadian is to sew a large Canadian flag patch on your backpack or put a Canadian flag sticker on your suitcase. The Canadian flag is red and white, with a red oak leaf in the center white stripe. To complete the disguise, end every sentence with the interrogative "eh?" Canadians are notoriously hard of hearing. However, do not pose as a Canadian while traveling in Afghanistan, as U.S. Air Force pilots on amphetamines will drop a 500-pound bomb on your head.

★ The ten best ways to kill an entire village of peasants and escape unharmed.

★ Which foreign agents are okay to sleep with, so long as your wife doesn't find out.

As a bonus, you'll receive the CIA's *Human Resource Exploitation Training Manual,* a veritable treasure trove of advanced torture techniques. First published in 1983, this book has been used successfully by sadistic military officers across Latin America in their ruthless persecution of leftist dissidents. Come on, admit it—you've wanted to know how to kill a man with nothing but an ordinary pencil ever since you saw G. Gordon Liddy brag to Johnny Carson that he knew how to do it. Now's your chance to find out!

EMPLOYMENT OPPORTUNITIES: When your vacation's over, if you've enjoyed your little taste of what it's like to control the actions of those around you and kill them if they transgress, then why not consider a career at the Central Intelligence Agency? We're looking for folks with travel experience. Don't call us, we'll call you.

★ THE WORLD IS YOUR TOILET

Foreign food is unreliable, awful, and downright dangerous. But if you're unable to pack several weeks' supply of healthy Pop-Tarts™ and Mountain Dew™, you might just be forced to sample the bizarre cuisine of foreign lands. Don't be surprised if it turns your peaceful American stomach into a chaotic war zone. However, relief is always close at hand. Since these foreigners can provide neither digestible food nor functional, comprehensible plumbing, it is perfectly acceptable for gastrointestinally stressed Americans to defecate in any location of their own choosing. You're an American, and that means you have the right to take a dump whenever and wherever you please. Streets and sidewalks, parks and park benches, the back seats of taxicabs, double decker buses, museums, royal palaces, halls of parliament, ancient Mayan pyramids, Greek temples, French cathedrals, public fountains, formal gardens, tropical beaches, coral reefs, volcanoes, zen rock gardens, Buddhist

monasteries, pagodas, cemeteries, national shrines for war dead...it's all there for you to shit on. Your comfort should be your only concern. As a courteous gesture, you can always pop one of your little American flags on top of the steaming pile to let the curious natives know the origin of the human dung that lies before them. When they see that it dropped out of the anal chute of a generous American tourist, they will understand, and be perfectly gracious as they gather it up to sell as valuable, protein-rich fertilizer.

Homesickness: Is It Patriotic?

by William J. Bennett
Co-Director, Empower
America™; Secretary-
Treasurer, Gamblers
Anonymous™

You're far from home, friendless, hungry, and alone. (Except for your family, and the folks who run the bed-and-breakfast, and those nice young newlyweds from Connecticut you met yesterday.) You're asking yourself the questions every American asks once they've spent a few days in a foreign land: "Why isn't this place more like America? Have these people no standards? No character?" Those are good questions, but five'll getcha ten that the answer will stun and upset you. You see, the fault lies not with the native foreigners, but rather with the millions of Americans who travel abroad each year. Call it a moral failing, call it stupidity, but whatever you call it, you're letting America down every time you say "thank you" in French, or pay for something with funny-looking currency. Bowing to the foreigner's ways is just another assault on the standards that give America her unique character. It's time for Americans to wake up and take charge. You don't have to struggle with strange foreign syntax or consonants that can only be pronounced by hocking up a load of phlegm. You must begin immediately the work of rebuilding America's place in the world. I'd lay odds that if you lead the way, Americans, the foreigners will follow.

★ Refuse to exchange currency. Insist on paying with American dollars wherever you go. Foreigners will do just about anything for those precious greenbacks.

★ Trace your travel itinerary on a map, then go online and check to make sure that there is at least one McDonald's and one KFC "restaurant" within a short drive of where you'll be staying. If there isn't one, you can visit my Empower America™ website at **www.empoweramerica.org**, and sign the petition demanding that the heads of the fast-food industry penetrate and conquer all foreign markets, bringing American quality-control standards to the food industry worldwide. Americans need fast food they can rely on, as

TERROR-TRAVEL ADVISORY

For reasons of personal safety, American citizens are advised not to visit these parts of Afghanistan: **Afghanistan** well as "restaurants" where they can read the menu and pay in good old American dollars. (Of course, if you're feeling adventurous, go ahead and try an ethnic restaurant, such as Chili's™.)

★ Try to eat only food that you recognize. Don't gamble, at least with your health. Hummus? Tabouleh? Barfi? No thanks, I'll take the Chicken McNuggets™. Even if you've heard of the unappetizing slop that passes for food overseas, pretend you don't know what it is. This will humiliate the foreign restauranteur, so that next time you'll be able to get your chili-burger and cheese fries.

★ Most important, speak only English. Everyone in the world should speak grammatically correct American English, and they should also understand that to resist the English language could one day result in tragedy and death. Foreign intellectuals will be offended, but the majority of average foreigners will understand that you're trying to raise their moral standards and help them to build character. Incidentally, the common belief that shouting does not help foreigners understand what you're saying has been disproved again and again. If a foreigner doesn't understand English, keep repeating your command at ever-increasing volume and intensity until your wish is carried out. Shout, if you must, for America.

TERROR-TRAVEL TIP

Dress appropriately for swift clearance through airport security! Each member of your family should dress identically in bright, jarring colors, so that they are easily identifiable to airport security personnel. It's best to choose a loose-fitting, easily frisked athletic suit of synthetic material, preferably one with the brand name prominently displayed on both top and bottom, and with no pockets. The head of the family should wear a large "fanny pack" in which he may place paper money, all required identification papers, and a container of non-alcoholic liquid refreshment. Wear chunky athletic shoes, also brightly colored and bedecked with brand logos, that are one or two sizes too large, and wear them unlaced for efficient removal and inspection. Into each shoe, place a Dr. Scholl's Odor Eater™ pad to avoid offending the delicate, finely-tuned nostrils of our homeland's shoe inspectors. (Today, the greatest health risk for airport security workers is not the terrorist bomb, but rather bronchial irritation caused by the sweaty feet of unwashed travelers.) No belts, no jewelry, no sunglasses, no watches, no medication, no dentures, no wigs or false moustaches, no reading matter in a foreign language (not even a phrase book), NO ALMANACS, no running, and no spontaneous displays of emotion. Stay in one spot (NEVER wander aimlessly), speak when spoken to, be polite and deferential to all security personnel, even the morons, and comply with any and all commands.

Franklin Delano Rosenfeld's biggest mistake, during a lifetime consisting almost exclusively of mistakes, was his famous proclamation, "The only thing we have to fear is fear itself." Yeah, right. In fact, the only thing we have to fear is that we're not scaring ourselves enough! Nothing to fear, indeed. Well, my fellow American, there's plenty to fear. Just think about it logically—in the relatively short life of our nation, we've managed to fill every available space in our culture with fear. And we're still in our national infancy compared to the Europeans, Chinese, Africans, and Arabs, for Gosh's sake, who've been on top of this fear game for literally *thousands of years!* With the head start these cultures have going for them, it's no wonder that the rest of the world has us beaten on fear of every imaginable variety: alarm, anxiety, trepidation, fright, dread, terror, horror, dismay, phobia, panic, angst, consternation, scare, worry, apprehension, foreboding, bête noire, you name it.

No matter where you go, fear is there waiting for you. Fear of contracting venereal disease in Paris; phobia about having to step through streets running with raw sewage in Baghdad; worry that you'll be served poisonous sushi in Tokyo; apprehension over the likelihood that you'll be captured and beheaded by African warlords; panic as the bus in which you're riding plunges thousands of feet off a cliff in the Peruvian Andes; dismay over the realization that the Russians you're having dinner with still want to bomb the hell out of us; anxiety over the likelihood that along with that interesting yak stew you just ate in Kathmandu, you've ingested parasites that will cause total blindness in less time than it will take to get you back to civilization for treatment.

Do you experience extreme fears such as these when vacationing in Orlando, Florida, or beautiful Branson, Missouri? Unfortunately, no. Whether they are actually manufactured or created out of thin air, we must envision new fears lurking around every corner of our homeland. It is a challenge, America, to examine our own fear-ridden society and make it even more excruciatingly alarmist, but this is a challenge that we must accept if we are to achieve world leadership in fear.

TERROR-TRAVEL TIP

Be sure to visit foreign countries only when Presidential Appointee George W. Bush is also visiting. You won't be able to travel very often this way, as George W. Bush has nothing but contempt and hatred for the rest of the world, but you will enjoy unparalleled safety and security during your trip. You'll love the peace of mind that comes with traveling beneath Bush's protective umbrella of Black Hawk helicopters, mobile missile launchers, and 16,000 rent-a-cops. There's no safer place on Earth.

★ TALES OF TRAVEL

On "Hunger" Overseas

by Rush Limbaugh
Conservative
Commentator and
Celebrity Drug Addict

If I have to look at one more liberal appeal showing some pleading urchin in Bagoogooland with a swollen belly, I'm going to puke! First of all, the pictures they use have to be at least twenty years old. And what was the photographer doing? What did he have for lunch? Did he offer a bite to the kid in the photo? Anyhow, nobody's that hungry anymore, not with the care packages and airdrops and all that good stuff we pay for so that people in other countries never have to worry about getting a job. I tell you, my friends, hunger is a luxury that you and I pay for with our tax dollars. Hunger is for lazy people.

You can't tell me that there's nothing to eat over there. I've been to their restaurants. Indian food is delicious! Go to an Indian restaurant and see for yourself. Huge portions of delicious, steaming food. Heaps of it. My mouth is watering right now. I'll tell you what's wrong over there. Picky eaters. They're like kids, they push away a full plate of perfectly good food and then whine because they're hungry. Have you ever seen what's in those food aid packages we dropped on Afghanistan? Delicious food, full of sugar and fat and starch. Keeps anybody alive and healthy.

Why are these starving people turning up their noses at a nice Pop-Tart™ spread with a thick layer of Jif™ peanut butter and grape jelly? What, are they afraid of keeling over from insulin shock? You know who's picky? The French. The pickiest eaters on Earth. They're even picky about cheese. What's not to like about cheese?

Here's what I propose, my friends—get out there in the world and show these people how real Americans eat. Pile on the food, stuff your face, throw plenty of leftovers on the ground, at least enough to feed one of those so-called starving families, and see how they react. If they go out and get a job, start supporting their families, and start buying their food at a clean, hygienic grocery store instead of rooting in the dirt all day and waiting for a handout, then, my friends, we will have done something worth doing that will just about drive our liberal buddies up the wall with envy and frustration!

TRAVEL ADVISORY

For reasons of personal safety, American citizens are advised not to visit these parts of Europe: **Europe.**

Are you a Friend of America™? Have you read and agreed with everything in this book? Then you need to learn this special handshake. (If you're not a Friend of America™, stop reading, put the book down, and turn yourself in immediately.) To help America's friends abroad avoid the embarrassment and inconvenience of finding themselves vacationing alongside terrorists and terrorist sympathizers, your government has devised the Friends of America™ Handshake, a quick and easy test that lets you know who your friends are. And why shouldn't you be able to tell, quickly and easily, whether those nice folks on the next beach blanket are the type to have dinner with, or the type who'll sneak into your room and slit your throat as soon as the hotel bar shuts down for the night? In the good old days, things were simpler. All you had to do was ask a fellow to recite the batting average of some obscure shortstop who played for the Yankees back in 1937. If he gave you the wrong answer, you shot him, quick and easy. Hell, even a dog can tell who his dog friends are just by sniffing around their howdydooyas. Today's American traveler deserves no less. Keep your trip safe, and help sniff out terrorists, by learning this secret handshake:

1 Proffer your hand as if you were an aristocrat whose ring is to be kissed, with the palm down and the hand hanging loosely from the wrist. This represents America's proper place in the world.

2 If the other person presents his or her hand in a similar fashion, spread and extend your fingers repeatedly like a spider, sensually stroking the other person's hand. This represents the octopus-like grip that America enjoys over the world's natural resources and peoples.

3 Finally, curl your hand into a fist and punch it repeatedly into the other person's hand. This represents the power of America that is righteously unleashed when other nations dare to oppose our Freedom™. Ideally, if the other person is also a Friend of America™, they are simultaneously punching your fist, creating a satisfying series of knuckle-smashing impacts. The first person that stops punching is the less patriotic American of the two, so be sure to toughen the skin and deaden the nerves of your hand by punching it into a bucket of gravel for at least thirty minutes every day.

★ A DEADLY JOURNEY

For many Americans, especially old, mentally confused ones, crossing the borders of our homeland to buy generic prescription drugs in Mexico or Canada can be a powerful temptation. This is a trip that you do not want to take. On behalf of the U.S. pharmaceutical industry, we would like to instill in you a powerful and irrational fear of these suspiciously cheap prescription drugs.

First of all, drug manufacturers in these countries are regulated under corrupt, socialistic health standards that allow up to 50 percent by volume of all medicines to consist of vomit, rat feces, decomposing human remains, and leper excrement. Second, when you buy drugs in America, you're paying not only for absolute purity, but also for the important service of prescription drug advertising, which shows you exactly how the drug works in brilliant, hyperrealistic detail. Which drug is better—the pure one that shows, *on television*, how its users stand proudly on towering columns of granite that thrust upward from a churning sea of discontent, and then float away like angels into a psychedelically beautiful sunset after consuming it? Or the contaminated one that just squats there on the shelf, reeking of putrefaction in its grim, black-and-white packaging? Obviously, the generic version of the drug has no such glorious, computer-animated effects to offer. And if it did feature animation, what would it show? Raw sewage flowing down your throat?

If this weren't reason enough to avoid these generic pharmaceuticals, consider that not only have millions of Mexicans and Canadians died instantly after taking their cheap pills, but many were also transformed into cannibalistic vampires before finally succumbing to a painful, slow, and extremely embarrassing death. If you're thinking of traveling to obtain these deadly drugs, *don't*. Stay at home, and try to keep your blood pressure down by watching television and taking frequent naps.

TERROR-TRAVEL TIP

In keeping with the "everything's changed" motif of post-9/11 travel, you must relearn even the most basic elements of trip preparation. The conscientious traveler once provided a full itinerary for family and friends, complete with addresses and phone numbers in case of emergency. No more. Today, the clever terrorist will stop at nothing to locate you. Do you have any idea how quickly a child will give you up under torture? If the terrorists know where you are, they'll know where to find you and kill you. Therefore, refuse to tell anyone when you are leaving, where you are going, or how you can be contacted. Don't worry—you're in good hands. The FBI, CIA, Defense Department Intelligence, and the Department of Homeland Security will track your location at all times, ready to strike with the might of our entire nation should you become a victim of terrorists (unless those terrorists are CIA assets who are being groomed for a "special operation").

Homeland
PRIDE

Welcoming Remarks by
Secretary of Homeland Security
and Head Fearleader,
Tom Ridge

When Presidential Appointee

George W. Bush asked me to be in charge of overseeing the security of this country, I wasn't sure I was up for the job. Prior to this, I was only the protector of Pennsylvania in a metaphorical, non-paranoia-inducing way. However, I decided that I love my country more than that crummy state, and the word "homeland" has always made me feel all tingly. I said that I would do it if I could issue constant terror warnings in a diverse palette of colors. I got my wish, and here I am today.

The charge of protecting this great nation is one I take very seriously, certainly more so than if I were put in charge of keeping, say, Guam or the Czech Republic safe from harm. Why? The answer is simple. Those countries don't matter, but the U.S.A. does. The U.S.A. stands for the

United States of America, but what does the United States of America stand for? It stands for liberty. It stands for Freedom™. It stands for justice. It stands for lip service to all of this and more.

Our country is the most diverse country in the world. You can take pride in the fact that white people, brown people, yellow people, white people, red people, and white people have come together to make up our diverse American stew. They come from all over to embrace the safe haven of the United States, only to be sent back to the country of their origin because we already have enough diversity on these shores. But at least for that brief moment, they've sampled American greatness, and maybe they'll take some of that home with them.

This diversity has led to a cultural landscape unparalleled in the world. We have scores of artists, hundreds of television channels, thousands of radio stations owned by one company, and millions of opportunities for anyone who wants to be the next Toby Keith or Jim Belushi. Any person, no matter how unappealing they may be, can find their way into our unending geyser of entertainment product to drench American minds with their gifts.

And resources? We've got them in spades! We have the third largest river, the largest freshwater lake, the largest mountain by volume, and the world's only palace made entirely of corn. Our forests are dense with lumber, our mountains rich with coal, and our ovaries swollen with scientifically induced fertility. We are unparalleled in military might, so we can spread righteousness to everyone. We've invented everything worth inventing, from blue jeans to the electric chair. We have a broad selection of delicious domestic bourbons and whiskeys, which I enjoy on a daily and nightly basis. We have Jesus in our corner and dollars in our wallets. We have unlimited night and weekend minutes. We have monster, monster, monster trucks and nitro-burning funny-car action roaring into a coliseum near you.

These are just some of the reasons I love our homeland and am proud to be its benevolent, squarely built guardian angel, able to swoop down on offenders without warning in the dead of night. I hope that you, too, cherish this land of ours and.... What was that noise? It sounded like terrorism. I smell falafel! Dear God, no! Orange Alert! Go to Red! Mayday! Mayday! I gotta go. You're all on your own!

"9/11 caused a groundswell of pride and patriotism for New Yorkers and for all Americans. It also caused my speaking fees to triple. It's a real shame that I won't be available to guide New York with my inspiring warmth and dignity when the next disaster occurs."

—Rudolph Giuliani
Former Mayor of New York City

★ PRISONS—YES, IN MY BACKYARD!

Manicured lawns, modern architecture, the bright banks of floodlights illuminating the night—prisons are a beautiful and welcome addition to any community. With a record-setting two million people now locked up in our prisons, the United States has overtaken Russia in the imprisonment race and has a higher percentage of its citizens behind bars than any other country in the world. Have you lost your manufacturing job at the auto factory to some Chinaman overseas? Your new career opportunity lies in controlling and imprisoning your fellow human beings. Working in a prison will soon be the best job left in "the land of the free," so grab an application for your local Supermax today. Being a prison guard sure beats being on the other side of the bars, getting yourself traded for a couple of cigarettes. And what loyal citizen wouldn't want to serve his country in one of America's dazzling new prisons of the future?

Cell doors open and close at the touch of a button. Gone are the days of the truncheon and the fire hose. Today's correctional officers now have an array of modern human-control technology at their fingertips, such as Tasers, concussion grenades, and prefrontal-lobe electronic implants—which can be used to convince even the most hardened criminal that he or she is a barnyard animal. In addition, all prisoners are extremely sedate and polite now, thanks to a wide range of mood-altering drugs added to prison food. You won't have to worry about being in danger when you're working in "the big house." With all of these advances in prison technology, you're more likely to be killed driving to work than having your throat slit in a prisoner uprising. Just in case, you'll be issued your own personal cyanide pill, to be used if you ever find yourself in an untenable position.

Prison jobs can bring you financial security, revitalize your community, and even revitalize your marriage. Husband-and-wife prison guard teams are no longer just a staple of hilarious television sitcoms. They really work in real life. You'll also be able to spend more time with your spouse when you take the helmets and body armor off at the end of a long day. With most communities boasting a medium- to high-security correctional facility within a twenty-minute drive of the downtown area, you and your wife will no longer need to commute for several hours to get to your jobs.

Prisoners providing plentiful custodial help at low rates to communities are another benefit of our police state. Are you sick and tired of seeing graffiti on your children's playground? Low-paid, well-mannered work squads will dutifully clean up every inch of that playground, under the watchful eye of your shotgun-toting neighbor. Prisons are so successful that they are always generating more prisoners, who can be outsourced to the general population if we can't pack any more into the cells. Soon, you might have your very own convict busily cleaning your garage or weeding your flowerbed.

With all the complaining about the economy, the prison-industrial complex is an economic model that has worked and thrived. The turning point was when we stopped looking at prison as just a rehabilitative system and realized that it was a golden moneymaking opportunity. By defunding educational programs, erasing drug treatment facilities, and aggressively stepping up police presence in inner-city communities, we're putting more men and women in jail than ever before, creating real jobs for imprisoned Americans. In addition, we're creating astronomically better-paying jobs for those executives who run our prisons. Crime does pay, at least if you're a white guy in a suit.

Our "three strikes and you're out" plan means that a person can get a life sentence for stealing $20 of groceries, but the Bush administration is also not ignoring corporate criminals who steal over $20 million from their investors and employee pension plans. We will soon pass tough maximum sentencing laws for white-collar criminals, which will consist of a grueling sentence of no more than four days of incarceration at a two-star resort hotel, with no chance of parole.

★ THE SEVEN WONDERS OF THE U.S.A.

The seven wonders of the ancient world were located primarily in the Middle East, but everyone knows that place has really gone to hell over the last 2,000 years. In our modern age, America has seized the torch of wonder, erecting monuments that have shocked and awed the world. Let us take you on a tour of the most marvelous landmarks of our proud homeland!

1 **THE MALL OF AMERICA** The name says it all. America does their mall shopping here, at the nation's largest retail and entertainment complex. This enclosed corporate space in Bloomington, Minnesota, one of the most visited destinations in our homeland, is an unprecedented mix of retail and entertainment. Consumers can shop their favorite stores as well as see a movie, ride a roller coaster, or meet famous celebrities such as their favorite Minnesota Vikings offensive lineman. The Mall of America is the pinnacle of American business ingenuity. While one could conceivably go to an Orange Julius franchise in any mall, what right-thinking American wouldn't want to get an Orange Julius from the *biggest* mall in the land?

2 THE KRISPY KREME FRANCHISE
From its humble start as a single donut shack in the Sweet South, Krispy Kreme Donuts is now the leading fried-pastry restaurant chain on the New York Stock Exchange. In the late 1990s, Krispy Kreme enjoyed explosive growth across the nation, ensuring that Americans from coast to coast could finally enjoy the Krispy Kreme touch on their daily pound and a half of sugar, fried dough, and precious cremes. If you haven't gobbled down six Krispy Kreme original glazed in one sitting, you don't know how good it can feel to be an American.

3 BRANSON, MISSOURI This wholesome music entertainment complex is timeless, like the Pyramids of Egypt. Branson is here to stay, for it has been built on a rock-solid foundation—spreading the pure joy of America through music while minting money, metaphorically speaking. The joy is real. The mint is metaphoric. The money belongs to Andy Williams. The shining jewels of Branson include Planet Branson, the Welk Champagne Theatre, the Waltzing Waters colored light show, the Moon River Theatre (Andy Williams and Glen Campbell *together!*), The Baldknobbers Jamboree, Gregory Popovich's Comedy Pet Revue, the Boxcar Willie Theater...and the list goes on so long, you know it's a wonder. Get out the ink and paper, and grease up the presses—we're printing hundreds tonight, Maw!

4 THE BIG DIG Under construction since 1991, the Big Dig in Boston, Massachusetts, is the largest, most complex, and technologically challenging highway project in American history. It is also the slowest-to-progress, most-over-budget, traffic-clogging sinkhole of corruption and graft in our fair land. They've been building "the pride of Boston" for thirteen years, they've spent $14.6 billion, and it still isn't finished. Who is behind this fiasco of modern municipal fiscal irresponsibility? Bechtel, the same construction corporation that we picked to "rebuild" Iraq! The Big Dig might not be much to look at, but it is truly amazing how much money this Republican-connected company has been able to suck out of taxpayers' pockets!

5 THE MISSILE SILOS OF NORTH DAKOTA Across the silent wastes of this cold, rectangular state, the prairie is dotted with the subterranean missile silos of our mighty nucular arsenal. Viewing this landscape of perpetual readiness to obliterate all human life on the planet, questions may come to the mind of contemplative Americans. How far can man reach? How deep can man go? We keep our eyes set on the stars, but toil toward hell.

6 THE WORLD'S LARGEST BALL OF TWINE There are no fewer than three World's Largest Balls of Twine in the United States, and each one is a testament to man's resolve and domination over jute fibers. The primary twine ball is housed in Darwin, Minnesota, where hundreds of people visit every year to pay their respects to this 17,400-pound stringy orb. Who can blame them? It is truly inspirational. Francis Johnson, who personally wrapped each piece of twine around his massive ball, was a man who ignored everything else—politics, culture, art—and dedicated his life to the sole purpose of rolling up a gigantic ball of twine. He is a model for all Americans.

7 **THE PENTAGON** Exactly sixty years before 9/11, on September 11, 1941, ground was broken in Arlington County, Virginia, for a huge new building to house the Department of War. This monument to our military might is the largest inhabitable non-parallelogram polygon in the world. Certain ancient tribes of the 1960s thought that the building's pentagon shape—a traditional emblem of the occult—trapped a demon inside that powered our military's success, but these rumors have never been proven.

★ FEDERAL DAY CARE

The family has always been the cornerstone of the American pyramid. Children can learn more from a stable family life than they can in any atheistic, state-run school. However, some realities must be faced. There's almost no way that the average family can raise a child without two incomes these days. How can the family survive in this environment? In order to help the less fortunate, we're instituting our new "Leave a Child, Take a Child" program. Sounds like wasteful big government spending, you say? It's exactly the opposite. Children at our Child Rearing and Indoctrination Facilities will not be a drain on your tax dollars. Instead, they will be paying their own way by patriotically assembling U.S. flags and cluster bombs.

Just drop off Junior on your way to work. While they're in our facility, they'll learn about the dangers of socialized medicine and the benefits of a flat tax system in our state-of-the-art hypno-learning center, as well as the virtues of an honest day's work in our fairly safe labor shops. Our program will ensure that the children all become basically identical, so you don't have to worry about keeping tabs on which one was exactly your child. At the end of the day, you can pick up a child that is most likely yours, safe in the knowledge that he received the best care he could earn during his stay. As an added bonus, he'll be too tired to raise much of a fuss at home, so you can watch your Fox News in peace.

★ GO TEAM!

The game of football captures the very essence of our aggressive, enraged nation. All across America, our boys are cramming as much beef, creatine, steroids, and human growth hormones into their guts as they can, then hitting the weight room to transform themselves into thickly muscled battering rams in the hope of "making the team." Smaller and weaker boys may volunteer to launder these players' jockstraps to save what little dignity they have left. From children's Pop Warner games all the way up to the NFL, it is every American's duty to watch as much football as humanly possible. This brutal, homo-sadistic reenactment of land-acquisition warfare, with opposing squads of strong young men crashing into each other with their "blitzes" and "bombs," is a fascinating reflection of the smash-mouth foreign policy that guides us in our new age of American empire.

However, the Green Bay Packers represent the worst that football has to offer. We must ask you to not root for this team from the smallest market in the NFL, a miserable little town in a cold, dreary state. Even worse, the Packers are publicly owned by the citizens of Green Bay. This Marxist scheme is a slap in the face to the wealthy owners of all the other NFL teams, who are free to pick up their teams and leave town if some other city offers to build them a bigger stadium. Instead of rooting for these pathetic, proletarian Packers, you should support the Houston Texans and the Dallas Cowboys, or Texan-millionaire-owned teams such as the Minnesota Vikings. Did you know that the Houston Texans actually had a 15-1 record this past season, went to the playoffs, and were barely defeated in the AFC Championship Game by a last-second field goal? It's totally true. Also, Enron posted record profits this past year and all the students in the Houston public school district got straight As on their report cards.

OUR NEW MASCOTS

For some reason, certain sensitive types take offense to athletic teams identifying themselves with American Indian mascots, such as the Braves, the Redskins, or the Savage White-Women Scalp-Hunters. Luckily, the United States has a new defeated foe to decorate the helmets and jerseys of our sports teams. We're perfectly fine with laying the Indian mascots to rest now that we have the Iraqis to caricature. Instead of mascots like Chief Illini, whooping it up on the basketball court while waving a plastic tomahawk, we soon may see Iraqi-styled mascots dancing for fans of the Ragheads or the Fighting Fedayeen, wearing a kaffiyeh and brandishing a rocket-propelled grenade launcher. Much like the Indians, the Iraqis are a once-proud race of warriors that we have nearly wiped off the face of the earth.

Unknown to most Americans, there exists a shadowy network of terrorists who have carried out violent attacks and operations across the globe for over fifty years. Along with the usual bombings and shootings, this terror group has carried out narcotics trafficking and experiments in mind control using LSD, PCP, and other drugs on unwitting American subjects. Some of these U.S. soldiers and civilians committed suicide after being given the drugs unknowingly.

In even more outrageous attacks, the terror group has taken out democratically elected governments around the world with coups d'état and assassinations, then installed murderous dictators who torture, rape, and kill millions of their own people. Many of these victims are on an "enemy list" that the terror group provides its dictator. Sometimes the dictator becomes too powerful through his connection with the terror group and goes out of control, forcing America to go to war to stop him. The reach, scope, and power of this terror group is unparalleled. They are a cold and vicious band of killers who are friends to tyrants and enemies of human rights, self-determination, free speech, and democracy.

You must be thinking, "So who is this incredible terror group, anyway?" Are we talking about al-Qaeda? The Al-Aqsa Martyrs Brigade? The Tamil Tigers? COBRA? No, no, no, and no.

We're talking about the CIA!

Yes, the true masters of terror can be found working for the good old U.S. of A. Isn't it great to know that in this global age of unrelenting terror that we've somehow gotten ourselves into, the professionals are on *our* side?

THE FREEDOM™ ZONE

Americans are in love with all fifty of our beautiful states, but now we have yet another piece of land that we can call our own—The Freedom™ Zone. This strip of land, running from the oil reserves of the Caspian Sea region, across Afghanistan and into India, is coincidentally where our oil pipeline is being built. American tourists will soon be flocking to this land for fun and good, safe times. But first, we all need to work together. We need strong men who can lay our pipeline, as well as guard it from evildoers who only want to destroy our Freedom™. Once we finish the grand pipeline, we'll all be living the good life! Come on, everybody pulled together back in the 1800s to build the Transcontinental Railroad, linking the east and west coasts of America. Where are the hardworking Irish and Chinaman slaves of the twenty-first century? The Freedom™ Zone is the next step in our manifest destiny. This pipeline will pump in a new era of prosperity and wealth for all Americans. You'll be able to afford bigger and bigger cars, year after year—until 2012, when the world's oil reserves dry up and we enter a new phase of global war to reduce the world's population to a more manageable level.

★ THE HALL OF CO-OPTED HEROES™

"History is written by the victors," they say. And who are "they"? Academicians. History professors. Democrats. *Terrorists.* The ones who would have our children believe the preposterous notion that America is a nation founded on racism, sexism, genocide, economic inequality, brutal expansionism, and imperialism. It's known as "The Big Lie," and no one sells it better than Democrat/terrorist academia. History has not been written by the victors. It has been written by the Communists.

No wonder history is no fun. For liberals and terrorists, history is a litany of complaints and crimes that need to be redressed. Okay, we killed off the Indians—excuse us!—the *Native Americans.* We enslaved Africa. We manipulated the politics of the entire Western Hemisphere, and a good chunk of the Eastern, using murder, assassination, open and covert warfare, espionage, the destruction of democratically elected governments, and installation of brutal dictatorships. We robbed millions of souls of their God-given right to self-determination, not to mention disenfranchising and oppressing huge segments of our own citizenry using prejudice and terrorism. We've nearly destroyed nature and mortgaged the future, all to make a buck for a privileged, powerful few. So say the Communists. Hit us over the head with it, why don't you? It's no wonder those Commies couldn't manage to provide their citizens with sufficient toilet paper. They were too busy wiping their behinds with our proud heritage.

The Democrats and terrorists use history as a bludgeon to hit us with our alleged mistakes. First of all, who says they're mistakes? Who says that it's a mistake to cut down all the trees and make everyone drive cars, which means that carbon dioxide levels skyrocket, which leads to global warming, which leads to worldwide catastrophic climate change? Who says—scientists? Scientists come from universities—*liberal* universities that still preach Marxism even after that pathetic ideology has been tossed on the ash heap of history. And finally, how can you even call our actions mistakes? Those "mistakes" have led to us being on top of the world. We consume 80 percent of the world's resources. Would you rather be some barefooted, dysentery-ridden Yanomani Indian being chased through the Amazon by corporate mercenaries? If we're making so many mistakes, how come we're the ones who are only paying $2 a gallon, bombing whomever we choose, and dictating international trade terms? No, I don't think we're the ones making any mistakes. Remember, mistakes are for terrorists and Democrats. Real Americans are filled with pride.

And that's what we're here to celebrate! *Symbolic,* not literal truth is what The *New* American History™ demands of us. Honoring, not denigrating, our achievements. Happy, not sad. And just as those pinkos of prostration bend history to suit their depressing purpose, we shall coax out of history the inspiring, the uplifting, the harmlessly heartwarming "facts" and "events" that will take the place of living memory and turn gloom and discontent into complacency and complicity. Move it, Professor Sad Sack Democrat! Out of the way, Mr. Muhammad al-Terrorist! We're making history! All across our homeland, Americans are coming out in support of a landmark that will leave a lasting impression on ignorant tourists for centuries to come. Citizen, behold Washington, D.C.'s latest historical monument—the Hall of Co-opted Heroes™.

In this great and patriotic theme park, visitors will discover an American history of inclusion—where the formerly outcast have been taken to heart and transformed into beloved icons. Once rebels, despised by society for their challenges to the social order, the laws of nature and of man, our heroes have been tamed, de-fanged, declawed, and neutered. They will be safe and friendly, stripped of meaning and commodified, the contexts of their real lives erased and reconfigured into narratives of dignity and patriotism, suitable for marketing to the widest possible cross section of the American public. These co-opted heroes will have some new friends, too!

With the magic of audio-animatronic technology, you'll see Malcolm X politely asking Richard Nixon if he can take Nixon's daughter Tricia out for an ice-cream cone. You'll see Lieutenant Colonel Oliver North patiently sewing traditional multicolored shawls with Nicaraguan women. You'll see FBI chief J. Edgar Hoover running up the stairs at the Lorraine Motel, pushing Jesse Jackson aside to cradle Martin Luther King's lifeless, bloody, audio-animatronic head in his lap. You'll see Strom Thurmond giving encouragement to Muhammad Ali as his ringside coach, rubbing the champ's shoulders and rinsing out his mouthguard in between rounds. You'll see a robotic dummy of Ronald Reagan bounding up the Olympic victory stand to raise his own fist of Freedom™ in support of Tommie Smith's and John Carlos's black power salute. At the Hall of Co-opted Heroes™, anything is possible!

FIX POTHOLES WITH PRAYER

Lord, fill this jagged hole,

As You have filled my broken heart.

Guide my giant car, so that its wheels will not be bent and pierced,

By the black asphalty sharpness of life's travails.

Protect the crumbling pavement of our streets,

Making heavy trucks find an alternate route.

Lift up and strengthen the concrete of our humble labor.

All praise unto You who maketh the holes,

And the amalgam that filleth them,

For Thine is the power that causeth all repairs on Earth,

Not our municipal governments.

———————————————————Amen.

Note: The power of prayer is most effective when it is delivered by all. Any citizen who fails to pray against potholes will be regarded with the highest suspicion.

★ FLAG CARE IN A POST-9/11 UNITED STATES

Wear It, Wave It, Stick It on Your Car

Nothing brought out our patriotic spirit like the terrorist attacks of 9/11. The towers may have fallen that day, but Americans responded by raising their hearts and their flags. However, people are far too busy putting America back on its feet to adhere to a code of flag care that was written when people had nothing but time to fuss around with these sorts of things. We're wiping the slate clean, updating our codes of flag care so that we have more time for vigilance.

The first rule of flag care is this— proudly bear at least one flag. Of course, the more flags you display, the more patriotic you really are. That being said, here are the new guidelines for maintaining your star-spangled banners:

DO have a flag for every occasion. Fly the flag in your front yard as well as your backyard. Hang a flag in every window. Make sure you have one primary flag pin for your daily clothes, and one backup pin for your pajamas.

DON'T worry about the conditions of laborers in the country that manufactured the flags you are displaying.

DO wear the flag proudly on your torso, particularly if it commemorates the tragedy of September 11, endorses the election of the Presidential Appointee, or is accompanied by a tacit threat should an asshole attempt to destroy it with fire.

DON'T wear the flag if your mission is to disgrace it by displaying unpatriotic sentiments of doubt or foolishly voting for Democrat John Kerry, a sworn enemy of our commander in chief.

DO attach multiple flags to your car's antenna, windows, bumpers, and doors, regardless of visibility issues. Your limited visibility will be compensated for by the protection your shield of patriotism offers against auto collisions.

DON'T create a traffic hazard by stopping abruptly to pick up your tattered flag when it is finally ripped from your car due to your high velocity. It belongs to God now, and he will do with it as he sees fit.

DO buy an extra flag and donate it to someone who is too poor to buy a flag of his own.

DON'T give that person anything else. He needs to learn self-sufficiency.

Terrorists hate and fear our Freedom™, so exercise yours by purchasing as many flags as you can. Osama will cry with fear when he sees how many flags are proudly flapping over our homeland!

Playtime with Condi

by Condoleezza Rice
National Security
Advisor

As your National Security Advisor, I have many duties in safeguarding our homeland. Besides protecting our country from the dangers of Arab self-determination, I am responsible for building up the strength and fitness of our children—our future foot soldiers in the Global War on Terror. To that end, I have devised several fun playground games for our children to enjoy, which provide not only physical conditioning but valuable mental conditioning as well. Learn these new playground games, kids, and start building strength and patriotism today!

Duck! Duck! Duck!

(5 to 12 players, ages 2–7)

Children, or "potential victims," sit in a circle. One child is the "Secretary of Homeland Security." The potential victims remain seated, cowering and immobile, while the Secretary circles around them, slapping everyone on the head and screaming, "DUCK!" When a child's head is slapped, he must duck down and protect his vital areas. This continues until the Secretary grows bored and screams, "ORANGE ALERT!" at which point everyone jumps up and runs around screaming in random directions. This continues until order is resumed, with all the children returning to the circle and the fetal position.

Anthrax Tag

(4 or more players, ages 5 and up)

One child, preferably a foreign-born one, is designated as "anthrax," and a location, such as a flagpole or swing set, is designated as "cipro." So long as the other children are touching cipro, they are safe from being tagged, or "infected," by anthrax. However, the moment the children leave cipro for any reason, including having to go to the bathroom, they are vulnerable to getting tagged by anthrax. If they are tagged, they become anthrax and must try to infect the other children. Once a child has been infected with anthrax, and after he has passed it on to another child by tagging him, he must lie down and play dead. The game ends when all the children are scattered, prone and motionless, across the playground.

Border Patrol

(10 to 24 players, ages 6–12)

Players divide into two equal teams facing each other across the playground, with each team standing side by side and linking arms. The team with the most blond children yells, "Foreigners, foreigners, try to get through these borders! We call [child's name]." The child from the opposing team who has been called on then has to charge toward the other side. If he manages to break through two linked players, or "the borders," he gets to do menial chores for the opposing team, such as washing the blackboards for them after class. If he fails, he is captured and "jailed" inside the jungle gym.

Republican Rumor Mill
(8 to 20 players, ages 7 and up)

The players sit or stand in a line. The first person makes up a rumor about a Democratic political candidate, such as "John Kerry has a huge, gruesome forehead." He whispers this rumor to the person next to him, who whispers it to the next person, and so on until the rumor reaches the end of the line. The last person then announces to the group what he has heard, such as "John Kerry had a threesome with Al Gore." The result is often hilarious, and teaches a valuable lesson about the importance of gossip and character assassination.

Smear the Frenchman
(3 to 10 players, ages 8–14)

One child, the "Frenchman," stands against the wall and everyone else—the "patriots"—takes aim at him with rubber playground balls for twenty minutes. Every time you hit the Frenchman in the arms or legs, you get one point. A blow to the abdomen or torso is worth two points, and a head shot gets you three points. The patriot who gets the most points wins. If someone actually knocks the Frenchman down with a well-placed throw, that child is the automatic winner, and gets the honor of standing above the prostrate Frenchman with his foot on his chest.

★ CORRECTING OUR CALENDAR

Holidays give shape and meaning to our lives. They are expressions of our deepest human emotions and experiences, such as birth, renewal, love, and togetherness. The Bush administration must establish dominance over these important symbols, so we have renamed our holidays in order to guide our citizens through the year along a proper path of patriotic paranoia and total obedience. For example, the twisted Communist celebration of workers' rights, May Day, will now be known as Loyalty Day. Arbor Day is now Enjoying Wood Products Day. Labor Day is now Be Happy You Still Have a Job Day. Valentine's Day is now Hallmark™ Day. Groundhog Day has been denounced as "pagan" by Attorney General John Ashcroft, who has ruled that groundhogs are evil servants of Beelzebub. Animals are not magical heralds of the cycles of nature, but rather our test subjects and food sources, so Groundhog Day will now be known as Meat Lover's Day. Halloween is an even more satanic holiday that has been changed to Angels' Day. Thanksgiving is now Thankstaking, in honor of our Pilgrim ancestors who thanked the Indians for their gifts of food by taking their land and slaughtering them all. On a similar note, Columbus Day will remain unchanged. This is a wonderful holiday that honors a great American. The triumph of the West over ignorant savages and the genocide of an entire race of people are always cause for celebration.

More important than all of these holidays combined is September 11—our new national holiday of grief and rage. Of course, this holiday commemorates the death of almost 3,000 Americans three years ago—OR HAVE YOU FORGOTTEN ALREADY?!?—but many other important events have happened on September 11 throughout our nation's proud history. Ground for the Pentagon was ceremonially broken on September 11, 1941. President Salvador Allende was murdered and the democratically elected government of Chile was overthrown in a U.S.-backed coup on September 11, 1973. President George H.W. Bush first used the term "New World Order" in his State of the Union address on September 11, 1991.

Under mysterious circumstances, a man named Frank Corder stole a small plane on September 11, 1994, in Washington, D.C., and flew it kamikaze-style into the White House, crashing into a wall two stories below the presidential bedroom. Corder's suicide attack was a valuable "test run" for the larger airplane attacks that occurred seven years later. Yes, 9/11 is a day of mourning for most Americans, but it is also a day of triumph for our military-industrial complex and the men who run it.

★ FAITH-BASED SERVICES

Picture, if you will, a public library for the whole family. A place you could go to be surrounded by the finest works of literature, without all the smut. No *Catcher in the Rye*, no *Romeo and Juliet,* no Noam Chomsky—absolutely no books that could possibly offend or challenge you. This vision is quickly becoming real. Given the success of our faith-based initiatives so far, such as using U.S. taxpayer money to support Reverend Franklin Graham's Bible distribution in Iraq, we're preparing to turn over even more government services you take for granted to private, Christ-centered religious organizations.

Everyone knows that a personal relationship with Jesus is much more important than a personal relationship with your congressman. The taxpayer no longer wants to be burdened with federal services he doesn't necessarily use, run by big bureaucracies that nobody wants. Instead, these services can be provided by religious institutions that already have a time-tested infrastructure in place. It's nonsensical for the atheists to protest about the separation of church and state—we're talking about federal services here, not state services. And a few state services too, but whatever.

Beginning in 2005, assuming that God's provenance is with us once again for the coming election, you can look forward to a host of new faith-based services. The U.S. Postal Service will be the Lutheran Postal Service. Municipal swimming pools will be separated by gender so Christian men and women won't be forced into close proximity while in a state of undress. Bus and subway schedules will be preprinted with biblical scripture. Only ordained garbagemen will pick up your garbage. The true moral authorities of the Roman Catholic Church will become the policemen of our communities. The only requirement for enjoying the benefits of these faith-based services is that you wear a crucifix necklace around your neck at all times.

★ PRIVATIZING OUR NATION'S TREASURES

In our brave quest to reduce the federal deficit, the Republican Party is always looking for new ways to save money. In going over the books, it's become apparent that caring for our national parks is too much of a strain on the federal budget. The solution? Private corporations will now take over the management of these formerly public areas. In return for their management assistance, these corporations will be granted the right to rename our natural treasures.

We've already lined up several sponsors to tend to our most prized resources. Visit the Pepsi™ Grand Canyon, especially during Pepsi™ Days, when the Colorado River will run with a refreshing rampage of Diet Pepsi™. Intel™'s Old Faithful geyser goes off with the precision of a Pentium™ chip. And the Applebee's™ Badlands are unprecedented in their home-cooked goodness.

If you're skeptical about the concept of private sponsorship of our nation's parks, look at the shining example of the Disney™ Corporation. Disney World™ is a model of efficient land management and is unparalleled in the science of people moving. Consider the case of tourists visiting Yellowstone National Park. Why would you want people just loafing in one place, taking in the cashless splendor, when they could be moving past the concessions and souvenir stands in an orderly fashion so they can pay for the privilege of looking at nature's beauty?

This isn't pie-in-the-sky talk here— we're ready to roll. Our government needs new streams of revenue, and selling off national monuments to Microsoft™ will get us the money we need to invade more countries. So unless you're willing to give up your tax cut, quit your bellyaching and get ready to embrace a whole new corporate park system. Enjoy a park and a smile!

The dark days of the Vietnam War, when journalists circulated unpatriotic images such as dead Americans and massacred Vietnamese peasants shot like dogs by crazed U.S. soldiers, are thankfully far behind us. Now, our journalists are on the winning side! We are so proud of our news media. It all started with television shows like *Cops*, where TV camera crews accompanied police officers in a nationwide search to arrest, film, and televise every single black man on PCP and in his underwear across the nation. After years of being embedded in the police, journalists took the courageous step of being embedded in our armed forces in foreign conflicts. No longer are TV crews stuck with filming the same old boring arrest sequences—now they have all the exciting footage they need of variously colored people being shredded by the firepower of our brave troops.

These two trends really came together at the protests during the Free Trade Association of America convention, held in Miami in November 2003. Governor Jeb Bush of Florida adopted his older brother's doctrine of preemptive war and transformed it into preemptive policing. The stormtroopers of Freedom™ in which the journalists were embedded were an unstoppable combination of riot police tactics and military technology. Their enemies were also thrillingly new. Instead of the tired visual clichés of young black men or swarthy, bearded terrorists being defeated, TV audiences were treated to novel images of white, middle-aged labor union members and peace-activist grandmothers being cut down with rubber bullets, sprayed with tear gas, and getting slammed in the face with nightsticks. Decked out in their own Darth Vader body armor and helmets, some news reporters even got in on the act, harassing and attacking protestors to provoke wonderful, extremely violent television news.

Just wait until you see what unfolds at the Republican National Convention, to be held in New York City in September 2004. The combination of massive protests and massive police repression in the media capital of the world will provide our bloodthirsty embedded reporters with their most explosive footage yet!

GLANCING AT THE ARTS

If there's one art form that we'd like to master, it's the art of the sell-off. Our country owns so much art! There's no reason to hold onto it all, as one painting looks pretty much like any other. Just imagine the *money* we could get for all of that art. For example, if we sold off the entire collection of the Metropolitan Museum of Art in New York City, we could make so much money that we could fuel our entire military operation in Iraq for two whole weeks! Of course, there's always a certain degree of wasteability you have to account for in military spending, so that figure might adjust downward to two or three days.

★ NO ELECTRICITY? NO PROBLEM!

As the great blackout of 2003 proved, our electric power grid is in desperate need of a major overhaul. Of course, such an undertaking would take a great deal of money that we'd rather give to our campaign contributors to "rebuild" Iraq. Privatization of the power grid is the obvious answer, but there are always a few nervous Nellies who make a big stink about Enron's "massive fraud of consumers" in California as soon as you mention the p-word. Until we can silence these pesky voices with extreme prejudice, we're going to have to make do with the existing grid that could plunge our nation into darkness at any moment.

If you think back, though, the 2003 blackout wasn't really all that bad. Neighbors came together to make sure the night (or nights, depending on how affluent a neighborhood you lived in) didn't end in tragedy. And of course, a whole lot of energy conservation was practiced during that time, which should make the treehuggers happy. Considering how well it all went, we've decided to look at blackouts and brownouts as blessings in disguise. From now on, these events will be called Hearth and Homestead Nights. We all need some emergency family time! We'll celebrate the pioneer spirit and a time before electricity, with our families huddled close around candles. If a Hearth and Homestead Night happens in January, we'll sleep with all of our family members in one bed so we don't freeze to death. We'll get to know our neighbors and eat like kings, so long as we have a refrigerator full of rapidly spoiling food and a barbecue grill to slap it on. The sooner we get used to this the better, since there will be a lot more Hearth and Homestead Nights to come as soon as we get our deregulation way.

A PRAYER FOR EDUCATION

Lord, open up the skulls of youth to learning,

So that no child is left behind in the darkness of Your ignorance.

Let bake sales and raffles fill our shelves with books,

And fund much-needed roof repairs.

Let volunteerism provide the leadership that once-big government,

In its sinful pride, tried but failed to bring.

Let worship of Your holy name fill every classroom,

Despite the killjoy courts and antics of their godless minions, the liberal lawyers,

Who dream of classrooms rife with smut, evolution,

And suchlike blasphemy of modern men.

For You are the teacher and we are the students, Lord,

And Thine is the ruler smacked across the knuckles,

That shall shape and bend and finally subdue our children,

Until they shall dwell in righteousness and productivity,

Self-sufficient, out of our houses, forever and ever.

—AMEN.

"The poor" is a phrase describing a class of people that is in urgent need of revision. Sympathy and pity are built into the phrase, conjuring such thoughts as "Oh, look at that poor child with no legs shivering on the heat grate." The poor do not need our sympathy; they need to be described more accurately. The new phrase for this parasitic underclass will be "the useless eaters." If the useless eaters would like to be called something else, they can either make some money or join the U.S. armed forces to protect our corporate interests, in which case they will be called "our brave troops."

Hunger is the useless eaters' fault. Hunger is for lazy people. We want to eliminate government except as a structure to kill people and to enrich our

corporate friends. Poverty is an issue of self-sufficiency—not the government's problem. Who creates the problem of poverty? The impoverished. They should be locked away and not allowed to vote. If these people could read, then we'd really be in trouble. That's why government literacy programs never work. Trust us.

In order to streamline operations and get the money flowing the right way, the government's War on Poverty will be handed over to Halliburton in a no-bid contract. Halliburton will then cut costs on food-service facilities for the useless eaters with inedible food and substandard building materials. Much like Halliburton facilities for our troops in Iraq, these shelters will be filthy and disease-ridden. If there is an outbreak of food poisoning or a building collapse, these shelters will serve double duty as mass graves. In time, this will eliminate the problem of the useless eaters, because they will know that if they walk into these Halliburton-operated shelters with their mouths open and their hands out, they might not come back out alive.

If one of these shelters does collapse

WE'RE PROUD OF YOU

It's about time we gave you some privacy. You're a big boy now, aren't you? We're leaving you alone to fend for yourself. Choose your own inadequate health care plan. Perform simple medical operations on your family at home by looking up surgery tips on AOL. Remove your own teeth—call a friendly dentist through a help-line in Bangalore and he will walk you through the procedure. Choose your own unaffordable prescription drug plan. Gamble away your retirement benefits in the stock market. Find your own way through the piles of rotting garbage we're not picking up. Nothing builds pride more than a Darwinian system where it's every man for himself!

or poison hundreds of useless eaters with botulism, it will be a cause for celebration. These events will save our children the cost of a bottle of lighter fluid, a book of matches, and the risk of going out late at night in dangerous neighborhoods. Of course, we're not monsters; we wouldn't want to see any sleeping, bearded derelicts doused with flammable liquid and ignited. Do you know how hard a mess like that is to clean up, much less how difficult it is to explain to the police?

★ WHAT WE HAVE LEFT

When you're out on the road and enjoying the sights of our new America, don't be surprised if you can't get too close to national monuments or famous landmarks anymore. You can still enjoy our beautiful country if you have a camera with a 400x digital zoom lens, but the eternal threat of terrorism means you won't be allowed anywhere near our beloved monuments. You just might be a terrorist yourself, hell-bent on blasting George Washington's nose off of Mount Rushmore by hurling a shoe packed with plastic explosives at it. To guard against such a tragedy, a Human Freedom™ zone, measuring 2,000 yards in diameter, will protect all national monuments and landmarks. This zone will be kept automatically free of any humans by our orbiting network of long-range laser and microwave weapons. On the perimeter of the Human Freedom™ zone, there will be the standard system of concentric concrete barricades and a heavy police presence, including aggressive bomb-sniffing K-9 units. Unfortunately, the presence of multiple Human Freedom™ zones in areas dense with national monuments, such as Washington, D.C., may create large, interlocking areas of instant death for all humans. Instead of visiting our nation's capital, why not enjoy exploring the sights of Washington, D.C., at your local IMAX theater?

DANGEROUS QUESTIONS YOU MUST NEVER ASK ABOUT 9/11

There have been many questions asked about the terrible events of 9/11, especially in France, but you must not ask them. Hopefully you've been so distracted by our frantic series of hysterical terror alerts for possible future attacks that you haven't thoroughly analyzed the one that actually happened, but some dangerous freethinkers out there may still harbor doubts about our official story of 9/11. As George W. Bush declared, "Let us never tolerate outrageous conspiracy theories concerning the attacks of September the eleventh; malicious lies that attempt to shift the blame away from the terrorists themselves, away from the guilty."

Our wise leader is right. To even call 9/11, planned in utmost secrecy for years by a small group of attackers, a "conspiracy" is laughable. It's much better for you to think of 9/11 as an unstoppable, natural eruption of terror, much like an earthquake, a mudslide, or a political assassination, that we could have never predicted or had any part in planning. Otherwise, the coincidences and unlikely circumstances of 9/11 might look to you like the standard procedures employed by the CIA in fabricating evidence of a conspiracy.

To avoid confusion and public unrest about the overwhelming events of 9/11, the Better Citizenship Bureau has compiled this list of questions, so that you can identify which inconvenient ideas you should drive out of your head as quickly as possible. Don't worry; after we have exposed you to these dangerous questions, we'll tell you what to think. Now, take a deep breath and read these questions that only a drug-addled, terrorist-loving lunatic would dare to ask.

THE BIG QUESTION

1 Why have George W. Bush and Dick Cheney done everything in their power to stop and derail any investigation into the events of 9/11? When Senator Tom Daschle called for a thorough investigation into 9/11, Bush and Cheney told him to drop the idea completely, insisting that a 9/11 probe would distract us from the War on Terror. Why wouldn't the Bush administration want the failures of 9/11 fully investigated and understood, so that future attacks might be prevented? When Bush finally relented, *fifteen months after the attacks*, and agreed to an "independent" probe, he chose Henry Kissinger to head the 9/11 inquiry commission. Was Kissinger picked to investigate this world of war criminals, mass murderers, international fugitives, and purveyors of terrorism because he is all of these things himself? Why did Kissinger almost immediately resign from this appointment, saying that leading a 9/11 investigation would lead to a controversy over the identities of clients served by his consulting firm? Who are these clients whose relationships with Kissinger could compromise an investigation into 9/11? Why the secrecy?

Why was the initial budget that the U.S. government allotted for investigating the biggest terrorist attack in history only $3 million, when $70 million was fruitlessly spent in the Whitewater investigation into Bill Clinton's obscure real-estate deals in Arkansas? Why have the Bush administration and the Federal Aviation Administration (FAA) refused to provide the 9/11 inquiry commission with requested documents, even under threat of subpoena? Why is the Bush administration stalling for months on producing documents, censoring and "cleansing" the documents they do turn over, and still withholding important information, especially on Bush family ties to Saudi Arabia? Why does Dick Cheney have to accompany George W. Bush when they appear before the 9/11 commission? Why did National Security Advisor Condoleezza Rice refuse to testify under oath or testify publicly before the 9/11 commission until the public outcry became overwhelming? Why would the Bush administration attempt to defeat and stonewall any inquiry into 9/11 if they didn't have something to hide?

THE HIJACKERS

2 If the U.S. government claims to have had absolutely no foreknowledge of the 9/11 terrorist conspiracy, how could they produce a detailed list of the perpetrators, including their multiple aliases, and confidently name Osama bin Laden as the mastermind of the operation, almost immediately after the catastrophic attacks?

3 Who exactly hijacked the planes, since British media have reported seven of the nineteen alleged hijackers to be alive since 9/11, and one other suspect was found to have died in a small plane crash in 2000? When these seven men came forward to state that they were obviously not aboard any suicide jets on 9/11, why was the official list of hijackers never revised to explain who *had* hijacked the planes? FBI Director Robert Mueller has twice been forced to admit on CNN that there is "no legal proof to prove the identities of the suicidal hijackers." Why does the FBI appear to have no interest in finding out who the actual perpetrators of 9/11 were?

4 Why is there no airport security-camera video footage showing any of the nineteen alleged hijackers passing through airport security at any of the three originating airports of the four doomed flights?

5 How did these Arab hijackers get on the planes if they're not on security-camera video in the originating airports? If they did somehow evade standard boarding procedures, why would any of the flight crews take off with four or five young Arabic men on the planes who lack any boarding passes or proof of fare payment?

6 One still-image frame of airport security video has been released from the morning of 9/11, showing hijackers Mohammed Atta and a man we are told is

Abdulaziz al-Omari in the Portland, Maine, airport. (Abdulaziz al-Omari is one of the alleged hijackers who has turned up alive.) They are flying out of Portland to Logan International Airport in Boston, where they will allegedly board Flight 11, the plane that crashed into the North Tower of the WTC. Why did Atta and al-Omari go to Portland and fly from there to Boston to hijack a flight? In fact, we are told that Atta and al-Omari almost missed their Boston flight. For such a meticulously planned series of attacks, why risk the possible delay of transferring flights?

7 On the morning of 9/11, a man in the Boston airport's parking lot got into an argument with five "Middle Eastern–looking men" over a parking space. Later in the day he reported the event to the police, and the car was discovered to have been rented by Mohammed Atta. Why would men who had lived quietly for years in the United States, avoiding suspicion while plotting an elaborate terrorist attack, start a screaming match over a parking space right before the attack, when keeping a low profile mattered most? Was this argument a staged event to draw attention to the car? Inside, police found Arabic-language flight manuals, a Koran, and an airport ramp pass, allowing access to restricted airport areas. Why would an airport ramp pass be left in the car instead of being used to board the airplanes? Did the five men want all of this evidence to be found?

8 On September 9, after checking out of the Panther Hotel in Deerfield Beach, Florida, Marwan al-Shehhi and two other unnamed hijackers left a flying school tote bag in the hotel's Dumpster containing a box cutter, aviation maps, and martial arts books. Why did these hijackers leave this evidence behind in such a concentrated and easily tracked manner?

9 Lead hijacker Mohammed Atta not only left rental cars in Boston and Portland, but also helpfully checked in a suitcase full of evidence at the Portland airport. Inexplicably, this suitcase was not transferred onto his doomed flight out of Boston— it was reported to be the only piece of luggage from Portland that was not transferred onto Flight 11. Atta's suitcase contained a slide-rule flight calculator, a handheld electronic flight computer, a flight instruction manual for Boeing 757 and 767 aircraft, two videotapes giving "virtual tours" of jumbo jets, another Koran, and a handwritten document in Arabic entitled "In the name of God Almighty, Death Certificate." Why would a man on a suicide mission go to the trouble of checking in a suitcase? Why would a man on a secret attack mission bring all of this incriminating gear that, if discovered, would result in his arrest—but then check in the suitcase to be sent through to his final destination, making his flight computers unusable for the attacks? What about the videotapes? When was he planning on watching them? What about all the 800-page flight manuals? Were these terrorists cramming on their drive to the airport, getting in that last twenty minutes of studying on how to fly a 757? Finally, why does Atta's Islamic suicide note/religious exhortation to his comrades seem to be written by someone who has very little familiarity with Islam, in the opinion of religious scholars?

10 If, as is claimed, the hijackers got on board the planes with fake IDs, how does that reconcile with the fact that the real passport of hijacker Satam al-Suqami was found in the rubble of the WTC one day after the attack? This is a piece of "smoking gun" evidence that the government produced to prove the existence of the terrorist hijackers. Why would a hijacker risk blowing his cover by bringing both a fake ID and his real passport on this top secret mission?

11 More incredibly, how does a passport gently float to the ground to perch atop twenty stories of smoldering rubble, miraculously unharmed and perfectly legible, considering the inferno that it had emerged from? Satam al-Suqami and his passport were supposedly on Flight 11, the jet that hit the North Tower. In that collision, the jet hit the tower squarely and was absorbed into the tower completely. How could a passport survive being on a plane that disappears into a skyscraper, which then explodes in an inferno hot enough to supposedly liquefy the steel frame of that skyscraper, which in turn powderizes itself and collapses into a massive cloud of dust? Was this passport planted evidence? Even if the passport somehow survived, is it likely that the authorities would find it so quickly in the chaos of Ground Zero?

12 If a passport can survive such catastrophic events without a scratch, why does the government claim that the flight data recorders of Flights 11, 175, and 77 were either never found or were so damaged that they were unusable? These indestructible "black boxes" are designed to withstand temperatures up to 2,000°F for one hour and impacts up to 3,400 Gs. Perhaps if the black boxes had been made out of paper with a laminated cardboard cover instead of titanium, they would have survived the crashes.

13 How did the terrorist pilots manage to fly their hijacked jets across the country at top speeds toward precise targets with the skill of seasoned military pilots when they had no piloting skills? None of the terrorist pilots had ever flown a jet before, much less a gigantic commercial airliner. They had only trained on Cessna prop-driven two-seater airplanes and flight simulators. Their flight instructors had judged all of them to be terrible pilots who were completely unable to fly even two-seater planes by themselves. For example, Hani Hanjour, the pilot who allegedly flew a 757 with incredible accuracy into the Pentagon, was refused permission to rent a small plane at Freeway Airport in Bowie, Maryland, one month before the attacks. Officials there said that he lacked any piloting skills. On May 4, 2002, the *New York Times* quoted two flight-school instructors on Hani Hanjour's piloting skills: "He didn't care about the fact that he couldn't get through the course," said one instructor. Another declared, "I'm still amazed to this day that he could have flown into the Pentagon. He could not fly at all." Nawaq Alhamzi and Khalid al-Midhar, two other supposed terrorist pilots, have been described as similarly clueless. "Their English was horrible, and their mechanical skills were even worse," said a flight instructor of the two men. "It was like they had hardly even ever driven a car.... They seemed like nice guys, but in the plane, they were dumb and dumber." Mohammed Atta, the alleged pilot of Flight 11, and Marwan al-Shehhi, the alleged pilot of Flight 175, both flunked out of their flight school.

How could Hani Hanjour have executed a tight 270-degree turn while descending 7,000 feet, given his total lack of flying skills? How could he have piloted the jet to within inches of the ground so as to crash into the first floor of the Pentagon at such a shallow angle that the plane penetrated through three rings of the building? This straight-on impact was accomplished apparently without doing any damage to the lawn in front of the Pentagon. He supposedly performed all this while flying a giant, extremely difficult-to-maneuver commercial airliner at 450 mph. How could Hanjour, a man incapable of flying a two-seater plane, pull off these amazing maneuvers?

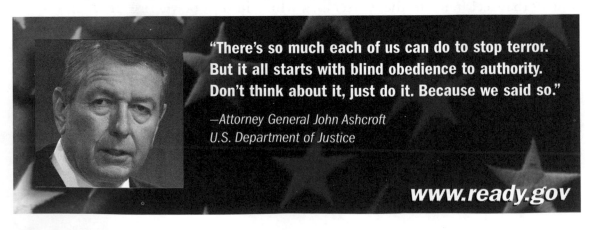

"There's so much each of us can do to stop terror. But it all starts with blind obedience to authority. Don't think about it, just do it. Because we said so."

—*Attorney General John Ashcroft*
U.S. Department of Justice

www.ready.gov

14 If, as the FBI claims, the hijackers boarded the planes with knives, guns, noxious gas, and gas masks, how did all of these weapons pass through airport security—not just once but nineteen times?

15 If the hijackers and their supporters were devout, fundamentalist Muslims, why were some of them spending $200 to $300 each on alcoholic drinks and lap dances at a strip club in Miami the night before 9/11? John Kap, the manager of the Pink Pony and Red-Eyed Jack's Sports Bar, described a loud and obnoxious group of Middle Eastern men in his club on September 10, 2001. "They were talking about what a bad place America is. They said, 'Wait 'til tomorrow. America is going to see bloodshed.'" These men paid their tabs with credit cards, leaving behind credit-card receipts and photocopied driver's licenses. One man also left a business card with his name on it, and, incredibly, *they left another Holy Koran on the bar, as if it were a dirty napkin*. Were these "devout Muslims" getting in a few minutes of Koran study between lap dances? Why are these "secretive terrorists" working so hard and planting so much evidence to remind everyone that they're fanatical Islamic murderers?

THE FLIGHTS

16 NORAD, the North American Aerospace Defense Command, is the vast and powerful defense shield of satellites, radars, and other sensors that normally protects the United States against all forms of airborne attack, including hijacked aircraft. The standard, automatic operating procedure is that whenever any flight even deviates from its pre-appointed flight path, *for any reason*, NORAD is notified within two minutes by air traffic controllers, who request a military intercept by supersonic jet fighters. In the year 2000, military jets were sent into the air, or "scrambled," 129 times to intercept errant airplanes. Why were these standard operating procedures of our national air defense not followed on 9/11?

17 For example, why was there an eighteen-minute delay in reporting to NORAD the takeover of Flight 11, the first airliner to be hijacked, then an unbelievable thirty-nine-minute delay in reporting the takeover of Flight 77, which supposedly crashed into the Pentagon? A full hour and eighteen minutes elapsed between the time when air traffic controllers lost contact with Flight 11 and when the Pentagon was struck. Why did air traffic controllers wait so long to report the Flight 77 takeover when two airliners had already crashed into both World Trade Center towers?

18 Despite normal intercept times of between ten and twenty minutes for airplanes that stray from their flight paths, how could the airliners that were hijacked on 9/11 roam the skies for over an hour without interference from the air defense network protecting the Eastern Corridor of the United States, the most heavily defended air space in the world?

FLIGHT	TAKEOFF	TAKEOVER	REPORTED TO NORAD	CRASH
11	7:59	8:20	8:38	8:46, WTC 1
175	8:14	8:42	8:43	9:03, WTC 2
77	8:20	8:46	9:25	9:38, Pentagon
93	8:42	9:26	not released	10:06, Pennsylvania

19 Why was there not only a failure to promptly report the hijackings to NORAD, but also a failure to put military jets in the air? Once notified, why did NORAD not scramble jets from the nearest air bases, but instead scrambled jets from air bases far away from New York City and Washington, D.C.? For example, radar showed that Flight 77 was heading toward Washington, but NORAD first ordered three F-16 fighters to fly out from Langley Air Force Base in Virginia to intercept Flight 77. Langley is 129 miles from Washington. Aircraft at Andrews Air Force Base, which is 11 miles away from Washington, were scrambled later and did not reach the Pentagon until after it had been struck.

20 Why was there not only a failure to report flight-path deviations and a failure to scramble jets, but also a failure to intercept? Why have some researchers, using NORAD's own numbers, calculated that the supersonic fighter jets, with a top speed of 1,875 mph, failed to reach their targets because they flew at roughly 25 percent of their maximum speed?

21 Why was there not only a failure to report flight-path deviations, a failure to scramble jets, and a failure to intercept, but also a failure to redeploy fighter jets? Why were fighters that were airborne and within interception range of the deviating aircraft not redeployed to pursue the hijacked jets?

22 After presiding over the complete, multilayered failure of U.S. air defenses on 9/11, why was Air Force General Richard B. Myers not tried by court martial, but rather confirmed by George W. Bush on October 1, 2001, as Chairman of the Joint Chiefs of Staff, the highest-ranking military post in the country?

23 Why did the hijacked flights all fly long, circuitous routes, which took them far from their targets before looping back, exposing them to certain interception given standard operating procedures? Why weren't aircraft hijacked from airports that were closer to their intended targets? For example, the airliners that hit New York City flew out from Boston. Wouldn't it make more sense, if you were a terrorist who wanted to successfully hit the World Trade Center without being intercepted, to hijack a plane flying out from one of the three airports in the New York City area? Is this evidence that the "hijackers," whoever they were, knew that U.S. air defenses would not oppose them and therefore took long, lazy flight paths in order to "hit their marks" on a preset schedule?

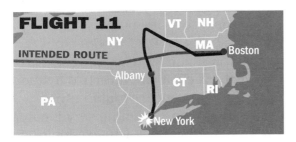

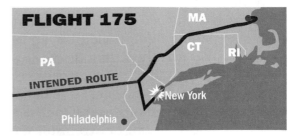

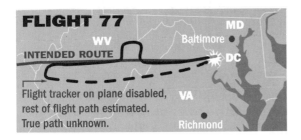

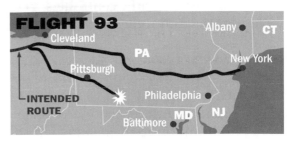

24 How could all eight pilots, four of whom were formerly in the military, some with combat experience in Vietnam, and all of whom were in superb physical shape, have been subdued by the hijackers without a fight or so much as a sound?

25 Why have the contents of the indestructible black boxes—the flight data recorders and cockpit voice recorders of the flights—not been released to the public, when it has been standard practice to release this data in the past? Why have none of the electronic monitoring records of the hijacked flights by air traffic control systems been released? Why have no interviews with air traffic controllers involved in 9/11 been released? The standard official response to such questions is that this information cannot be divulged "for national security reasons." The terrorists, whoever they were, knew exactly how to penetrate our national security system without any problems. Withholding this information from "the terrorists" does us no good, because they've already proved they know how to defeat all of our security strategies. Therefore, the only reason to withhold this information is to conceal it from the American public. Why would that be?

26 Why did none of the four pilot crews radio air traffic controllers that hijackings were in progress? Why did none of the pilot crews punch in the four-digit hijacking code—the buttons for which are located in four places throughout the cockpit, including right on the control stick—an operation that would have taken only a second? For example, in the case of Flight 11, a transcript of a phone call that was made by flight attendant Madeline Sweeney states that the hijackers had stabbed two flight attendants and slit the throat of a business-class passenger, killing him. In addition, an FAA memo produced on 9/11 reported one passenger had even been shot dead with a pistol. According to Sweeney's highly detailed account, all of this violence occurred *before* the cockpit was breached by the hijackers. Could this violence have happened in complete silence? Wouldn't the stabbed flight attendants, as well as the passengers, have been screaming very loudly? There's the noise of one or two pistol shots as well. Why didn't—or why couldn't—the pilots alert air traffic controllers, given the fact that they must have heard the violent noises and were still free to communicate?

THE WORLD TRADE CENTER

27 Given the fact that NORAD was notified that Flight 175 was hijacked at 8:42 a.m., and that Flight 11 crashed into the North Tower at 8:46 a.m., why were public announcements made in the South Tower after these times telling World Trade Center employees that the situation was safe and that they should return to their desks?

28 If the World Trade Center towers were built to withstand a direct hit from a passenger jet, which both did successfully, shouldn't that design insure survival from the fires that would erupt? The official theory for the collapse of the towers is that the heat of the burning jet fuel (refined kerosene) weakened steel components essential to the towers' support. James Quintiere, a professor of fire protection engineering at the University of Maryland, College Park, states that the jet fuel fires did not bring down the Twin Towers, and that the jet fuel in fact burned up within minutes. Steel does not lose its elasticity until it reaches 1,022°F, and melts at 2,795°F. To melt steel, a pressurized blast furnace or white-hot oxygen torch is normally needed. Did the jet fuel create fires in the Twin Towers hot enough to compromise their steel structure?

29 Why has fire never caused the collapse of a steel-framed building except on 9/11, even though there have been high-rise building fires that lasted longer and appeared to be much more severe than those in the Twin Towers? In these precedents, the fires consumed multiple floors, produced extensive window breakage, exhibited large areas of emergent flames, and went on for several hours—yet the buildings did not collapse. In the case of the February 23, 1991, fire in One Meridian Plaza, a thirty-eight-floor skyscraper in Philadelphia, the fire raged for *eighteen hours* and gutted eight floors, causing window breakage and cracking of granite. The fires in the Twin Towers did none of these things. Instead, the WTC fires died down fairly quickly and began producing large amounts of black smoke, which is a sign of a low-burning fire that is starved of oxygen. Why then did One Meridian Plaza not collapse while the Twin Towers powderized themselves?

30 The North Tower was struck first, at 8:46 a.m. The airplane hit it squarely at a head-on angle, depositing its entire fuel load inside the building. The South Tower was struck next, at 9:03 a.m., but this airplane came in at an angle, striking the corner of the tower. Much of the plane's fuel load evaporated in a few seconds in a massive fireball that exploded outside of the building—the dramatic image that defines the WTC attack. However, the South Tower collapsed first, at 9:59 a.m. The North Tower did not collapse until 10:28 a.m. How did the South Tower, which was struck seventeen minutes after the North Tower, did not sustain damage to its core structural column, internally absorbed much less jet fuel, and whose fires were much less severe, collapse twenty-nine minutes before the North Tower did?

31 An audiotape of radio transmissions released by the FDNY proves that at least two firefighters, Battalion Chief Orio Palmer and Fire Marshal Ronald Bucca, made it to the impact zone of the South Tower before it collapsed. Seven minutes before the collapse, Orio Palmer said: "Ladder Fifteen, we've got two isolated pockets of fire. We should be able to knock it down with two lines." Why didn't these firefighters find a blast furnace capable of melting steel?

32 How did the forty-seven-story WTC Seven building collapse later in the day on 9/11? A plane did not strike it, and it did not suffer significant fire damage—there were only small, isolated fires that did not break a single window. Nor was WTC Seven significantly damaged by the collapse of the North Tower—WTC Six and Vesey Street separated the two structures. No other surrounding buildings across the street from the WTC collapsed, including the buildings on both sides of WTC Seven. Even WTC Six, right next to the North Tower, was still partly standing after suffering fires and damage much greater than WTC Seven's. How, then, did WTC Seven powderize itself and collapse evenly and precisely, straight down into its footprint, just like the Twin Towers? For WTC Seven to collapse in this fashion, some researchers believe that all of the load-bearing supports on the ground floor would have had to fail at exactly the same time. If the collapse of WTC Seven was the result of a fire, they reason that this fire would have to be equally distributed throughout the entire first floor of the building, providing equal heat for an equal amount of time to the entire floor, so that all the load-bearing supports would fail at the exact same moment. However, WTC Seven suffered only small, isolated fires, none of which consumed an entire floor. If fire did not cause the collapse of WTC Seven, what did? After the collapse, why were the remains of WTC Seven immediately carted away and destroyed without any real effort made to determine this unprecedented building collapse? In "America Rebuilds," a September 10, 2002 PBS documentary, the owner of the World Trade Center Complex, Larry Silverstein, makes this statement regarding WTC Seven: "I remember getting a call from the fire department commander, telling me that they were not sure they were gonna be able to contain the fire, and I said, 'We've had such terrible loss of life, maybe the smartest thing to do is pull it.' And they made that decision to pull and we watched the building collapse." What did they mean by "pull," and why did WTC Seven collapse after this decision was made?

33 Why was the full investigative team set up by the Federal Emergency Management Agency (FEMA) not allowed to enter Ground Zero to collect potentially critical evidence in the weeks after the attack? Why did this federal investigative team not even receive a copy of the World Trade Center blueprints until early January, 2002? Why was there so much confusion over which federal agency was in charge of the World Trade Center collapse inquiry? By March, 2002, FEMA had only invested $600,000 to determine how the Twin Towers collapsed. Why was the effort to understand the collapses of the Twin Towers and WTC Seven so mismanaged and muddled?

34 How did the three WTC buildings collapse in such an even, symmetrical fashion, straight down into their footprints? The fires were not distributed evenly throughout an entire level of the buildings, especially in the cases of WTC Seven and the South Tower, which was struck at its corner. If the fires did cause a localized deformation of the steel frames, why didn't the Twin Towers sag or collapse first on their weakened side, leading to an asymmetrical collapse like a tree that had been toppled?

35 The unimpeded collapses of the Twin Towers were extremely rapid. Both towers were transformed into pillars of dust in identical, explosive detonations that lasted approximately fifteen seconds from start to finish.

Researchers state that this is basically the speed of free fall—that is, a rock dropped from the top of the World Trade Center would take about fifteen seconds to hit the ground, if the only force slowing its descent were air. The official story is that the tops of the towers smashed down through the lower levels like a pile driver, obliterating them. How can eighty stories of reinforced concrete slab floors, the steel grids of the outer walls, the steel lattice of the massive core structure, and all other contents of the building put up no more resistance than thin air?

The atomized concrete of the World Trade Center.

36 How did all of the concrete of the Twin Towers transform into a fine dust? No large chunks of concrete were found at Ground Zero, only twisted steel. All of that concrete turned into towering waves of dust that traveled outward at estimated speeds of 35 mph. Powderized concrete begins to appear in the air in enormous quantities during the very earliest stages of the collapses. Why is all of this concrete immediately transforming into a fine dust and being ejected laterally from the building at high speed? Many researchers have pointed out the horizontal explosions from the Twin Towers that look much like "demolition squibs" seen in controlled demolitions of buildings (see photo at right). Steel parts of the towers were also thrown 500 feet laterally. Can the downward force of a gravity-driven collapse account for this energetic lateral ejection of heavy debris?

The collapse of the South Tower. Examine the explosive, lateral ejection of debris, as well as the horizontal row of explosions well beneath the collapse zone, noted by the arrow. Video footage of the collapses shows this horizontal explosion and others like it going off in a progressive sequence, from top to bottom, as the towers vaporize above them.

37 Why were the claims of numerous eyewitnesses, including New York City firefighters, that there were a series of detonations inside of the Twin Towers never investigated?

38 Is there a pattern of rapid destruction of evidence between the attacks on the World Trade Center and the Murrah Federal Building in Oklahoma City? A firm called Controlled Demolition, Inc., or CDI, was contracted to deliver a plan to remove the WTC debris a few days after the attacks. At the request of General Services Administration, which owns and operates federal buildings, CDI also demolished the ruins of the bombed Murrah Federal Building in Oklahoma City in 1995. The government thereby prevented independent investigators from pursuing evidence on leads suggesting that there were bombs set off inside the building. The remains of the Murrah Building were carted away and buried in a hole in the desert. The buried evidence was then surrounded by a security fence and patrolled by armed guards from Wackenhut, a private security corporation.

39 In order to figure out how the Twin Towers held up during the jet impacts and fires, but then somehow disintegrated into rubble, why wasn't a careful analysis of the steel that made up the Twin Towers undertaken? Instead, the authorities carted away the key evidence of this vast crime and unprecedented engineering failure and recycled it. They trucked it away as quickly as they could and sold it as scrap to foreign countries. Why was nearly all of this crucial evidence destroyed?

40 Given that the people in charge considered the WTC steel garbage that was useless to any investigation, why did they go to great lengths to make sure the steel didn't end up anywhere besides a smelting furnace? They installed GPS tracking devices on each of the trucks that were carrying loads away from Ground Zero, at a cost of $1,000 each. This measure was taken so that every truckload could be tracked, making sure that all of the contents were destroyed.

THE PENTAGON

41 Why was a preparedness drill simulating an airliner crashing into the Pentagon scheduled for September 11, 2001?

42 The official story is that Flight 77 crashed into the Pentagon. However, the initial hole created in the Pentagon, before the surrounding segment of wall collapsed twenty minutes later, appeared to be approximately 15 feet in diameter. Flight 77 was a 757 airliner, which has a wingspan of 125 feet. How does an airplane with a wingspan of 125 feet disappear into a 15-foot-wide hole?

A wide view of the impact hole at the Pentagon. Note the undisturbed cable spools sitting squarely in the flight path of the alleged jet.

A closer look at the hole. The white substance being sprayed by firefighters across the bottom of the photo is a fire-retardant foam. Note the foam coating the unbroken windows immediately above the impact hole. Why weren't these windows broken by a 100-ton aircraft traveling at 450 mph?

43 Since Flight 77, or something else, struck the Pentagon at an oblique angle, researchers state that the impact profile of a 757 against the building would have actually been 177 feet. Again, the initial hole created in the Pentagon, before the surrounding segment of wall collapsed, was apparently 15 feet wide. How does a plane that should leave a 177-foot-wide hole instead make a 15-foot-wide hole? Even after the collapse of the surrounding walls, the width of the broken-away walls at ground level was apparently 90 feet, which still falls short of the size of the hole that should have been created. Structural columns of the Pentagon remained standing near the center of the impact hole. This is where the fuselage, the densest, longest section of the aircraft, would have had to have penetrated. The wings of the WTC planes sliced through steel—why didn't they damage the concrete of the Pentagon? Why does the damage to the Pentagon not appear to match the impact profile of a 757 airliner?

The initial fire at the Pentagon. Again, note the undisturbed cable spools, as well as the unmarked lawn.

A close-up view of the indestructible cable spools.

44 Why was there initially one concentrated fire that burned at the Pentagon, centered in the impact hole, where the fuselage of the plane supposedly entered? (See photo on this page.) The two fuel tanks of a 757 are located on its wings—why weren't there two separate fire zones on either side of the central damage?

45 Proponents of the official story explain the suspiciously small damage to the Pentagon by claiming that Flight 77 first hit the ground in front of the building, which absorbed much of the force of the crashing plane. Why, then, as many have pointed out, was the grass lawn in front of the impact hole apparently undisturbed after the attack? How can a 100-ton aircraft plow into a lawn and not leave a single mark? Also, lightweight cable spools were on the lawn before the attack, directly in the flight path of the plane. (The Pentagon was undergoing renovations at that time. See photos on previous page.) Why were these objects completely unaffected as well?

46 Why was no significant debris of a 757 apparently found at the Pentagon, besides one small, conspicuous piece with a clean paint job, found a good distance from the impact point, that showed no signs of burning or abrasion? What happened to the other 100 tons of the airplane? Is it easier to vaporize 100 tons of airplane than it is to peel and blacken paint?

47 Why is there no video footage or photographs showing Flight 77 approaching or hitting the Pentagon? Don't you think that the nerve center of the American military would have several hundred security cameras rolling at all times? What about the highway traffic

The beautiful and pristine Pentagon lawn.

A not-so-nice-looking lawn from a real plane crash.

The remains of Flight 77 at the Pentagon.

cameras that were set up in dozens of locations underneath the flight path of the alleged jet, or the security cameras of businesses across the highway from the Pentagon? If footage of a 757 hitting the Pentagon actually existed, don't you think the media would have broadcast it repeatedly, like they did the footage of the WTC strikes?

48 The only evidence of the Pentagon crash that has been released to the public is a set of five video still-image frames from a Pentagon security camera. (Between this and the one frame of Mohammed Atta in the Portland airport, why are we shown only still frames of video instead of actual footage?) This set of video frames is incomplete—the frames that would clearly show the object that hit the Pentagon have not been released. The first frame in this set shows a fragment of some sort of airborne object approaching the Pentagon that is largely obscured by a parking-lot structure. This airborne object is emitting a thick, white vapor trail from the rear. The other four frames show an explosion.

Do these video frames prove that a 757 airplane hit the Pentagon or that a missile hit the Pentagon? The mostly obscured object seems much too small to be a 757. Also, 757s have turbofan engines. Turbofan engines do not emit vapor trails at low altitudes. Have you ever seen a commercial airliner take off at the airport leaving a thick vortex of white vapor behind? However, rocket engines do create dense vapor trails at all altitudes because they produce water vapor in a concentration that causes it to condense immediately. Missiles, not commercial airplanes, have rocket engines. As researchers have pointed out, the remaining frames show an explosion revealing all the characteristics of a detonation of an explosive, not a combustion of jet fuel. The features of the explosion seen in these frames are that it is white-hot, so bright it illuminates surrounding objects, rapidly grows in a nearly spherical shape, and appears to be about 130

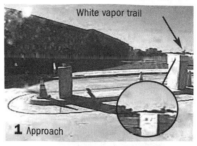
White vapor trail

1 Approach

White vapor trail

2 White-hot explosion

3 Spherical explosion

4

5

feet high while still white-hot, showing no yellow or orange coloration. However, jet fuel fireballs are not white, go from yellow to orange to black in color, expand slowly compared to explosives, and have a shape determined by momentum, not a spherical shape. Look at these Pentagon video frames in color on the Internet and compare them to images of the jet fuel fireball from the WTC South Tower impact. Do the fireballs at the World Trade Center and the explosion at the Pentagon look the same?

49 Why was the internal damage inflicted on the Pentagon in the shape of a long, narrow tunnel that punched its way through three of the building's concentric rings? The official explanation is that an engine from Flight 77, which weighs six tons, detached from the plane and hurtled forward through six walls of reinforced concrete. How can an engine, which is 6 percent of the weight of the airplane and travelling at a lesser speed than the plane was when it hit, punch through six walls of reinforced concrete, when the other ninety-four tons of the plane hit the wall and vaporized, hardly penetrating the Pentagon? Where is this indestructible engine now, and why has it never been produced as evidence? Is there a more plausible explanation for this unusual damage?

An aerial view of the damage done to the three rings of the Pentagon. The path of the object that penetrated the Pentagon is shown by the white arrow, which points to the exit hole of the damage.

Exit hole

A close-up view of the exit hole.

Another view of the exit hole, which shows the size of the hole more clearly.

READ THEN BURN

50 Why were security-camera video recordings from businesses near the Pentagon seized by the FBI shortly after the attack and never seen since? The FBI seized videotapes that had captured the Pentagon strike from a gas station directly under the flight path of the missile and also from a nearby hotel. (Security-camera videotapes in the vicinity of the Murrah Federal Building in Oklahoma City were also seized after that attack and have never resurfaced.)

Souvenir hunters?

51 After the Pentagon strike, a column of fifty FBI officers walked across the south lawn of the Pentagon, picking up debris and stuffing it into bags. Why did these FBI officers remove evidence from the scene of the crime before a real investigation by safety engineers could begin?

52 One explanation for the reason why there are no remains of a 100-ton aircraft to be found at the Pentagon is that Flight 77 was completely vaporized in a huge explosion. If so, researchers say there must have been an intensely hot fireball at the Pentagon reaching temperatures over 2,467°C, the boiling point of aluminum—the primary structural component of the airplane. However, the government also tells us that they have successfully identified 98.4 percent of the DNA remains of all the passengers of Flight 77. Human remains are completely destroyed at temperatures over 150°C. How can there be any human remains from Flight 77, which disappear at 150°C, if a fireball of 2,467°C supposedly vaporized 100 tons of aluminum?

53 If Flight 77 did not crash into the Pentagon, where did it go? What happened to the passengers aboard Flight 77?

FLIGHT 93

54 Why did air traffic controllers report that an F-16 fighter jet was trailing Flight 93 and was in visual range at the time of the crash—and why does the government now deny that there was any F-16 in the area?

55 What was the mysterious, unmarked white jet that was trailing Flight 93 before it crashed, and witnessed by people on the ground? At least six eyewitnesses have come forward to say that they saw a small, white, military-type jet following Flight 93 in the air above the Shanksville, Pennsylvania, area immediately before Flight 93 crashed.

56 If the FBI insists there was no F-16 or any other type of military jet in the Shanksville area on the morning of 9/11, why then was a sonic boom—caused by a supersonic jet—picked up by an earthquake monitoring station in southern Pennsylvania sixty miles away from Shanksville at 9:22 a.m. on 9/11?

57 If the U.S. government insists that Flight 93 exploded on impact with the ground, how is it possible that plane debris was scattered over so wide an area? Debris was found shortly after the crash up to eight miles away, on the other side of a mountain ridge. How did human remains, metal scraps, books, clothing, seat cushions, and other debris—so much material that residents and FBI agents were filling up garbage bags with it—float up out of a thirty-five-foot-deep muddy hole and across wet, muddy fields up to eight miles away on a still, calm day? Why did workers at the Indian Lake Marina, nearly six miles from the crash site, report a cloud of confetti-like debris floating down onto Indian Lake within minutes of the crash? Other eyewitnesses reported burning debris falling from the sky. Has this wide, immediate dispersal of debris ever happened before in any other airplane crashes that did not suffer midair traumas—such as bombs exploding onboard the plane or the plane being shot down by a missile?

58 Authorities stated that the destruction of Flight 93 was so total that most of the airplane was found in pieces "no bigger than a briefcase." However, one of the plane's six-ton engines was found intact over a half mile from the crash site. A 1,000-pound turbofan was found over a mile away from the crash site as well. If Flight 93 was completely obliterated by its impact with the ground, how can such large, heavy pieces be found intact so far away from the crash site if they didn't fall off the airplane in midair, *before* the crash? Or did the breeze blow the six-ton engine and 1,000-pound turbofan away from the crash site as well?

59 How can debris be thrown for miles out of a plane's impact crater in Pennsylvania, but no debris was found scattered across Washington, D.C., after Flight 77 supposedly hit the Pentagon? Why weren't six-ton engines or 1,000-pound turbofans thrown all over Washington, D.C.? For that matter, why did Flight 93 turn into a confetti cloud of debris that littered the ground for eight miles, while Flight 77 yielded up one scrap?

60 Passenger Edward Felt made the last cell-phone call from Flight 93, to a 911 operator named Glenn Cramer. At 9:58 a.m., Felt frantically said that he had locked himself inside the plane's bathroom, and told Cramer that there had been an explosion and that he saw white smoke coming from the plane. Ground witnesses also report hearing several explosions. Why has the tape of this 911 call been seized by the FBI, and 911 operator Glenn Cramer instructed by the FBI to not talk about this call with anyone?

61 The government has never asserted as fact the story that "the heroes of Flight 93" stormed the cockpit and fought for control of the plane with the terrorists. They also will not release to the public the cockpit voice recorders that might prove whether or not this actually happened. However, there were military jets in the air, noted by both eyewitnesses and air traffic controllers, that the government denies; eyewitnesses heard several explosions in the air; the 911 call described explosions and smoke on the plane; and most important, Flight 93 broke up in the air, scattering large amounts of debris for miles. Is it possible that Flight 93 was deliberately shot down?

62 At the crash site of Flight 93, how did investigators find a copy of Mohammed Atta's suicide note, the same document that was left in the suitcase in Portland? The crash destruction was so complete that the largest piece of human remains found was an eight-inch fragment of spine. How did the letter survive the devastating crash and incineration in perfect condition?

GEORGE W. BUSH

63 Why can't George W. Bush recall exactly where he was when he first heard the news that an airliner had struck the North Tower of the World Trade Center? Why has he changed his story several times? Can't any normal person tell you exactly where they were when they first heard that America was under attack on 9/11?

64 Why has Bush said on several occasions that he saw the first crash of Flight 11 on television at 9:01 a.m. on 9/11, when videotape of the Flight 11 crash did not surface and was not broadcast until the next day? Is Bush far more confused than his handlers should allow him to admit?

65 Why did George W. Bush sit quietly and listen to a little girl read a story about a goat at Booker Elementary School in Saratoga, Florida, after he was told that a plane had crashed into the World Trade Center? Bush's photo op appearance at the school was publicly known and had appeared in newspapers and TV media several days before 9/11. If terrorists were hijacking airplanes and crashing them into buildings, wouldn't it be reasonable to assume that the terrorists would try to kill the Presidential Appointee of the United States, especially when the Saratoga airport is only minutes away by plane from the elementary school? Why didn't the Secret Service agents guarding Bush hustle him immediately to a secure, undisclosed location? Three aircraft had already been reported to NORAD as hijacked while Bush was sitting in the classroom. Bush did not leave the school until 9:34 a.m. Why did Bush and his team act as if they were in no personal danger?

66 When Bush and his team took off from the Saratoga Airport in Air Force One at 9:56 a.m., why did they fly off without any military fighter jet escorts? There were still 3,520 commercial planes in the air over the United States that could have been hijacked. Why would being up in the air, unprotected, in the large target that is Air Force One, be a better choice than going to an undisclosed location on the ground? The lack of fighter escorts is especially strange given that Dick Cheney circulated a false story on the morning of 9/11 that Air Force One was a target of the terrorists.

OSAMA BIN LADEN AND AFGHANISTAN

67 Why did Osama bin Laden say he had nothing to do with the 9/11 attacks? There is no doubt that Osama bin Laden is a murderous terrorist. He and his followers claimed responsibility for the bombings of the American embassies in Africa in 1998 and the bombing of the USS *Cole* in 2000. But he did not claim responsibility for 9/11. Instead, bin Laden reportedly issued this statement on September 14, 2001:

> *"After the recent attacks on the United States of America, its leaders have indicted us and accused us for standing behind these events. We are accustomed to America's accusations as we are blamed on every occasion, even though America has many enemies. On this occasion, I confirm that I did not do this action that appears to have been done for personal motives of America."*

If bin Laden had orchestrated the 9/11 attacks, why wouldn't he proudly claim responsibility for such a terribly successful strike against his sworn enemy? By capturing the attention of the world, why wouldn't he issue a list of his demands, as he and other terrorists have done in the past? Why has no terrorist group come forward to claim responsibility for 9/11? Normally, Middle Eastern terrorist groups scramble over each other to claim responsibility for attacks. However, the true perpetrators of 9/11 apparently wish to remain hidden. Everything we've heard about these terrorists has come from our own government. The Bush administration has told us who the terrorists are, what they believe in, and where they come from. As for their causes, we're told simply that the terrorists "have targeted our way of life" because they "hate our freedom." Why haven't the terrorists spoken for themselves?

68 The United States produced a "smoking gun" videotape of Osama bin Laden supposedly taking credit for the 9/11 attacks. Why does the man on the videotape identified by the U.S. government as Osama bin Laden look so little like Osama bin Laden? Here are a few ways that these two faces appear to not match up:

X **OSAMA HAS A MUCH LONGER AND NARROWER NOSE.**

X **OSAMA HAS A LESS ROUNDED BROW RIDGE.**

X **OSAMA LOOKS FIFTY POUNDS LIGHTER.**

X **OSAMA HAS LOWER AND LESS FULL CHEEKS.**

X **OSAMA'S FOREHEAD SLOPES BACK MORE.**

X **OSAMA'S FACE IS WIDER AT THE LEVEL OF HIS EYES.**

X **OSAMA'S COMPLEXION IS PALER.**

Some guy we're told is bin Laden.

A real photo of bin Laden.

69 Why was the "mountain of evidence" that the United States and Britain trumpeted would conclusively tie Osama bin Laden to the 9/11 attacks never produced?

70 Is it a little too convenient to blame a terrorist attack on a country that you've already announced you're going to invade, and already made preparations to invade? Niaz Naik, a former Pakistani foreign secretary, was told by senior American officials in mid-July 2001 that military action against Afghanistan would begin by mid-October 2001, before the winter snows began to fall. Right on schedule, the American invasion of Afghanistan began on October 11. The governments of Tajikistan, Uzbekistan, Russia, and India were also notified of the U.S. military plans. It was especially obvious to Tajikistan and Uzbekistan, as U.S. forces were massing in those countries on their borders with Afghanistan as early as June 2001. Afghanistan is made up of some of the most inhospitable, rugged terrain on Earth, and it's on the opposite side of the planet from the United States. Even the United States can't transport and assemble the soldiers, vehicles, and matériel needed to invade and occupy such forbidding and distant terrain in one month. Was the war in Afghanistan not a direct response to 9/11, but rather a planned event? Did the terrorist attacks of 9/11 just make the invasion look good to the American public?

71 Why did six chartered flights rush scores of Saudi Arabian citizens out of the United States shortly after 9/11, including many members of Osama bin Laden's family? These Saudis were flown out of the country and beyond the reach of U.S. law enforcement agencies. Members of bin Laden's family and other prominent Saudis—a total of 142 people—were driven or flown, under FBI supervision, to a secret assembly point in Texas and then to Washington, from where they left the country on private chartered flights.

OTHER QUESTIONS

72 Why did some people receive advance warnings about flying on 9/11, including many people associated with governmental and national security operations? On September 10, a group of top Pentagon officials suddenly canceled air travel plans for the next morning because of security concerns. San Francisco Mayor Willie Brown admitted to having received a warning from his airport security late Monday evening, just hours before the attack. Writer Salman Rushdie, who is under the continuous protection of British intelligence services, was prevented from flying on September 11, 2001. John Ashcroft was told by the FBI to stop flying commercial

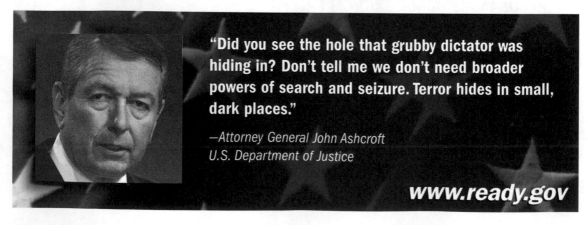

"Did you see the hole that grubby dictator was hiding in? Don't tell me we don't need broader powers of search and seizure. Terror hides in small, dark places."

—Attorney General John Ashcroft
U.S. Department of Justice

www.ready.gov

airplanes in July 2001 because of a "threat assessment." (This is the same FBI that claims they didn't "connect the dots" before 9/11.) There are more cases such as these.

73 Why were several million dollars in United and American airline stocks short-sold by unidentified traders a few days before 9/11? All four planes involved in 9/11 were operated by United or American. "Put options" on American Airlines totaled 4,516 the day before the attacks, compared with an August daily average of 269. Were these unidentified traders using criminal foreknowledge of the attack to reap huge profits when the stock of these two airlines fell disastrously? Why has there been no effort to name these unidentified traders?

74 Is Donald Rumsfeld a gifted psychic? At 8:44 a.m. on the morning of 9/11, Rumsfeld happened to be delivering a speech about terrorism in the Pentagon. "Let me tell ya," he said, "I've been around the block a few times. There will be another event." He then repeated himself for emphasis: "There will be another event." Two minutes later, the first plane hit the World Trade Center. At 9:38 a.m., Rumsfeld was still in the Pentagon meeting with Representative Christopher Cox (R-CA), and was apparently completely oblivious to the approaching Flight 77. As he watched TV coverage of the World Trade Center, he said, "Believe me, this isn't over yet. There's going to be another attack, and it could be us." Moments later, the Pentagon was struck.

75 Why were members of Dick Cheney's staff and other unnamed White House personnel given ciproflaxin, the antidote to anthrax, by the White House Medical Office on the evening of 9/11—three and a half weeks before the first anthrax attacks occurred? Is it reasonable to assume that if Dick Cheney's staff were put on cipro, that Dick Cheney himself and George W. Bush were among the unnamed White House personnel that were also put on cipro? Why wasn't Congress put on cipro if the White House already knew there was cause to take it, and why weren't the postal workers?

76 Why was the investigation into the anthrax attacks dropped when it was revealed that the military-grade anthrax spores most likely came from Fort Detrick, a U.S. Army biological weapons laboratory? Why has our government been unable to find out who was sending anthrax through the mail?

77 Is the concept of the U.S. government permitting or orchestrating a terrorist attack on its own people for ulterior motives really so impossible, given the historic precedent of Project Northwoods? Project Northwoods was a secret plan drawn up by the Joint Chiefs of Staff, the leaders of America's military, in 1962 and presented to President John F. Kennedy, who rejected it. In these documents, recently declassified by the Freedom of Information Act, the Joint Chiefs of Staff proposed launching a secret and violent war of terrorism against their own country, then blaming the terrorist attacks on Fidel Castro and Cuba. Cuba would be framed as the evil aggressor to an outraged American people. With the public's backing, independent, communist Cuba could then be invaded by U.S. troops and turned back into an American-run fiefdom. Project Northwoods called for innocent American civilians, soldiers, and Cuban refugees to be killed; for American ships to be blown up; for a "terror campaign" of bombs to be detonated in major American cities, including Washington, D.C.; for innocents to be framed for these bombings; and for military and commercial planes to be destroyed in elaborate and deceitful ways. Consider this excerpt from Project Northwoods that advocates recreating a USS *Maine* incident, referring to the mysterious explosion aboard the American battleship *Maine* in Havana Harbor in 1898, which killed 266 American sailors and provided an excuse for the United States to go to war with Spain and take over its empire:

> A "Remember the Maine" incident could be arranged in several forms:
> a. We could blow up a U.S. ship in Guantánamo Bay and blame Cuba.
> b. We could blow up a drone (unmanned vessel) anywhere in the Cuban waters....
> The U.S. could follow up with an air/sea rescue operation covered by U.S.
> fighters to "evacuate" remaining members of the non-existent crew. Casualty
> lists in U.S. newspapers would cause a helpful wave of national indignation.

Project Northwoods also proposed a number of elaborate "false-flag" attacks on American aircraft, with U.S. fighter jets disguised as Cuban MIG fighters:

> Use of MIG type aircraft by U.S. pilots could provide additional provocation.
> Harassment of civil air, attacks on surface shipping and destruction of U.S. military
> drone aircraft by MIG-type planes would be useful as complementary actions. An F-86
> properly painted would convince air passengers that they saw a Cuban MIG....

One Northwoods plan called for replacing an American aircraft with an identical drone aircraft, flown by remote control. The real plane would land at a U.S. Air Force base, where the passengers, boarded under prepared aliases, would be evacuated. The drone, packed with explosives, would then fly the original route, and when it passed over Cuba, emit a distress signal before being destroyed by a radio signal.

Do you still find it impossible that the U.S. military elite could countenance an attack on American soldiers and civilians? They started making these plans forty years ago. If you consider the attack on the USS *Maine*, which Project Northwoods pays homage to, these tactics have been in use for over one hundred years, since the dawn of the age of American empire.

78 Have the men currently in power been looking forward to something like 9/11 for years? The Project for the New American Century, or PNAC, is a conservative think tank that was formed in 1997. Founding members include Dick Cheney, now vice president; Donald Rumsfeld, now secretary of defense; Paul Wolfowitz, now deputy secretary of defense; Richard Perle, former chairman of the Defense Policy Board; Lewis Libby, Cheney's chief of staff; and Zalmay Khalilzad, Bush's ambassador to Afghanistan. In their position papers, PNAC advocated the unlimited use of American military power around the globe in order to dominate the world's resources and prevent the rise of any potential rivals. However, the PNAC acknowledged that the American people would have to be pushed along in order to support this eternal war. They stated that *"the process of transformation, even if it brings revolutionary change, is likely to be a long one, absent some catastrophic and catalyzing event—like a new Pearl Harbor."* Before going to bed on the evening of 9/11, Bush dictated for his diary, *"The Pearl Harbor of the 21st century took place today."*

79 Why has all the real evidence that could conclusively answer questions about 9/11—such as the flight data and cockpit voice recorders, video or photographic evidence of the Pentagon strike, and the steel of the World Trade Center—either been suppressed or destroyed or is seemingly nonexistent? Why can't our government provide better evidence than phony passports, planted luggage, and what looks like an amateurishly faked videotape of an Osama bin Laden impersonator claiming responsibility for the attacks?

Congratulations! The madness is over. Now that you've

finished reading this traitorous list, tear these pages out and burn them. Readers under the age of twelve should have proper parental supervision. As the paper turns to ash, imagine these foolish questions also burning away in your mind, leaving a clear, confident state of absolute trust in our wise and compassionate leaders.

If you got some crazy ideas from this list—like the hijackers weren't who you thought they were, that the planes could have been flown by remote control, that the World Trade Center was possibly demolished by explosives planted inside the buildings, that the Pentagon could have been hit by a bunker-buster missile, or that Flight 93 was shot down—we think it's time you called 911 and committed yourself to the lunatic asylum! Come on, get a grip on reality. The terrorists obviously teleported onto the planes. The Twin Towers were vaporized by the hot breath of Satan, whose evil face *everybody* saw in that thick, black smoke. And a six-ton engine floated away on the breeze and skipped a merry half mile from the crash site of Flight 93, while a similar six-ton engine transformed itself into an armor-piercing missile that punched through three rings of the Pentagon. It all makes perfect sense.

If you still have doubts about 9/11, ask yourself this: Who benefits from the crime? This is a question that detectives normally like to ask when conducting an investigation. Who's in a better position now that the evil deed has been done? Well, George W. Bush's approval ratings went from 40 percent to nearly 100 percent right after the attacks, ending any lingering doubts about his "election." We were able to ram the USA PATRIOT Act through Congress thirteen days after the 9/11 attacks without your elected representatives even reading it, fulfilling our long-held dreams of the end of personal privacy, omnipotent law enforcement, and extra-legal detention camps. (Ever wonder how John Ashcroft slapped together a 1,200-page document that modified hundreds of pre-existing laws in thirteen days? Stop wondering!) We can stifle any dissent and spy on any opponent who dares to question us while we are "at war." We've created the new global enemy of "terrorism," now that the big, scary Soviet Union doesn't exist, to justify massive hikes in military spending. We were able to take "the peace dividend," the money that you thought could be spent on silly little things like schools and health care after the Cold War was won, and put that money right back in the pockets of our covert spy agencies and weapons manufacturing corporations, where it rightfully belongs. The 9/11 attacks gave us a good reason to invade Afghanistan, install a puppet government, and build the ultra-profitable oil pipeline that the Taliban had so foolishly rejected. The 9/11 attacks also gave us a good reason to invade Iraq, sort of, and secure the second-largest national oil reserves on the planet all for ourselves. And we now have the Bush Doctrine, which makes no distinction between terrorists and the countries that harbor them—which means we can conquer and occupy any country we want, whenever we want, just by claiming there are terrorists over there, even if you can't see them. Remember, those terrorists are a real slippery bunch. They don't even show up on airport security cameras.

Clearly, the U.S. government immediately took on these solemn duties as the proper responses to terrorism. We don't look at our actions as benefits, but rather what needed to be done to prevent the evildoers from benefiting from their crime. Perhaps our government was more prepared for 9/11 than any of us even knew.

Now let's look at the other side of the coin and examine what al-Qaeda got out of 9/11. Unfortunately, even the vast arsenal of anti-terror policies that we enacted after 9/11 were unable to stop the evildoers from enjoying the true benefits of their crime. Obviously, al-Qaeda are the big winners here. They're the ones who really came out on top. Why? *Because they're all dead!* We killed them all! They *love* that! Getting 5,000-pound bombs dropped into their caves in Afghanistan means they get to hang out with Ali Baba and the Forty Virgins in Paradise that much quicker!

SOURCES

Following the example of forthrightness and integrity set forth by our honest leaders, the Better Citizenship Bureau presents these sources that verify many of our amazing accomplishments. For our ideas and programs that have not been achieved in reality yet, you'll just have to wait until George W. Bush is reappointed in November 2004!

p. 11, rich dressed as poor for tax cut rallies: Julian Borger, "Why America's Plutocrats Gobble Up $1,500 Hot Dogs," *Guardian,* November 5, 2003.

p. 13, budget cuts: Edmund L. Andrews, "Bush Budget Cuts a Variety of Programs," *New York Times,* February 4, 2004.

p. 17, shadow government: Barton Gellman and Susan Schmidt, "Shadow Government Is at Work in Secret," *Washington Post,* March 1, 2002.

p. 21, Diebold CEO's quote: Paul Krugman, "Hack the Vote," *New York Times,* December 2, 2003.

p. 24, tips on running for class president: John Nichols, *Jews for Buchanan: Did You Hear the One About the Theft of the American Presidency?* (New York: The New Press, 2001).

p. 31, the Babylon Project from DARPA: Paul Eng, "A Few Good Machine Translators," ABC News, June 12, 2002.

p. 32, Unocal Vice-President John J. Maresca's statement: *World Press Review* background documents. http://www.worldpress.org/specials/pp/unocal.htm

p. 32, pipeline in Afghanistan: BBC News, "Afghan Pipeline Given Go-Ahead," May 30, 2002. http://news.bbc.co.uk/2/hi/business/2017044.stm

p. 32, Afghanistan forgotten in 2003 budget: BBC News, "Afghanistan Omitted from U.S. Aid Budget," February 13, 2003.

p. 33, Meet Our Troops: *9/11: The Road to Tyranny* is a film by Alex Jones that includes footage of U.S. troops engaging in martial law simulations with civilian role players. The film is available through Jones's website, http://www.infowars.com, or by calling 888-253-3139.

p. 34, Colonel Randolph Alles quote: James W. Crawley, "Officials Confirm Dropping Firebombs on Iraqi Troops," *San Diego Union-Tribune*, August 5, 2003.

p. 36, Iraq sanctions: National Network to End the War Against Iraq, "The Deadly Effects of Sanctions on Iraq." http://www.endthewar.org/frontps/factsheet.htm

p. 38, form letters from troops in Iraq: Ledyard King, "Newspapers Sent Same Letter Signed by Different Soldiers," Gannett News Service, October 12, 2003.

p. 39, "Baghdad is getting better" billboard: Alex Berenson, "U.S. Case for Helping Iraq Suffers a Setback," *New York Times*, October 27, 2003.

p. 40, wounded troops charged for hospital food: Ed Howard, "Hospitalized Troops Are Charged for Meals," *Nebraska State Paper*, September 17, 2003.

p. 41, transfer tubes: Tim Harper, "Pentagon Keeps Dead Out of Sight," *Toronto Star*, November 2, 2003.

p. 43, Carlyle Group, including Shafig bin Laden, met on 9/11: Ed Vulliamy, "Dark Heart of the American Dream," *Observer* (London), June 16, 2002.

p. 44, Dick Cheney, Halliburton, and war profiteering: Kevin Phillips, *American Dynasty: Aristocracy, Fortune, and the Politics of Deceit in the House of Bush* (New York: Viking, 2004).

p. 44, gay Arab speakers fired by the U.S. military: Associated Press, "U.S. Army Linguists Fired for Being Gay," November 15, 2002.

p. 50, unequipped U.S. soldiers lacking modern body armor: Jonathan Turley, "Full Metal Jacket," *Los Angeles Times*, September 29, 2003.

p. 51, birth defects in Iraq: http://www.web-light.nl/VISIE/extremedeformities.html

p. 53, filthy conditions in Halliburton facilities: NBC News, December 12, 2003.

p. 55, Karl Rove talking about George W. Bush's tight blue jeans: Nicholas Lemann, "The Controller: Karl Rove Is Working to Get George Bush Reelected, but He Has

Bigger Plans," *New Yorker*, May 12, 2003.

p. 61, Karl Rove's dirty tricks: James Moore and Wayne Slater, *Bush's Brain: How Karl Rove Made George W. Bush Presidential* (New York: John Wiley and Sons, 2003).

p. 64, Donald Rumsfeld approving U.S. airstrikes which would kill Iraqi civilians: Michael R. Gordon, "U.S. Attacked Iraqi Defenses Starting in 2002," *New York Times*, July 20, 2003.

p. 65, Asea Brown Boveri selling nuclear reactors to North Korea: Randeep Ramesh, "The Two Faces of Rumsfeld," *Guardian*, May 9, 2003.

p. 76, sodomites making jokes about Rick Santorum's name: http://www.spreadingsantorum.com

p. 84, praying for God to "remove" pro-choice Supreme Court justices: Sheryl McCarthy, "Pat Robertson Loses It in Attack on High Court," *Newsday*, July 17, 2003.

p. 87, execution of labor union leaders: Juan González, "Bottling Coke and Spilling Blood," *New York Daily News*, November 11, 2003.

p. 88, ice sculptures that urinate premium vodka: Kevin McCoy, "A Birthday Party for the Ages," *USA Today*, October 27, 2003.

p. 90, honoring our fathers: Bob Fitrakis and Harvey Wasserman, "Siege Heil: The Nazi Nexus," *Columbus Free Press*, October 6, 2003. http://www.freepress.org/departments.php?strFunc=display&strID=386&strYear=2003&strDept=20

p. 100, privatization of Iraqi economy: Rajiv Chandrasekaran, "Economic Overhaul for Iraq," *Washington Post Foreign Service*, September 22, 2003.

p. 101, Policy Analysis Market: Carl Hulse, "Pentagon Prepares a Futures Market on Terror Attacks," *New York Times*, July 29, 2003.

p. 103, Wal-Mart's toy manufacturers in China: Jim Hightower, "How Wal-Mart Is Remaking Our World," *Hightower Lowdown*, April 26, 2002. http://www.alternet.org/story.html?StoryID=12962

p. 104, Wal-Mart's treatment of female employees: Liza Featherstone, "Wal-Mart Values," *The Nation*, posted November 26, 2002. http://www.thenation.com/doc.mhtml?i=20021216&s=featherstone

p. 108, how to avoid paying overtime: Leigh Strope, "Bush's Labor Department Offers Employers Tips to Avoid Overtime Pay," Associated Press, January 6, 2004.

p. 109, Afghanistan's prewar opium trade: BBC News, "Afghanistan's Opium Industry," April 9, 2002. http://news.bbc.co.uk/1/hi/world/south_asia/1840182.stm

p. 109, effects of Taliban ban on Afghan opium trade: United Nations Drug Control Programme, Afghanistan, Annual Opium Poppy Survey 2001.

p. 110, worldwide annual sale of narcotics: Douglas Keh, "Drug Money in a Changing World," technical document no. 4, Vienna United Nations Drug Control Programme, 1998, p. 4.

p. 113, Tamimi Company paying workers $3 a day: Nicolas Pelham, "Contractors in Iraq Accused of Importing Labor and Exporting Profit," *Financial Times,* October 14, 2003.

p. 113, Halliburton pipeline in Burma: Peter Waldman, "Pipeline Project in Burma Puts Cheney in the Spotlight," *Wall Street Journal,* October 27, 2000.

p. 122, picking cotton for 4¢ an hour: Joel Stein, "The Lessons of Cain," TIME.com. http://www.time.com/time/reports/mississippi/angola.html

p. 123, metabolism of aspartame produces methanol: Ann Endo, "To Your Health: How Sweet It Is," *Daily Yomiuri* (Tokyo), February 20, 1999.

p. 123, removal of tumors from Searle test animals: Gregory Gordon, "NutraSweet Approval Marred by Controversy," United Press International Investigative Report, 1987. http://www.dorway.com/upipart2.html

p. 123, FDA urged grand jury investigation of Searle for possible law violations in aspartame testing: *Wall Street Journal,* April 9, 1976. Copyright 1976 The New York Times Company: Information Bank Abstracts.

p. 124, government lawyers decide against prosecuting Searle: Andy Pasztor and Joe Davidson, "Two Ex-U.S. Prosecutors' Roles in Case Against Searle Are Questioned in Probe," *Wall Street Journal,* February 7, 1986.

p. 124, Rumsfeld said he would "call in his markers": Gordon, "NutraSweet Approval Marred by Controversy."

p. 124, Rumsfeld using political connections to win aspartame approval: Eric

Swanson, "Rumsfeld's Folly: National Missile Defense," *Pittsburgh Post-Gazette,* January 14, 2001.

p. 124, Searle reapplying for aspartame approval the day after Reagan's inauguration: Gordon, "NutraSweet Approval Marred by Controversy."

p. 124, Arthur Hull Hayes Jr. accepting free rides on General Foods jet: Gordon, "NutraSweet Approval Marred by Controversy."

p. 124, Arthur Hull Hayes Jr. and Burson-Marsteller: Jane E. Brody, "Sweetener Worries Some Scientists," *New York Times,* February 5, 1985.

p. 124, 8,000 consumers complain about aspartame: Greg Gordon, "The Artificial-Sweetener Debate; FDA Repeatedly Opposed Studies on Aspartame," *Minneapolis Star Tribune,* November 22, 1996.

p. 124, FDA forced to release list of aspartame complaints through the Freedom of Information Act: http://aspartametruth.com/92symptoms.html

p. 124, Original 1995 DHHS document of consumer complaints on aspartame: http://www.321recipes.com/symptoms.html

p. 125, Dr. John Olney and aspartame's history: Greg Gordon, "Aspartame Is a Suspect in Rise of Brain Tumors; But FDA, Manufacturer Dispute New Study About Sweetener," *Minneapolis Star Tribune,* November 5, 1996.

p. 125, when heated or stored in acidic liquids, aspartame breaks down into methanol: Nancy Jenkins, "Aspartame Issue Goes On," *New York Times,* August 1, 1984.

p. 125, 100 percent of NutraSweet research positive and 92 percent of independent research negative: Catherine Brown, "Sweet and Sour: Concern Mounts over Synthetic Sugars, with Attention Heavily Focused on the Market Leader, Aspartame," *Glasgow Herald,* August 26, 2000.

p. 126, usage restrictions lifted for aspartame in 1996: *Houston Chronicle,* "FDA Gives NutraSweet OK for All Foods," June 28, 1996.

p. 129, Taliban massacred in boxcars: Mahvish Khan, "Documentary Alleges U.S. Complicity in Afghan Massacre," *San Jose Mercury News,* December 23, 2002.

p. 140, the Preemptive Proactive Operations Group: William M. Arkin, "The Secret War," *Los Angeles Times,* October 27, 2002.

p. 140, Terror Tip—Back Off: Greg Palast and David Pallister, "FBI Claims Bin Laden Inquiry Was Frustrated," *Guardian,* November 7, 2001.

p. 140, John O'Neill frustrated in attempts to investigate terrorism: Robert Kolker, "O'Neill Versus Osama," *New York,* December 17, 2001.

p. 150, Afghan children killed by U.S. warplanes: *Guardian,* "Six Children Die in Fresh U.S. Blunder," December 10, 2003.

p. 166, Canadian soldiers killed by U.S. pilots on amphetamines: CBC News Online, "Go-Pills, Bombs & Friendly Fire," October 22, 2003. http://www.cbc.ca/news/background/friendlyfire/gopills.html

p. 196; Kissinger, 9/11 panel, and conflicts of interest: Michael Kranish, "Kissinger Quits as Chairman of 9/11 Panel," *Boston Globe,* December 14, 2002.

p. 197, hijackers turning up alive: BBC News, "Hijack 'Suspects' Alive and Well," September 23, 2001. http://news.bbc.co.uk/2/hi/middle_east/1559151.stm

p. 197, more hijackers turning up alive: David Harrison, "Revealed: The Men With Stolen Identities," *Telegraph* (London), September 23, 2001.

p. 197, even more hijackers turning up alive, and dead, before 9/11: CNN correction, CNN.com, September 13, 2001. http://www.cnn.com/2001/US/09/13/america.attack/

p. 198, argument in parking lot; evidence in hotel Dumpster: Curtis Morgan, David Kidwell, and Oscar Corral, "Prelude to Terror," *Miami Herald,* September 22, 2001.

p. 198, Atta's luggage the only luggage not transferred onto Flight 11: Paul Sperry, "Airline Denied Atta Paradise Wedding Suit," WorldNetDaily.com, September 11, 2002. http://www.worldnetdaily.com/news/article.asp?ARTICLE_ID=28904

p. 198, contents of Atta's suitcase: James K. Lechner, FBI affidavit, September 12, 2001. http://www.abc.net.au/4corners/atta/resources/documents/fbiaffidavit10.htm

p.199, religious oddities of Atta's letter: Brian Whitaker, "Chilling Document Hints at 'Armageddon,'" *Guardian,* October 1, 2001.

p. 199, terrorist's passport found in rubble of WTC: ABC News, September 12, 2001.

p. 200, piloting skills of Nawa Alhamzi and Khalid al-Midhar: William Booth and Rene Sanchez, "San Diegans See Area as Likely Target: Three Hijackers Drew Little

Notice in City of Many Transients," *Washington Post,* September 24, 2001.

p. 200, Mohammed Atta and Marwan Al-Shehhi flunking out of flight school: Steve Fainaru and Peter Whoriskey, "Hijack Suspects Tried Many Flight Schools: 'Polite, Quiet' Men Stirred No Concerns," *Washington Post,* September 19, 2001.

p. 201, terrorists carousing at strip club: Associated Press, "Manager: Men Spewed Anti-American Sentiments," *USA Today,* September 14, 2001. www.usatoday.com/news/nation/2001/09/14/miami-club.htm

p. 201, military jets were scrambled 129 times in 2000: Linda Slobodian, "NORAD on Heightened Alert: Role of Air Defence Agency Rapidly Transformed in Wake of Sept. 11 Terrorist Attacks," *Calgary Herald,* October 13, 2001.

p. 202, aircraft at Andrews Air Force Base: Sylvia Adcock, Brian Donovan, and Craig Gordon, "Air Attack on Pentagon Indicates Weaknesses," *Newsday,* September 23, 2001.

p. 202, flight speed calculations: Jim Hoffman, "NORAD Stand-Down," 911research.wtc7.net. http://911research.wtc7.net/planes/analysis/norad/indcx.html#ref3 See also: Glen Johnson, "America Prepares: The Investigation Military Response; Timeline Shows Fighters Were Closing on Jets," *Boston Globe,* September 19, 2001.

p. 202, failure to redeploy fighter jets: Associated Press, "Sept. 11 Fighter Pilot Thought World War III Had Started," August 21, 2002.

p. 204, James Quintiere's statements: James Quintiere, "A Fire Prevention Engineer Asks: Why Did the WTC Towers Fall?," *Baltimore Sun,* January 3, 2002.

p. 206, investigation of Ground Zero underfunded and confused: Eric Lipton, "Mismanagement Muddled Collapse Inquiry, House Panel Says," *New York Times,* March 7, 2002.

p. 208, delivery of debris removal plan for WTC: Nadine Post and Debra K. Rubin, "Debris Mountain Starts to Shrink," *Engineering News-Record* (New York), October 1, 2001.

p. 208, demolition of the shell of the Murrah building in Oklahoma City: http://www.controlled-demolition.com/default.asp?reqMode=1&reqLocId=7&reqItemId=20030317124730

p. 208, demolition and removal of Murrah building prevented independent

investigators: Christopher Bollyn, "Eyewitness Reports Persist of Bombs at WTC Collapse," *American Free Press*, December 2, 2001.
http://www.rense.com/general17/eyewitnessreportspersist.htm

p. 208, WTC steel sent abroad for recycling: Reuters, "WTC Scrap Sails for India, China," *Daily News* (Sri Lanka), January 22, 2002.
http://origin.dailynews.lk/2002/01/22/wor02.html

p. 208, airplane crash simulation drill at Pentagon on September 11, 2001: John J. Lumpkin, "Agency Planned Exercise on Sept. 11 Built Around a Plane Crashing into a Building," Associated Press, August 22, 2002.

p. 208, Pentagon facade intact after strike: George Edmonson and Mei-Ling Hopgood, "Attack on the Pentagon: Breach Was in Structure, Not Defense," *Atlanta Journal-Constitution*, September 12, 2001.

p. 213, FBI seizing videotapes of the Pentagon attack: Bill Gertz and Rowan Scarborough, "Notes from the Pentagon," *The Gertz File* [connected to *Washington Times*], September 21, 2001.
http://www.unansweredquestions.org/timeline/2001/gertzfile092101.html
See also: Bill McKelway, "Three Months On, Tension Lingers Near the Pentagon," *Richmond Times-Dispatch*, December 11, 2001.

p. 213, FBI officers removing debris: Mary Beth Sheridan, "Loud Boom, Then Flames in Hallways; Pentagon Employees Flee Fire, Help Rescue Injured Co-Workers," *Washington Post*, September 12, 2001.

p. 213, F-16 jet trailing Flight 93: United Press International, "Hijacked Jets Nearly Collided," September 13, 2001.

p. 214-215, eyewitnesses describe white jet trailing Flight 93; sonic boom caused by a supersonic jet in Shanksville area; Edward Felt's mobile phone call: Richard Wallace, "What Did Happen to Flight 93?," *Daily Mirror*, September 13, 2002.
http://www.mirror.co.uk/news/allnews/page.cfm?objectid=12192317&method=full&siteid=50143

p. 214, widespread debris of Flight 93: Tom Gibb, James O'Toole, and Cindi Lash, "Investigators Locate 'Black Box' from Flight 93; Widen Search Area in Somerset Crash," *Pittsburgh Post-Gazette*, September 13, 2001.

p. 214, burning debris falling from sky: Reuters, "FBI Does Not Rule Out Shootdown of Pennsylvania Plane," September 13, 2001.

p. 215, George W. Bush seeing Flight 11 on television on 9/11: Stephanie Schorow, "What Did Bush See and When Did He See It?," *Boston Herald,* October 22, 2002.

p. 216, Osama bin Laden denies responsibility for 9/11: CNN.com, "Bin Laden Says He Wasn't Behind Attacks," September 17, 2001. http://www.cnn.com/2001/US/09/16/inv.binladen.denial/index.html

p. 217, U.S. produced videotape of Osama bin Laden: David E. Sanger, "A Nation Challenged: The Evidence; Another Tape Ties bin Laden to Hijackings," *New York Times,* December 10, 2001.

p. 217, Niaz Naik, as well as Tajikistan, Uzbekistan, Russia, and India, were notified of U.S. military plans in Afghanistan: George Arney, "U.S. 'Planned Attack on Taleban,'" BBC News. http://news.bbc.co.uk/2/hi/south_asia/1550366.stm

p. 218, U.S. forces were massing on the borders of Afghanistan in June 2001: "India in Anti-Taliban Military Plan," *India Reacts,* June 26, 2001. http://www.indiareacts.com/archivefeatures/nat2.asp?recno=10&ctg=

p. 218, bin Laden family flown out of the United States by the FBI: Patrick E. Tyler, "Fearing Harm, bin Laden Kin Fled from U.S.," *New York Times,* September 30, 2001.

p. 218, Pentagon officials suddenly canceling travel plans for 9/11 on 9/10: Evan Thomas and Mark Hosenball, "Bush: 'We're At War,'" *Newsweek,* September 24, 2001.

p. 218, Willie Brown warned against flying on 9/11: Philip Matier and Andrew Ross, "Willie Brown Got Low-Key Early Warning About Air Travel," *San Francisco Chronicle,* September 12, 2001.

p. 218, Salman Rushdie prevented from flying on 9/11: James Doran, "Rushdie's Air Ban," *London Times*, September 27 2001.

p. 219, Ashcroft stops flying on commercial planes: Jim Stewart, "Ashcroft Flying High," CBSNews.com, July 26, 2001. http://www.cbsnews.com/stories/2001/07/26/national/main303601.shtml

p. 219, short-selling of stocks before 9/11: David Roeder, "Terrorists Trailed at CBOE," *Chicago Sun-Times,* September 20, 2001.

p. 219, Rumsfeld's prediction: Robert Burns, "Pentagon Attack Came Minutes After Rumsfeld Predicted: 'There Will Be Another Event,'" Associated Press, September 11, 2001.

p. 219, Rumsfeld predicting the Pentagon would be struck: William Langley, "Revealed: What Really Went on During Bush's 'Missing Hours,'" *Telegraph,* December 16, 2001.

p. 219, Cheney's staff were put on cipro on 9/11: Sandra Sobieraj, "White House Mail Sorters Anthrax-Free," Associated Press, October 24, 2001.

p. 219, anthrax most likely from Fort Detrick: Oliver Burkeman, "U.S. Scientist Is Suspect in Anthrax Investigation," *Guardian,* February 20, 2002.

p. 219, Operation Northwoods: David Ruppe, "Friendly Fire: Book: U.S. Military Drafted Plans to Terrorize U.S. Cities to Provoke War with Cuba," ABCNews.com, November 7, 2001.
http://abcnews.go.com/sections/us/DailyNews/jointchiefs_010501.html

p. 220, original Operation Northwoods document: National Security Archive, George Washington University. http://www.gwu.edu/~nsarchiv/news/20010430/

p. 221, Project for a New American Century: "The Plan: Were Neo-Conservatives' 1998 Memos a Blueprint for Iraq War?," ABCNews.com, March 10, 2003.
http://abcnews.go.com/sections/nightline/DailyNews/pnac_030310.html

p. 221, a new Pearl Harbor: The Project for a New American Century, "Rebuilding America's Defenses," September 2000, p. 63.
http://www.newamericancentury.org/defensenationalsecurity2000.htm

p. 221, Bush linking 9/11 and Pearl Harbor for his diary: Dan Balz and Bob Woodward, "America's Chaotic Road to War," *Washington Post,* January 27, 2002.

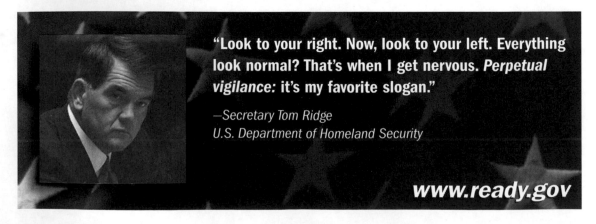